MW01708537

Implementing Configuration Management

Hardware, Software, and Firmware

Second Edition

Implementing Configuration Management

Hardware, Software, and Firmware

Second Edition

Fletcher J. Buckley

IEEE COMPUTER SOCIETY PRESS
50 YEARS OF SERVICE • 1946-1996

Los Alamitos, California

Washington • Brussels • Tokyo

IEEE Press

New York

The Library of Congress has catalogued the hard cover edition of this title as follows:

Buckley, Fletcher J.
Implementing configuration management: hardware, software, and firmware / Fletcher J. Buckley, — 2nd ed.
p. cm.
Includes bibliographical references and index.
ISBN 0-8186-7186-6 (case)
1. Configuration management. 2. Computers. I. Title.
QA76.76.C49B84 1996
004' .068 ' 5—dc20
95-23409
CIP

Copublished by:

IEEE Computer Society
10662 Los Vaqueros Circle
P.O. Box 3014
Los Alamitos, CA 90720-1264

IEEE Press
445 Hoes Lane
P.O. Box 1331
Piscataway, NJ 08855-1331

IEEE Computer Society Order Number BP08932
IEEE Press Order Number PP5629
Library of Congress Number 95-23409
ISBN 0-8186-8932-3

Additional copies may be ordered from:

IEEE Computer Society Press
Customer Service Center
10662 Los Vaqueros Circle
P.O. Box 3014
Los Alamitos, CA 90720-1314
Tel: +1 714-821-8380
Fax: +1 714-821-4641
Email: csbooks@computer.org

IEEE Service Center
445 Hoes Lane
P.O. Box 1331
Piscataway, NJ 08855-1331
Tel: +1 732-981-0060
Fax: +1 732-981-9667
mis.custserv@computer.org

IEEE Computer Society
Watanabe Building
1-4-2 Minami-Aoyama
Minato-ku, Tokyo 107-0062
JAPAN
Tel: +81-3-3408-3118
Fax: +81-3-3408-3553
tokyo.ofc@computer.org

IEEE COMPUTER SOCIETY

IEEE

To My Wife, Betty

CONTENTS

Illustrations

TABLES

Preface

This is a book about configuration management, an engineering discipline and a process whose purpose is to maintain the integrity of products (hardware, software, and firmware) as these products evolve through the development and production cycles. It is based on the experience of the author at the GE Government Electronic Systems Division (now Lockheed–Martin) and the experiences of others in different organizations who have been faced with the same concerns.

This book is aimed at the implementers in both commercial and government environments who, faced with immediate challenges, must make decisions, implement them, and live with the results. To assist the implementers, the material provides both an overview of configuration management itself and specific guidance on implementation that can be tailored to specific organizational needs. The view is that it is much easier to change details to fit a particular environment than to implement general principles in an undefined manner. Recognizing that the emphasis in this book is on cost-effective implementations of the process, the reasons for various actions are provided so that readers can make knowledgeable choices to fill their specific needs.

This book will be of use not only to those on large and medium-sized projects but also for those on small projects who can easily tailor downward to an implementation which fits their needs.

It can be a long jump from statements of configuration management principles to cost-effective implementations. This book is aimed at helping to bridge that gap.

This revision has been driven by the suggestions from readers who liked the first edition but who wanted still more. Reflecting those suggestions, this edition has been expanded to:[1]

(a) Include a detailed decomposition and further descriptions of the configuration management process into separate executable steps to the point where individual procedures can be written to support each step. This supports the need to improve all of our engineering processes (including CM) and which has been expressed in many forms including the Software Engineering Institute's Capability Maturity Model and the International Standards Organization 9000 series of standards.

(b) Provide additional details on the configuration management aspects of computer-aided design/computer-aided manufacturing (CAD/CAM). The CAD/CAM world has been literally exploding and is suffering from all the penalties of success, one of which is the need for a regulated process that will maintain the integrity of the products as they evolve to hardware. This revision is aimed at serving that need.

(c) Add both guidance and detailed examples of generic configuration management plans and procedures that can be directly tailored to meet the requirements of individual projects. In this case as with most endeavors, one size does not fit all; cultures are different, products are not the same, and the processes that produce the products all have local variations. To develop a cost-effective configuration management implementation requires tailoring to individual projects, and in this regard it is much easier to tailor downward (for example, remove material) than it is to compose it while under schedule and cost pressures. For this reason, the first edition has been expanded to provide details of generic plans and procedures as well as a strategy for producing these documents locally.

(d) Provide exercises at the end of each chapter. This allows the book to be used as a supplementary text in engineering management, industrial engineering, and software engineering courses.

(e) Ensure the material is up to date with the latest editions of the approved standards; for example, notice 1 of MIL-STD-973.

---

[1]Material on pages 156 through 159 is based on similar material on pages 64–66 in *Implementing Software Engineering Practices*, F. Buckley, 1989, John Wiley & Sons, Inc. Reprinted with permission of John Wiley & Sons, Inc.

Acknowledgments

This book would not have been possible without the help of many others. Many hours were spent discussing these issues with the members of the General Electric Aerospace Group Configuration Management Subcouncil: Miki Dekany, Gary Eagle, Kraig Lenius, Patricia Miglino, Warren Scofield, Jeff Stay, and Mark Whistler. Those dialogues illuminated many of the practical considerations I have attempted to replicate in this book.

Ron Berlack, Susan Dart, Henry Miller, and Dave Schultz spent many hours reading the drafts of this edition to correct and clarify items contained therein. If their efforts did not completely succeed, the fault lies with me.

The appearance of this book should not be construed to indicate that its contents state official Lockheed–Martin policies or positions on the topics covered herein.

1

INTRODUCTION

As technology continues to increase along Toffler's curves, both the products themselves and the processes used to produce those products have become increasingly complex. As the complexity increases, opportunities for the introduction of errors increase, as do the impacts of these errors if they remain uncorrected.

Over the past 50 years an engineering discipline has arisen, the purpose of which is to maintain the integrity of the product throughout the development and production cycles. This discipline, *configuration management*, was initially applied to hardware production, principally in association with engineering drawings. Today, configuration management is increasingly applied not only to hardware, but also to software, the merger of hardware and software into firmware, and the documentation that supports the development and production processes.

Applying configuration management to a project is similar to buying insurance. The amount of money and effort to be spent on configuration management should be based on the value of the product, the perceived risks, and the impact on the product if one of the perceived risks should actually materialize. The question to be answered for each project is then: What is required to obtain a reasonable degree of assurance that the integrity of the product will be maintained?

1.1 GOAL

The goal of this book is to provide sufficient information and examples so that the reader can immediately begin to implement a configuration management operation that will meet the needs of a commercial or government organization.

1.2 INTENDED AUDIENCES

This book will be useful to five different audiences. The first consists of those who know nothing about configuration management and need to obtain a basic understanding of the field. That audience should read the chapters in the order in which they occur and then refer to individual chapters for reinforcement on desired topics.

The second audience is one which is familiar with configuration management in general but want detailed information on a specific topic. Those readers should either consult the table of contents and go directly to the chapter that is of direct concern, or review the index for pinpoint references.

The third audience is one which is looking for immediate help in a specific implementation of the process. Those readers could go directly to Appendix D, review the example configuration management plan, and refer to the index for the locations at which specific items are discussed.

The fourth audience is one which is engaged in CM process improvement. Those readers should review the flow charts and associated text that delineate the CM processes and associated processes for application to an individual company's process. Then, using the CM process steps, they can tailor the associated material (for example, the example plan in Appendix D, or the generic CM plan in Appendix F) for their individual usage.

The fifth audience includes those tasked with the evaluation or selection of automated CM tools and those tasked with preparing for registration under ISO 9001 and 9000-3 relative to the CM requirements. Those readers should use this material to provide a comprehensive identification of all the CM criteria that should be considered in each of those tasks.

1.3 ORIENTATION

This book is oriented toward the implementer—the person or group that must implement a configuration management (CM) system for hardware, software, and/or firmware in a commercial or government environment. The implementer is assumed to be on the firing line, with little use for untried techniques. Overall, the implementer is viewed as the person who has the problem of trying to initiate and maintain a configuration management system in an environment in which the product is actively changing, and who is looking for practical solutions.

To serve the implementer best, this text provides a detailed tutorial on the configuration management field together with illustrative examples. The examples used to illustrate the applications are drawn from efforts on Digital Equipment Corporation (DEC) Alpha machines operating under the VMS operating system and the operations of UNIX on a SUN platform. These examples should not be construed as indicating that these are the only machines for which CM systems are implemented; rather, they are used to provide a consistent set of implementation examples at the level of detail required to illustrate the points being discussed. The reason for this approach is to ease the pain of establishing a useful configuration management system that will provide immediate service to the users. With examples at the machine level, the theory can more easily be implemented by the reader.

The examples and practices illustrated are not the only ways to accomplish the individual CM tasks. Different practices can be used to accomplish the same ends—to maintain the integrity of the products—and the evolution of CM has been the result of a constant search for more cost-effective ways to accomplish these tasks. The practices illustrated in this book show at least one practical way to accomplish specific tasks if a better way that can be used is not immediately available. This, then, can furnish a first step toward improving local CM processes.

1.4 SCOPE

The scope of the applications to be controlled includes both commercial and government implementations. There is a great debt owed to the government from those in the configuration management field, as the government has led the way in the development and application of configuration management. In order to enable the commercial implementer to apply configuration management cost-effectively, this book emphasizes understanding the underlying rationale, the tradeoffs that can be made, and how the configuration management process is applied in a cost-effective manner.

CM interacts with other specialty fields (for example, reliability, quality assurance, purchasing, and manufacturing). In most cases, it is difficult to state precisely where one specialty field stops and another begins. The approach taken in this book is the larger view; this permits the user to tailor downward (to reduce scope), rather than requiring the user to extend the configuration management effort into uncharted fields.

Configuration management is an established specialty field of engineering expertise with a stated purpose, a defined scope of operations, and established methods for accomplishing its purpose. As such, there are certain core activities that are part of every configuration management implementation. Other actions (for example, the use of a standards-checking tool) may be added onto a configuration management effort based on the needs of a specific organization and the capabilities of the individuals concerned. These actions are interesting, and serve useful purposes, and they are discussed in the book as the occasion arises.

For the person just starting out, the configuration management vocabulary can be a major source of confusion. Viewed another way, configuration management is a foreign language, and fluency in the usage of configuration management terms is sometimes only acquired after practice. Furthermore, recognizing that configuration management is an established field, the terms must be used in very precise ways; otherwise, confusion will result. To help the reader, a complete glossary of configuration management terms is provided in Appendix A.

1.5 WHAT IS IT?

Configuration management is a discipline applying technical and administrative direction and surveillance to:[1]

(a) Identify and document the functional and physical characteristics of configuration items (CIs)

---

[1]A note to the reader on definitions.

(a) Each term (for example, configuration management) is normally defined in the text at the point of first usage. All these definitions are further collected in Appendix A for ease of reference.

(b) Definitions come from a variety of sources; the source used for each term is provided with that term in Appendix A.

(1) Where any substantive differences have been found in specific definitions from two or more sources, both definitions are provided in Appendix A.

(2) Where the definitions were sufficiently alike between two different sources (for example, between MIL-STD-973 and IEEE Std 610), the better definition was chosen and used herein.

(b) Audit the configuration items to verify conformance to specifications, interface control documents, and other contract requirements
(c) Control changes to configuration items and their related documentation
(d) Record and report information needed to manage configuration items effectively, including the status of proposed changes and the implementation status of approved changes

In turn, a configuration item is a collection of hardware, software, and/or firmware, which satisfies an end-use function and is designated for configuration management. (The system engineering processes that result in the designation of a particular collection of hardware, software, and firmware as a configuration item are beyond the scope of this book.)

As shown in Figure 1-1, configuration management consists of four major divisions:

(a) Configuration identification
(b) Configuration change control
(c) Configuration status accounting
(d) Configuration audits

Each of these core operations is covered in detail in the chapters that follow.

Another way to look at configuration management is that it is a process, and this is the view shown in Figure 1-2. As shown therein, the process consists of five subprocesses with the first subprocess being that of CM planning. Each of these subprocesses is discussed in depth in the material that follows. The number of the chapter in which that process is discussed appears in the right-hand side of each process box.

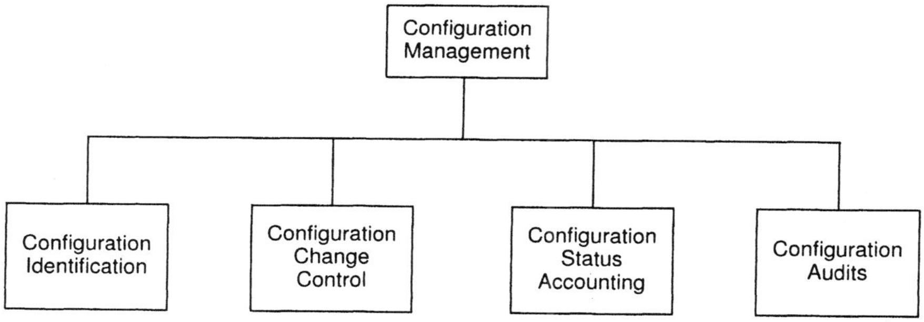

FIGURE 1-1. The Major Divisions of Configuration Management.

The benefit of looking at CM as a process is that it places all the CM actions in context with each other. Further, each subprocess can then be decomposed into subordinate processes until a level of detail is reached such that one or more procedures can be written to specify that subprocess. Even more important, however, the processes and subprocesses can be examined to see how they should be changed, rearranged, and/or augmented to improve the overall process.

1.6 STANDARDS

The world of standards is turning over very rapidly even as this text is being written. The US Department of Defense has initiated a policy of reducing the number of unique military standards and announced a preference for the use of commercial standards. Toward this end, working groups have been established to revise some of the commercial standards and to initiate new commercial standards where none currently exist. In some places, standards

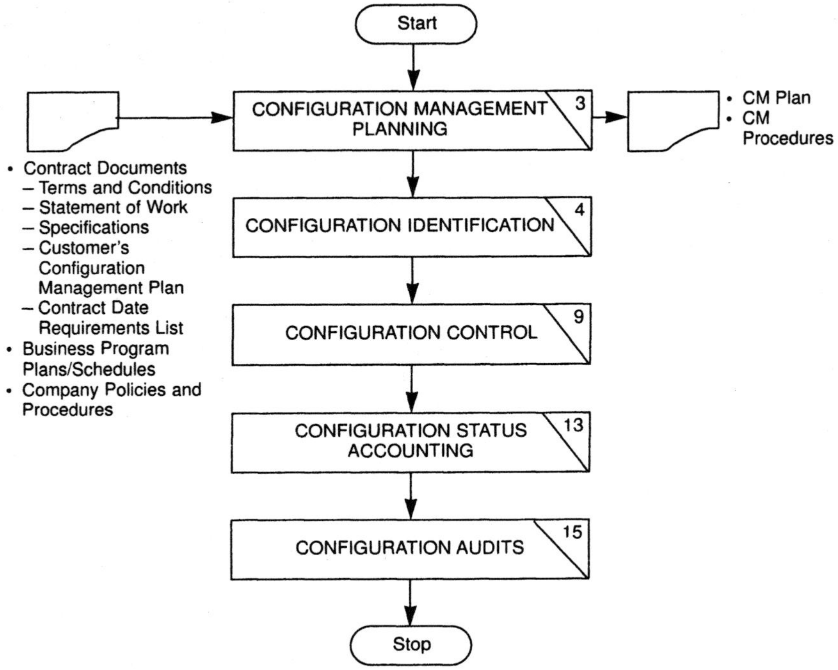

FIGURE 1-2. The Configuration Management Process.

such as DOD-STD-2167A have given way to MIL-STD-498, which in turn is projected to be replaced by a new commercial standard being drafted by a joint committee of the Electronic Industries Association (EIA) and the Institute of Electrical and Electronic Engineers (IEEE).

Pending the replacement of those standards and their associated implementations into new contracts, the current standards will remain a part of the repertoire of those in the CM field for two reasons: (1) they are embedded in the field and provide part of the working culture on those for whom they are requirements, and, more importantly, (2) they provide workable solutions to problems that have been previously encountered. In this context, caution should be exercised. The fact that a particular solution is embedded in a standard (military or commercial) should not imply an automatic acceptance of that solution. Rather, that solution should be examined with the view that it worked in one context and may be applicable to resolve a similar problem that occurs in the context of the reader.

Throughout this text, references are made to various standards where appropriate. These are for the aid and assistance of the readers who are in those worlds and for the information of those readers who are not. In either case, if they do not apply to the problems that the reader is trying to solve, they should be cheerfully ignored.

1.7 THE PURPOSE OF CONFIGURATION MANAGEMENT

The purpose of configuration management is to maintain the integrity of products as they evolve from specifications through design, development, and production. Configuration management is not an isolated endeavor; it exists to support product development and maintenance. Applying configuration management techniques to a particular project requires judgment to be exercised: too little configuration management and products will be lost, requiring previous work to be redone; too much configuration management and the organization will never produce any products, because everyone will be too busy shuffling paperwork.

1.8 INTRODUCTION TO THE REST OF THE BOOK

The book is divided into major sections as follows:

(a) Chapter 2 identifies the configuration management environment. This includes a brief description of the development and production processes as they apply to the items controlled by configuration management (hardware, software, and firmware).

(b) Chapter 3 covers configuration management planning, including the production of a configuration management plan and the associated procedures. This chapter is placed prior to the beginning of the discussion of the other four processes (subprocesses) to avoid confusion to those who are following the sequence in Figure 1-2. For those who are new to CM, the reminder of the book should be reviewed to obtain an appreciation of the overall CM effort before beginning the planning activities.

(c) Chapters 4 through 8 cover configuration identification. Chapter 4 discusses baselines and the identification of items to be controlled, while Chapters 5 through 8 apply the concepts of configuration identification separately to hardware, software, and firmware, and also to drawings and other documents.

(d) Chapters 9 through 12 cover configuration change control. Chapter 9 discusses the change-control process itself while Chapters 10 through 12 apply the concepts to hardware and software, and discuss the documents that support the change process. Firmware is covered in its components (hardware and software), so a separate chapter on firmware is not provided.

(e) Chapter 13 covers configuration status accounting.

(f) Chapter 14 discusses the subprocess of acquiring a configuration management facility. This is a generic subprocess and is placed in a separate chapter to avoid confusion with the rest of the configuration status accounting subprocesses in Chapter 13.

(g) Chapter 15 covers configuration audits, including common audit actions and the major concern associated with blindly applying hardware configuration audit practices to software without understanding the rationale behind these hardware audit practices.

(h) The index provides pinpoint references to specific topics covered in this book, and also provides detailed subject references to places where authoritative guidance is provided in the government standards. Those on whom these government standards are contractually binding should refer to the standards that apply to their efforts. Caution should be used in this regard, because contracts vary and the requirements are not always consistent among the standards. Furthermore, the standards themselves are changing as revision efforts proceed, so the reader should check the currency of the standard being consulted.

(i) Appendix A is a centralized collection of definitions that apply to the configuration management world. While terms are defined in the book at the point where they are first used, Appendix A provides a point for easy reference. Recognizing the difficulties in communicating with others when terms are used ambiguously, every effort has been made not only to provide authoritative definitions but also to provide the source from which each definition has been abstracted.
(j) Appendix B identifies all the acronyms and abbreviations used in the text as well as in the configuration management community. As noted above, communication difficulties can also be encountered when an acronym is used to indicate two different items.
(k) Appendix C identifies standards and other documents that apply to the configuration management field, as well as a selected set of references to ongoing configuration management work.
(l) Appendix D is an example of a project-specific CM plan. This takes the implementation of configuration management down to the working level and should ease the pain always encountered in the initial establishment of a configuration management capability.
(m) Appendix E is an example of a plan for producing a generic CM plan (one that could be provided at a company level and then tailored downward to fit the needs of individual projects).
(n) Appendix F is an example generic CM plan.

Two types of exercises are provided at the ends of the chapters. The first includes those that extend the material discussed in that chapter. At times these exercises require access to materials (for example, specific standards) that should be on the book shelf of the individual dealing with those topics. It is recommended that such material be acquired and be used to support the discussions contained herein.

The second type of exercise involves situation problems. These are provided from real-life situations which provide a basis for discussion with others. Recognizing that there are many ways to solve CM problems, these provide a way in which solutions can be shared among those reading this and other texts.

2

THE CONFIGURATION MANAGEMENT ENVIRONMENT

As shown in Figure 2-1, configuration management operates in the environment of two separate processes (development and production) which are applied to three different products (hardware, software, and firmware) and to the documentation that supports the definitions of these products. To understand configuration management, each of these processes and products requires separate discussion.

2.1 HARDWARE

2.1.1 The Hardware Production Process

Figure 2-2 provides a configuration management view of hardware production. As shown therein, smaller items are joined to larger items, which in turn are joined to still larger items, and so forth. Beginning at the bottom, the granularity levels of the hardware are:

(a) *Parts*—A part is defined as one piece, or two or more pieces joined together that are not normally subject to disassembly without destruction or impairment of the part's designated use (for example, a composition resistor, a screw, or an outer front wheel bearing of a truck).

(b) *Subassemblies*—A subassembly is defined as two or more parts that form a portion of an assembly or a unit replaceable as a whole, but having a part or parts that are individually replaceable (for example, a telephone dial or a terminal board with mounted parts).

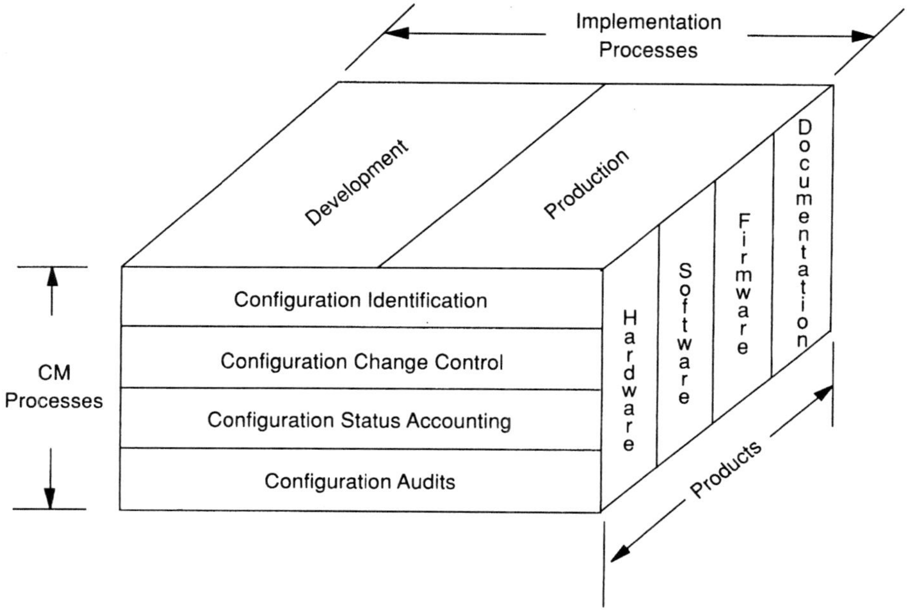

FIGURE 2-1. The Configuration Management Environment.

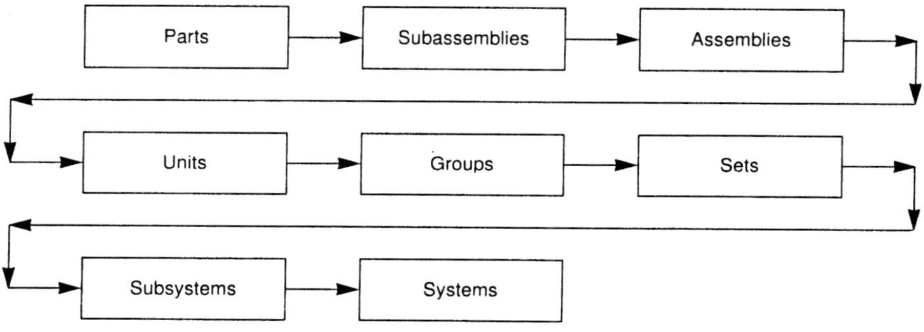

FIGURE 2-2. A Configuration Management View of the Hardware Production Process.

(c) *Assemblies*—An assembly is defined as a number of parts or subassemblies or any combination thereof, joined together to perform a specific function (for example, a power shovel-front, a fan assembly, or an audio-frequency amplifier).

(d) *Units*—A unit is defined as an assembly or any combination of parts, subassemblies, and assemblies mounted together, normally capable of independent operation in a variety of situations (for example, a hydraulic jack, an electric motor, or a radio receiver).

(e) *Groups*—A group is defined as a collection of units, assemblies, or subassemblies that is a subdivision of a set or system, but is not capable of performing a complete operational function (for example, an antenna group).

(f) *Sets*—A set is defined as a unit or units and necessary assemblies, subassemblies, and parts connected or associated together to perform an operational function (for example, a sound measuring set, which includes such parts, assemblies, and units as cable, microphones, and measuring instruments). (*Set* is also used to denote a collection of like parts such as a tool set or a set of tires.)

(g) *Subsystems*—A subsystem is defined as a combination of sets, groups, and so on that performs an operational function within, and is a major division of, a system (for example, a data processing subsystem or a guidance subsystem).

(h) *Systems*—A system is defined as a combination of parts, assemblies, and so on joined together to perform a specific operational function or functions (for example, a piping system, an air conditioning system, or a telephone carrier system).

The details of how each level is to be fabricated, assembled with the next higher level, tested, and so on are provided through the use of engineering drawings and other documents, all of which must also be identified and controlled.

2.1.2 The Hardware Development Process

From a configuration management viewpoint, the hardware development process can be visualized through the use of a *specification tree* (or document tree), a reference diagram that depicts the indentured relationships of the various specifications and other documents that define a system. These documents, which define and specify the design of the resulting end-item hardware, are the initial and intermediate products produced by the development process. To control the characteristics of the products when they are finally built, the development documentation itself must be identified and controlled.

An abbreviated specification tree is shown in Figure 2-3:

(a) The overall requirements for a system are normally expressed in a document entitled a *system specification*, which describes the essential technical requirements for the system and includes the procedures for determining whether or not the requirements have been met.
(b) The system requirements are normally decomposed into configuration item specifications, in which a configuration item is defined as an aggregation of hardware, software, or firmware designated for configuration management. It is immaterial to configuration management how the decision was made that designates a particular aggregation as a configuration item; what is important is that the aggregation is now identified and controlled in a cost-effective manner.
(c) The hardware configuration item is initially defined in a *hardware unit specification* with further definition provided in a *hardware design specification*. (For simplicity, Figure 2-3 shows the documentation for only one hardware configuration item and one software configuration item. There would usually be several of each.)

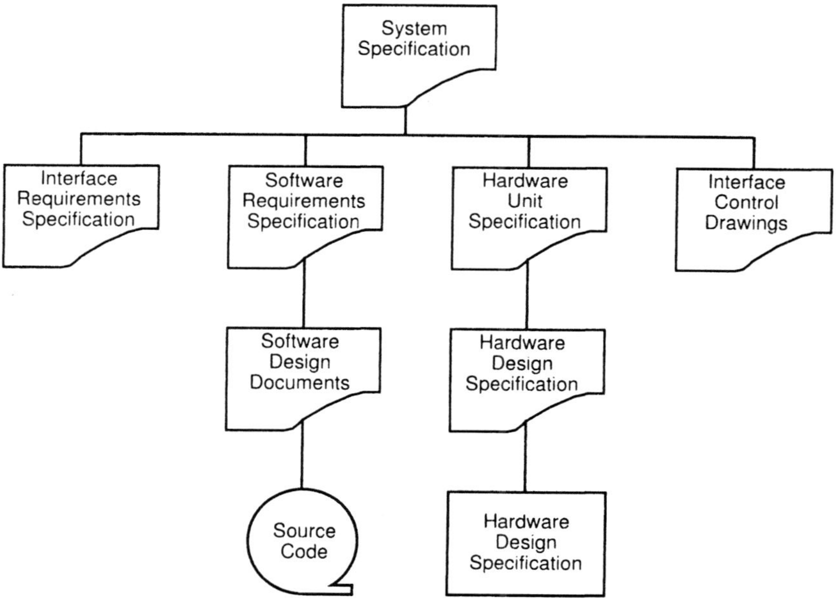

FIGURE 2-3. An Example Specification Tree.

As the hardware development proceeds, the design activity will build *breadboards* (prototype hardware) and take other actions to come to decisions on how a particular item should be built. Those "build-to" decisions are reflected in a *technical data package* (sometimes known as an *engineering drawing package*), a collection of the technical data or documents (such as engineering drawings and associated lists, specifications, standards, performance requirements, quality assurance provisions, and packaging details) from which the item can be manufactured. *Interface control drawings* are established concurrently with the hardware unit specifications and define the detailed interfaces between the hardware items. The early establishment of the interface control drawings is required to permit parallel development of the individual hardware items; otherwise each hardware item, as it was developed, would affect the other hardware items.

If there are software interfaces between software items and hardware items, those interfaces will be specified in the *interface requirements specifications.*

2.1.3 Hardware Considerations

The hardware production and development processes can be very complicated, and many more topics could be considered, for example:

(a) The allowance for intermediate decomposition of systems into subsystems and then into configuration items
(b) The documents that describe the interfaces between configuration items, subsystems, and systems
(c) The documents that describe specific manufacturing processes as well as the instruments and processes that perform higher-level calibrations of test instruments
(d) The need to control the software that supports the hardware development and production processes
(e) The need to flow down established CM requirements to subcontractors and vendors.

All of these (and more) will be covered in later chapters.

2.2 SOFTWARE

Software (or *computer software*, as it is sometimes called) is a combination of computer instructions and computer data definitions required to enable computer hardware to perform computational or control functions.

2.2.1 The Software Production Process

Figure 2-4 portrays a configuration management view of the software production process:

(a) The production process starts with files of source code (source files), where the source code is generally a high-order language such as BASIC, ATLAS, FORTRAN, COBOL, or Ada.
(b) The source files are transformed by an assembler or compiler into files of object code (object files) in which the code statements in the high-order language have been changed into machine language code (a series of "1s" and "0s").
(c) A number of object files are then merged by a linking program to produce an executable file, which can then be directly loaded and executed by a computer.

2.2.2 The Software Development Process

Figure 2-5 shows an abbreviated view of the software development process:

(a) This software development process is similar to that shown in Figure 2-3, in which a system specification is decomposed into hardware and software requirement specifications.
(b) Figure 2-3 shows the hardware development taken down to the technical data package to be used to produce the hardware. As shown in Figure 2-5, the software development process uses intermediate controlled documentation to reflect the top-level design of the software configuration item and the associated detailed design.

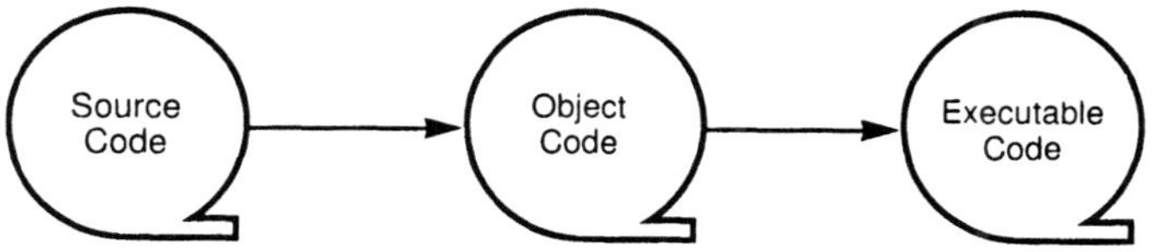

FIGURE 2-4. A Configuration Management View of the Software Production Process.

(c) Next, the detailed design is translated to source files of code, which, as described in the previous section, are converted to executable files for the test and integration phase of the development cycle.

2.2.3 Software Considerations

It is not just the deliverable software products that need to be identified and controlled, but also the software that supports the development and production of the software end products. This includes vendor-provided software, in-house software that supports various categories of test activities, and software that is being reused. Furthermore, the electronic media itself, on which the software resides, also requires identification and control. Each of these (and more) requires a different approach to its identification and control, and each will be discussed in later chapters.

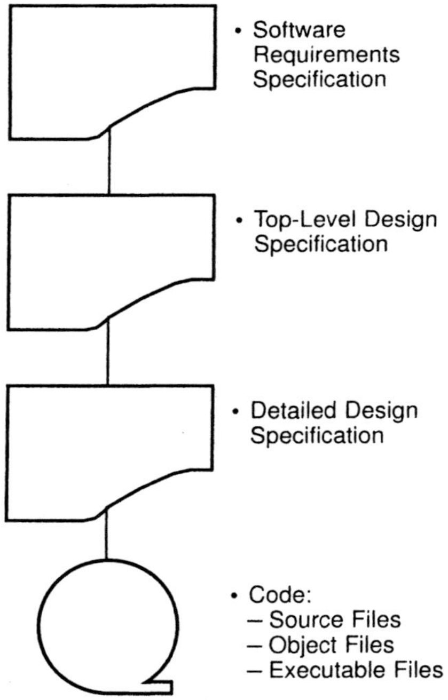

FIGURE 2-5. A Configuration Management View of the Software Development Process.

2.3 FIRMWARE

Firmware consists of a combination of a hardware device and the software that resides on the hardware device, where the software cannot be readily modified under program control.

2.3.1 The Firmware Production Process

As shown in Figure 2-6, the firmware production process includes both the hardware and software production processes:

(a) The software that is to reside on the hardware component is initially produced in a manner identical to the manner described in Section 2.2.1. An additional process is then used to transform the executable file into an image file, the precise alignment of bits to be placed on the hardware.
(b) The hardware on which the software is to reside is produced in unprogrammed form, as is any other item of hardware.
(c) The unprogrammed hardware and the software are then merged to produce an *altered item*. (The term "altered item'' is a configuration management term in wide usage in the field. It is derived from the view that the original hardware part, the unaltered item, has been altered by the addition of the software.)

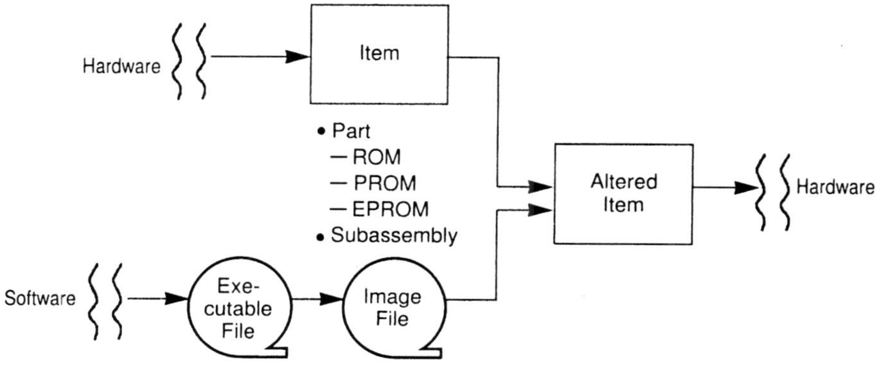

FIGURE 2-6. A Configuration Management View of the Firmware Production Process.

2.3.2 The Firmware Development Process

The firmware development process shown in Figure 2-7 is a direct derivative of the hardware and software processes. The hardware component is derived through the use of a hardware unit specification, a hardware design specification, and a technical data package. The software component of the firmware (down to the executable software file) has been derived through the use of a software requirements specification and a software design document. The only significant difference is that the requirements specification for the software component of firmware is usually a derivative of the hardware unit specification.

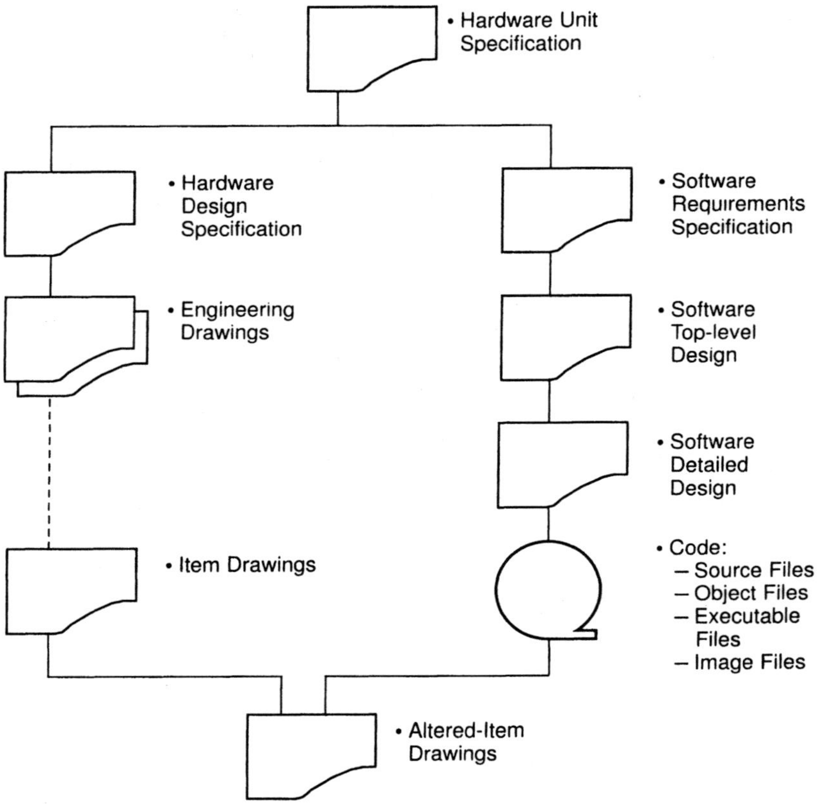

FIGURE 2-7. A Configuration Management View of the Firmware Development Process.

embedded systems

2.3.3 Firmware Considerations

The hardware components of firmware may be:

(a) *Read-only memories* (ROMs), solid-state memory storage devices that are programmed at the time of manufacture and cannot be reprogrammed.
(b) *Programmable read-only memories* (PROMs), solid-state memory storage devices that are not programmed at the time of manufacture but, once programmed, cannot be reprogrammed.
(c) *Erasable programmable read-only memories* (EPROMs), solid-state memory devices that, after being programmed, can be reprogrammed. These can include those EPROMs whose contents are erased using ultraviolet (UV) light and those that can be remotely reprogrammed using communications lines. The latter are usually referred to as *electronically erasable programmable read-only memories* (EEPROMs).

Difficulties in the identification and control of firmware are arising as the technology of erasable memories increases. Specifically, the ease with which the software component of firmware can be replaced is increasing rapidly. Currently, for selected items the software can be replaced at remote sites from communications lines. This presents challenges and concerns for the identification and control of firmware that will be covered in later chapters.

2.4 SUMMARY

Configuration management identifies, controls, and provides the status of defined end items of hardware, software, and firmware. To determine how the configuration management process is to be implemented, the processes (and associated intermediate products) must be defined and understood. In order to provide the context in which the remainder of the text is placed, this chapter has presented an overview of the development and production processes of hardware, software, and firmware from the configuration management viewpoint.

2.5 EXERCISES

1. Using Figure 2-2 as an initial top-level view of the hardware assembly process for a lawn mower: (1) list the types of engineering drawings and associated parts list identified in MIL-STD-100E associated with the processes of combining; (a) parts into subassemblies; (b) subassemblies into assemblies; (c) assemblies into units, etc.; and, (2) state the purpose of each type of engineering drawing used.

2. Repeat Exercise 1, but use ASME Y14.24-1989 in place of MIL-STD-100E.

3. Expand Figure 2-4 to show all the support software (such as operating system, compilers, and so on) that would be required to transform FORTRAN source code into executable code. Identify this support software using actual vendor names that would be required on an IBM PC clone.

4. Repeat Exercise 3, but in place of FORTRAN, use (1) Ada, and, (2) COBOL.

3

CONFIGURATION MANAGEMENT PLANNING

The first step in managing a collection of items is to plan the activities that should be done. As shown in Figure 1-2, the process of configuration management planning is one of the five subprocesses of configuration management. As a process (or subprocess), configuration management planning is the determination of who is going to do what, when, where, and how. This is then expressed in written form in a configuration management plan with its supporting procedures.

3.1 WRITE THE CM PLAN

The normal course of action in defining what is going to be done and how it will be accomplished is to write a plan. In this case, a configuration management plan is written for each project. The configuration management plan establishes the detailed specifics of what is to be done for a particular project. The plan builds a foundation for configuration management activities on the company culture, includes by reference the existing company policies and instructions, and tailors the application of those items to contract requirements. For example, a particular customer may want to use an identification scheme that will integrate this product with the customer's organization. This identification scheme should then be identified in the configuration management plan as an item needing special treatment.

The major gain from writing the plan is the establishment of common methods of doing business. By putting them in writing, these methods are stabilized and become an easy point of reference. As a result, the configuration management manager can take time to look ahead, see what problems are coming down the pike, and solve them before they would have any effect on cost or schedule.

There is a culture that states that plans are to be written only if required by the customer. As they say in the late, late movies on television when the expedition is about to start off into the deep, unexplored jungle, "that way lies only madness." The result of this failure to prepare a written plan is that the actions to be taken are then expressed only in view graphs, which change from presentation to presentation. Furthermore, failing to write a configuration management plan causes the configuration management manager to become completely absorbed in the day-to-day operations of the configuration management group; he or she is thus driven by day-to-day events in an uncontrolled manner.

3.1.1 Strategic Considerations

The process of developing a CM plan is critical to overcoming customer concerns. To some, configuration management is a service organization, the purpose of which is to maintain the integrity of the product. To others, the least mention of configuration management causes children to scream, women to faint, and brave men to turn pale. The fear is real; it is a blind unreasoning fear that some faceless bureaucrat will preclude the implementation of absolutely required changes unless endless amounts of paper are filled out, and then only with great delays.

As a result, part of the job associated with any successful configuration management operation is to sell the idea of configuration management to all those who are going to be affected. It is necessary to have top-level direct support, but more than just support is required. What is required is the general understanding and acquiescence of those who will be affected. (There will never be 100% enthusiastic approval, so it should not be expected.)

For this reason, the process of developing a CM plan becomes very important; it is one of the major ways to communicate comprehensive understanding on what should be done to maintain the integrity of the products.

One approach to ease these fears is to develop a configuration management plan, stamp it "draft" at the top and bottom of every page, and send it out for formal coordination, with a 30- to 45-day requested turnaround. Then, about 15 days after it has been dispatched, the author should make the rounds of all those who received a copy, explaining the need for a CM plan (a half-dozen briefing charts will work wonders to improve communications), and gathering comments about the CM plan. Part of the ensuing discussion will focus on control, and should include such statements as "How would you like to control it yourself up to the point that ...?" and "Oh, by the way, you will, of course, be able to delegate that control to your engineers, as long as you do it in writing."

When the comments come in, each comment should be examined in detail to see how it can be implemented. Those comments that cannot be implemented should get special treatment, as follows: (1) identify the unacceptable comments and enclose each in quotation marks, (2) underneath each one, provide a written positive response in detail, stating why each could not be implemented, (3) take the unacceptable comments and the written responses around to each of the persons whose responses could not be accepted, discuss why they could not be accepted, and attempt to gain an understanding of the basis of the original comment, (4) try to devise alternative wording to satisfy the underlying concerns leading to the comments; and finally, (5) see if the person still wishes to retain the comment. In almost all cases, alternative wording will resolve unacceptable comments.

The next step in the process is to iterate on the previous formal coordination. This implies the preparation of a package that contains: (1) the original draft that was previously circulated, (2) a copy of the revised draft (the one in which all the changes were made), with each change marked on the side of a page with a bar, (3) a list of all the changes that were made, arranged in the order in which they were implemented in the revised draft, and, (4) a list of all the comments that were provided. The accepted comments should be annotated by a reference to the change that was made, and those that were not accepted should be accompanied with detailed reasons why they could not be accepted. The entire package is then sent out for one more round of coordination, with a formal request for comments to be provided in 30 days.

Further disagreements may be resolved by talking with those who submit any further unacceptable comments. It may be necessary to refer a firm disagreement up the chain of command for a decision in those cases wherein a previous position of nonconcurrence is maintained.

3.1.2 Format Considerations

Almost any format will work as long as it contains the required contents. The best CM plan format is probably the one that was previously approved in your organization. This presents the topics to the audience in a familiar order and enables the customers to compare what had been projected to be done previously, with what is now being projected.

If the organization has not previously produced a CM plan, then consideration should be given to reviewing the several common formats that are in widespread use, comparing them and choosing the format which contains elements best suited to the organization's needs. The ones that form an initial basis for choice include:

(a) IEEE Std 828-1990, "IEEE Standard for Software Configuration Management Plans," is one of a series of software engineering standards approved by the Institute of Electrical and Electronics Engineers (IEEE). It is supported, particularly in the configuration management field, by IEEE Std 1042-1986, "IEEE Guide to Software Configuration Management," and IEEE Std 610.12-1990, "IEEE Standard Glossary of Software Engineering Terminology." IEEE Std 1042 has four example plans for software configuration management as appendices to the document itself, and these should be reviewed for applicability prior to establishing a format. These standards are particularly valuable because they are volunteer standards; as such, they reflect the consensus of concerned professionals in the field on what should be done.

(b) MIL-STD-973, "Configuration Management," April 17, 1992, specifies the format and content of a configuration management plan. The level of detail in Appendix A of that standard provides an overall structure from which to begin but is inadequate for detailed planning.

(c) DOD-STD-2167A, "Defense System Software Development," takes the approach of dispersing software configuration management planning information throughout the contents of a software development plan. While it is good that the necessity for configuration management planning information is recognized, its dispersal throughout another document is not considered preferred practice. If forced by contract to use this approach, for continuity it is recommended that the configuration management planning information be placed in an appendix and attached to the software development plan itself. DOD-STD-2167A has recently been overtaken by DOD-STD-498 which refers back to MIL-STD-973 for CM matters.

Appendix D provides an example project CM plan to further ease the pain of composition.

3.1.3 Contents

As noted above, the first choice to be made for a configuration management plan is the coverage; specifically, is the plan going to cover hardware, software, or firmware, two of them, or all three? The coverage will determine the format to some extent, but with the exception of the first section, the material can be placed in any reasonable logical order.

3.1.3.1 Introduction

In writing any configuration management plan, the following items should be covered in the introduction section:

(a) The purpose of the document should be clearly stated at the very beginning of the document. This allows the reader of the plan to quickly determine whether the document is of interest. Often, if the purpose of the document cannot be quickly determined, the response of a busy reader will be to place the document in the trash can.

(b) The second item should be the scope of the plan; what it includes and, even more important, what it does not include. If, for example, the configuration management plan is to cover software, this should be definitively stated as part of the scope. This allows the reader to determine whether the document covers material in which the reader is interested.

The scope statement is sometimes expanded to provide a definitive listing (that is, a table) of the configuration items to be controlled. If not provided as a part of the scope statement itself, such detailed identifications will be required later in the plan.

(c) References, definitions, acronyms, and abbreviations should follow. If any of these are very lengthy, they should be relegated to appendices and an appropriate statement provided.

(d) The last item in such an initial section would be an introduction to the remainder of the document, identifying each section and appendix with a short statement about the contents of each.

By placing these items in an initial section, the document becomes immediately useful to readers who, depending on their needs, can either read the plan itself in depth or proceed directly to the specific areas of interest.

3.1.3.2 Organization

The CM plan is to serve many readers, not all of whom will be familiar with all the organizational nuances of the company. To place this plan in perspective for all readers, a section is needed to identify the top level of the company organization, the top level of the organization of the project that this effort is to support, and the supporting organizations (for instance, drafting, quality assurance, and data management). This should include pinpointing the individuals (including location and telephone number) in those organizations who have been designated as the responsible individuals for this project and, even better, the individuals who have responsibilities that interface with the configuration management aspects of this project. Some organizations are very large; much time can be spent attempting to discover the specific individual to handle a particular problem.

One of the important elements to cover in detail is the portion of the company's organization that provides common configuration management support across the entire company. For example, there will probably be a department that handles drawings and supports their identification, control, and status accounting. This is normally done on a company-wide basis because of the need for a common interface between the drawing community and the factory. Most likely, there will be a department that handles duplication and distribution of data. There may also be a common computer library established to store archival data for the entire organization. All of these organizational details are important; all should be identified in the plan and put into writing so that later, when someone else is performing a configuration management action, the learning time can be shortened.

Having placed the entire effort in perspective, the organization of the project configuration management element (the CM group) should be delineated in detail. The configuration management element can be *functionally organized* (groups assigned according to the functions to be performed) or *product-oriented* (groups assigned to support different elements). The ultimate result will probably be some mixture of the two.

A typical organization of the CM group inside a project is shown in Figure 3-1. This is functionally organized with each element of the organization responsible for specific tasks. The appearance of such a chart should not be construed to indicate that separate people exist inside each box. For a small program, one person may take care of all the CM operations; in a much larger organization the load may be such as to require several persons to perform one function (for example, change control). What this type of organization does do is to highlight the tasks to be performed. Thus, for example, if the problem reporting system is to be operated by another organization (that is, reliability engineering) then it is relatively easy to identify that function and remove it from this organization.

Figure 3-1 also illustrates another point common to most organizations; the group that handles engineering drawings and associated lists normally

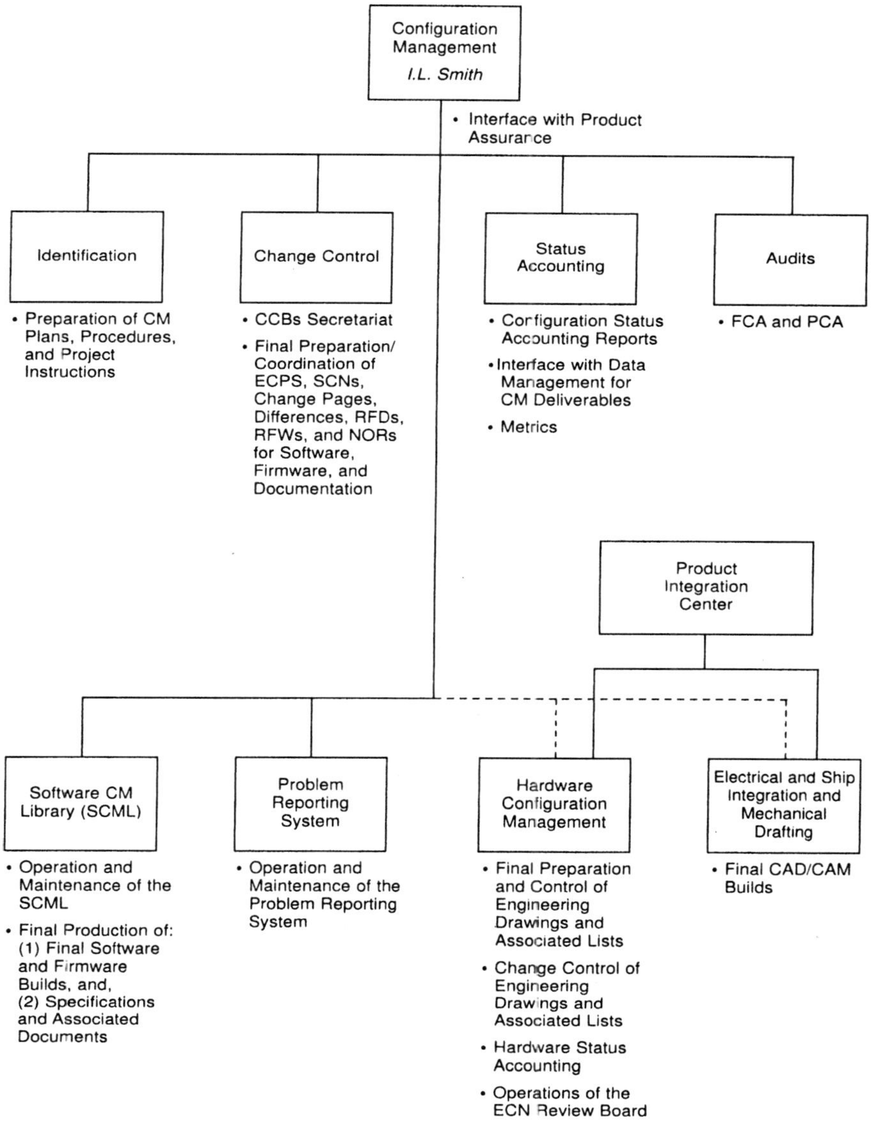

FIGURE 3-1. A Typical Configuration Management Organization.

provides support across all the projects in a particular location. In this organization the Product Integration Center (PIC) provides direct support to the project office. This direct support relationship can also exist for other functions (for example, the Problem Reporting System, the Software Configuration Management Library, and so forth) depending on the local organizational concepts.

3.1.3.3 Tasks

The next items to be defined are the tasks that configuration management is to perform. The natural way to express this is to first identify in detail the products to be managed (if not identified in detail in the scope portion of the introduction). Following that, the processes used to maintain the integrity of those products should be covered in terms of configuration identification, change control, status accounting, and audits.

Following those topics, or perhaps interposed with them, it might be appropriate to cover the other related topics (such as the problem-reporting system) which might be sufficiently large to require a separate section.

It is at this point that a series of tradeoffs should be considered. The first of these is how much detail to put into the configuration management plan and how much to relegate to the supporting configuration management procedures. As with most tradeoffs there are a number of options, and the decision on which approach to take is situation-dependent.

The first approach is to place all the details in the configuration management plan. This would go, for example, to the level of stating exactly how to complete the entries in an engineering change proposal. This is known as the exhaustive approach and is used when there might be a question of credibility on the part of those who are to review the configuration management plan. By placing all the details in the configuration management plan itself, reviewers will be confident that the person who wrote the configuration management plan did a thorough job. The difficulty with this approach is that as some of the details change, either the plan itself must be changed or a series of memos must be issued to indicate the changes.

A second approach is to relegate details, such as how to fill out an engineering change proposal, to individually named procedures. This permits the configuration management plan to be smaller and more useful as a management document. This is a better approach in a well-established configuration management culture. The danger associated with this second approach is that the plan becomes a shell with little or no specific contents that pertain to the specific project. To avoid this problem, the supporting procedures should be issued concurrently with the configuration management plan itself, and the individual who will be responsible for keeping the configuration management procedures current should be firmly identified.

3.1.3.4 Schedules

Having identified the tasks to be done, the next step is to identify when these tasks are to be accomplished. This part of the plan is very closely tied to the overall project schedule, and the configuration management milestones should track to the overall project milestones.

In this context, there are really two different types of milestones that are required. The first milestones show when a required configuration management functional capability has been achieved (for example, the production of the first configuration status accounting report, the completion of the testing on the standards-checking tool, and the demonstration of the interchange of data with the factory by transfer of electronic media). These show a capability of the configuration management system itself, and are prerequisites for what follows.

The second type of milestones are those that show accomplishment of specified project tasks (such as, completion of delivery of PROM image files for specified hardware devices).

3.1.3.5 Resources

Having stated what is to be done, how it is to be done, and the associated schedules, the next items to identify in the configuration management plan are the resources required to implement the plan. These resources include people, equipment, and space.

Defining the personnel resources needed requires defining how many people are needed, when they are needed (not all are required at the start of the project), and the associated skill requirements. In establishing these needs, one of the classic traps is considering that configuration management will be just a series of clerical tasks. The recommendation is that the resources required include the level and skills required to: (1) build small software tools (large tool efforts can be spun off to the project tools group), (2) interface tools from different vendors, and, (3) solve problems associated with the day-to-day execution of the configuration management tasks. These tasks can include everything from reformatting a configuration status accounting report and modifying the control language to allowing data to be abstracted directly from specified files to resolving why a certain compile operation did not execute properly.

Equipment will be needed to perform configuration management tasks. These are best identified as early as possible. Later, when the project has become sensitive to funding problems, declaring the need for additional items to be purchased is unadvisable. The equipment needs should dovetail with the personnel schedules and should include such things as computer terminals, desks, laser printers, file cabinets, telephones, copying machines, file cabinets, and tape racks. One way to develop a comprehensive list of these items is to make a sketch of a configuration management area, place the people in the sketch, and visualize how work will be accomplished. For example, if the nearest copying machine is located 500 yards away, a short time and motion study will show the need for a low-capability copier nearer to the configuration management area.

Space is required; it is easy to obtain at the beginning of a project, and almost impossible to obtain after projects have solidified and people have moved in. There are severe negative consequences if the configuration management people are not contiguously located (such as loss of control, inability to cross-train so that one person can do another's job in times of emergency, and lack of communication between people doing elements of a common job).

To do the configuration management job as it has been defined, adds up to a real cost in dollars. This cost, time-phased with the acquisition of the resources, should be in the plan. Assuming that the budget is approved, all is well. Now the configuration management manager has to live within the budget, which is a constant challenge. Difficulties can arise when the configuration management manager is told that the configuration management plan is approved, but the configuration management budget is being cut by some arbitrary amount. In this case, there are a number of strategies. In the best of all possible worlds, the configuration management manager would review the configuration management budget, fine-tune the estimates, find the money, and accept the cuts. In that case, all is well. (Some managers, in tune with the manner in which budgets are treated in that culture, may already have built in the money that now must be taken out.)

Difficulties can arise in those cases where the money cannot be removed without affecting the tasks to be performed. In that case, for the sanity of all concerned, the configuration management manager should revise the plan, deleting functions that, while not absolutely essential for the execution of the configuration management job as narrowly defined, would have provided assistance to the project as a whole. These could include such things as the development and use of a standards-checking tool, the development of documentation templates, and the acquisition and publication of project metrics. These tasks can be removed without serious harm to the project. In one view, the project would be run much more efficiently if these tasks were accomplished, but those who apportion the funds make the final judgment on what tasks are to be done.

If there is still a shortfall between what is required to be done and the funds to support those activities, major cuts should be considered. For example, identification and control of vendor-provided software could be deleted. This is getting very close to home and requires deep thought and careful consideration. It is best done after briefing all concerned on what is to be done so that there are no surprises. The point to remember here is that paying for a configuration management capability is akin to buying insurance. How much is to be purchased depends upon the assessment of the probability of the occurrence of the risk and the impact of a failure.

There is a school of thought that believes in continuing to promise to get the job done, no matter what funding cuts are received. This is not a recommended approach. What it states is that the original estimates have no value, and that further cuts could continue to be made without any negative consequences.

3.1.4 Special CM Planning Topics

Two topics that have been ignored in the standard outlines for CM plan are: (1) training, and, (2) metrics. These should be added to the plan.

3.1.4.1 Training

Configuration management training has several aspects. The first type of training is the recognition that configuration management is an engineering discipline which is currently only mentioned lightly in academic circles. To operate effectively, people need training; shoveling untrained people into a configuration management process as operators is unproductive.

Training comes in many layers; the initial layer is the overview of the entire process. There are many three-day courses that teach the basics of configuration management and every person assigned to the field should attend at least one of these. The short courses should be given off-site so that the training cannot be interrupted to resolve a momentary panic back at the plant.

The second type of training is organizational training. Individuals need to work together to accomplish desired ends. The organization as a whole, when first established, will be inefficient, and an allowance should be made for this factor. One successful approach to this portion of the training effort is to establish the configuration management organization, with a nucleus of people, three months prior to the actual projected need. This permits the nucleus to organize the shop, establish the detailed written procedures by which the shop is to operate, try the procedures out, and modify them to a workable solution. Configuration management procedures need to be comprehensive and complete. Establishing these procedures to the point which a person who was unfamiliar with the operation could use these procedures to produce the desired products is a time-consuming task and is best done in a no-stress environment.

The third type of training is specific tool training. Again, this is best initially done off-site at the vendor's location, and one of the primary criteria for the choice of a vendor is that such training can be done at the vendor's site. In order to avoid severe learning-curve problems as the tools are put into initial operation, this initial training must be supported by the vendor with on-call service or telephone support.

Vendor tool training should take place during the initial month of the establishment of the configuration management task, and not everyone has to go. However, the students selected should include those who will be using the tool and those who can transfer their knowledge.

A word of caution on training: no training course is perfect and all of them must rely on the students learning through application of the course material. The corollary is that training, like auto parts, should be delivered "just in time" to be applied. Otherwise, two unfortunate items can occur: (1) the people who have been through the training course may be diverted to other tasks and never apply what they have been taught—in this case the money spent on training has been wasted, or, (2) the people who have been through the training course may be assigned at some later time to the project, and may have forgotten much of what they knew when they finished the training. The bottom line is that the application of the training should take place immediately after the training course has been completed.

3.1.4.2 Metrics

Metrics are a bonus from an automated configuration management system that astute program managers can exploit. For those who are interested in metrics, the efforts of the configuration management organization provide easy access to worthwhile material. The configuration management electronic media libraries are rich sources of data and can easily be mined to obtain significant management insight, not only into the configuration management process itself, but also into the overall project operation.

A word of caution: there are a number of traps and snares associated with any metrics effort. The worst trap is to attempt to use a metrics program to produce data that is outside its range of validity and usefulness. Metrics should be used to provide indicators of where improvements can be made. For example, any metrics effort that is used as a basis for personnel actions (favorable or unfavorable) will quickly lose all validity.

3.1.4.2.1 Configuration Management Metrics

In terms of configuration management, process metrics are directly available. This is concerned with the intermediate products produced by the configuration management group and help to define the workload groups. This includes such items as: (1) the number of changes processed by the configuration management group and the status of these changes plotted against time, and, (2) the number of problem reports and the status of these problem reports plotted against time.

3.1.4.2.2 Project Metrics

One immediate source of raw data for project metrics is the configuration management library. The configuration management library holds the source files (documents and source code). By examining the documentation source files, the following can be easily obtained:

(a) *Documentation sizes*—These sizes can be easily measured in words using any standard word-counting program (such as WC on the VAX/ VMS SHELL facility). Metrics can then be provided for: (1) individual documents (the XXX unit specification), (2) individual types of document (the total of the sizes for all the unit specifications in the project), and, (3) documents grouped by configuration item (the total of all the sizes of the individual documents produced for a specific configuration item).

(b) *Documentation changes*—These are the actual number of changes for each document identified above, where one change is defined as one formal issue in a set of changed pages to an original document. In some organizations, these are issued through the use of specification change notices or document change notices. In turn, this data can be provided by individual document (for example, ZZZ changes in the XXX unit specification) and so on.

(c) *Size of documentation changes*—These consist of the actual size, in words, for the changes for each document identified above.

With some further efforts, additional insight can be obtained on requirements stability.

In a similar manner to documentation metrics, the following source code metrics can be easily obtained:

(a) The number of source files of code, which could be further grouped by source file size (the number of source files containing less than 101 executable lines of code, the number of source files in the computer program containing more than 100 lines of source code but less than 201 source lines of code, and so on). This could be further grouped by computer program and by project.
(b) Number of revisions to source code files, where a revision is defined as the issuance of a new version of a source code file after the issuance of the initial version. This can be grouped by the source file size granularity identified above and then by the number of revisions. For example, of 440 source files, each of which contained less than 101 source lines of code, 200 were never revised, 40 were revised once, and so on. This in turn could be used to provide some in-house numbers on the validity of the speculation that more changes are made in larger source files.
(c) Actual number of source lines of code, grouped by computer program and by project.

All of this assumes the following: (1) the organization has some common set of standards for source code, (2) a standards-checking tool (computer program) is used when a source file is entered into the library, and, (3) as part of that standards-checking effort, the number of source lines of code in a source file is automatically provided.

If there is an automated problem report system, its associated metrics are easily elicited. The initial data is the number of open and closed problem reports, arranged by computer program. However, if the data on the problem report can be processed, much more insight can be obtained.

The determination of the cause of the problem is of direct interest. If we can find some objective evidence of the causes of the problems in our shops, we have a valid basis for improvements. (Pronouncements about industry-wide problems have little credibility when it comes to establishing projects to provide cures. Without an ability to provide hard data on local problems, the rest may be dismissed as idle speculation.)

Tables 12-II and 12-III provide example sets of categories that could be placed on the initial issue of a problem report form. This data, in turn, can be arranged by problem cause, by configuration item by problem cause, by project by problem cause, and so forth. More elaborate categories can be developed. The categories shown in Tables 12-II and 12-III are simple and immediately usable, and can provide a basis for more elaboration as experience is gained.

Caution should be used, however, in using data from the problem report (for example, an entry indicating the cost or time used to fix the problem). That data is notoriously inaccurate and will probably be different from the data in the cost accounting system. Reconciling this data with the cost accounting system data is a thankless task, done after the fact, and accompanied by much anguish and pain.

The data from the configuration management library can be merged with data from a cost accounting system; and, in the best of all possible worlds, this merge would be used to provide cost metrics and productivity. Details of this type of merge are beyond the scope of this text, but a few words should be said to point out what a configuration management library can offer:

(a) With a minimal effort, data on the cost can be provided by computer program and by development phase. This may take some negotiation by the project office with the cost accounting system for the entries to be made by phase by computer program; and, if so, some of the details may have to be left to the next implementation. However, the organization will now be able to determine accurately how much money is really being spent, for example, in integration and test.

(b) Near and dear to the heart of upper management is increasing the productivity of the processes. Productivity measures are required in order to do more than just talk in vague generalities. Looking at this from a very simplistic viewpoint, software people produce two things, code and documentation. Building from the previous efforts, a code productivity metric can be obtained by dividing the total number of source lines of code delivered at the end of the project by the sum of all the costs of all the software efforts (from the start of the preliminary design phase through the completion of the computer program testing phase). A documentation productivity metric can be computed in a similar manner.

Rework metrics are well-recognized in hardware quality assurance and have become a popular topic in the software field. As possibilities, consider the following preliminary definitions:

(a) *Requirements rework*—This is computed by dividing the current sum of the requirement specifications size changes by the sum of the sizes of the requirement specifications that were initially established as part of the allocated baseline.

(b) *Interface rework*—This is computed by dividing the current sum of the interface specification documentation size changes by the size of the interface documentation that was initially established as part of the allocated baseline.

(c) *Code rework*—This is computed by dividing the total number of revisions to all the source files of code by the total number of source files that completed their initial tests.

Others can be developed (for example, test documentation).

The bottom line to all this is that, assuming the configuration management operation has a minimal library on electronic media, the project office can piggy-back onto those efforts to obtain meaningful management metric indicators. From those metrics, significant insight can be gained on where to apply further effort to make substantial improvements in the project's operations.

3.1.5 CALS

CALS (or Computer-aided Acquisition and Life-Cycle Support) is an initiative that originated with the US government in 1985 and has since spread to Europe and the Pacific Rim. Its purpose is to automate the millions of pages of technical data and drawings needed to support weapons systems by providing a common digital data base on the design, development, manufacturing, distribution, and manufacturing of products. This common digital data base is being provided by developing: (1) standards for storage and exchange, and, (2) automated systems to store, manage, and distribute this technical information.

The interest of the CM community in this effort is in two parts: (1) for those who are involved in this initiative, this will be an order-of-magnitude increase in workload for CM, and, (2) for those who use MIL-STD-973, Section 5 in the CM plan format in Appendix A of that standard has been set aside to cover CALS actions.

For more details on CALS, reference should be made to two periodicals: the *CALS/CE Report*, and the *CALS Journal*. The April 1994 issue of the *CALS Journal* is a reference issue and includes organizations, telephone numbers, and so forth of those involved with CALS.

3.2 DEVELOP THE SUPPORTING CM PROCEDURES

The purpose of CM procedures is to ensure that the actions taken to maintain the integrity of the products are performed in an objective, repeatable manner. In this context then, CM procedures can be placed into three different categories. The first are those procedures that deal with the flow of CM actions outside the CM organization, such as problem report flows, composition and operation of configuration control boards, and so on. These are necessary for the efficient implementation of business. Otherwise, the CM personnel will be taking much time to repeatedly tell individuals, for example, how to initiate a problem report rather than to provide an abbreviated response and a copy of the appropriate procedure.

The second type of procedures are those that state the flow of work inside the CM organization; for instance, these show how to put together a software change package or a version description document. These can be involved topics and work proceeds much faster when there is a written document to which the workers can refer if there is a question. The existence of the written document also helps ensure that there is only one answer to a question, and that if the answer is incorrect, there is a manner to ensure that future answers are correct.

The most difficult procedures to write and yet those that are most needed, are those that deal with specific CM tool activities. For example, given CM tool XYZ that compares two graphic documents and provides an overlay of the changes, a detailed step-by-step procedure at the level of "Enter the directory name" will preclude much anguish on the part of all concerned.

There are two approaches to writing procedures: the first (and the one that we all started off doing) is to write the procedures as they are needed. This has the benefit that no effort is wasted in writing unneeded procedures. The disadvantage of this is that the procedures are being written in the stress of the moment when many other things need to be done. As a result, conflicts arise and there is always an incentive to delay writing the procedures (or their review and correction) while the immediate work is done. As an example of preventing problems before they occur, the CM organization needs to establish a standard way of naming source files of documentation. For instance, long before the files are ready to come into the SCML, the originators are going to be working on the documents. If, all of a sudden, after much work has been done on the part of the users (files have been named and developed), a file-naming procedure is established requiring the users to rename their files, much resistance can be expected.

The second way is to look ahead and see what procedures are going to be needed and plan the development of those procedures as part of the overall CM planning. This permits the procedures to be identified in the CM plan and the effort to produce them can be allocated in a meaningful manner. It also provides a certain amount of publicity so that others are not surprised when the procedures do emerge.

3.3 GENERICS

The next step in process improvement, after writing several project CM plans and supporting procedures, is to prepare a generic CM plan and a set of generic CM procedures that could be tailored and adapted to meet individual project needs. This requires an investment (as it is not being done on project funds) and considerable thought; however, it will result in overall savings to the individual projects as it is much more cost-effective to tailor downward than it is compose from scratch.

This effort is normally produced in four increments: (1) a plan for producing a generic CM plan, (2) the generic CM plan itself, (3) a plan for producing the generic CM procedures, and, (4) the generic CM procedures themselves. Appendix E provides an example of a plan for producing a generic CM plan while an example generic CM plan itself, is provided in Appendix F. The plan for producing a generic CM plan is easily modifiable to provide a plan for producing the generic CM procedures and so is not provided herein. Tables 3-I through 3-VI provide shopping lists of procedures for a large project arranged by topic. Caution should be used in reviewing this list. Not all of these procedures will be required for all projects and certain of the procedures could be very easily combined in the implementation.

3.4 SUMMARY

Initiating the work leading to the establishment of a configuration management activity is best done by preparing and coordinating a configuration management plan. The plan can vary by coverage of the type of product being covered (hardware, software, or firmware), format, and other considerations. Overall, the plan should state who is going to do what, when,

TABLE 3-I. GENERAL CM PROCEDURES

No.	Title
1.	General instructions

where and how, and should provide a firm basis for the actions to follow. To help the writer, an example of a plan is provided in Appendix D of this text.

Three different types of training will be required for those who will be operating the configuration management system: overview training, so that all know what configuration management is and what they are to accomplish; organizational training, so that the individuals merge their specific efforts to achieve the organizational goals; and training on specific tools.

Establishing a configuration management operation provides an opportunity to provide management metrics at little or no cost, as a by-product of the on-going CM activities.

After the CM process has stabilized inside an organization and a number of project CM plans and associated procedures have been developed, the overall process can be improved by developing a generic CM plan and associated generic CM procedures that could then be tailored to fit the nuances of specific projects.

TABLE 3-II. CONFIGURATION IDENTIFICATION PROCEDURES

No.	Title
101.	Establishment of project baselines
102.	Establishment of the developmental configuration
103.	Types of software to be managed in each category
104.	Configuration item identification
105.	Configuration documentation identification
106.	List of configuration documentation
107.	Software external identification
108.	Software internal identification
109.	External labeling
110.	Engineering release of software
111.	SCML organization
112.	Processing new software into the SCML
113.	Processing approved changes into the SCML
114.	Releasing products from the SCML
115.	Version description documents
116.	Archiving products

TABLE 3-III. CONFIGURATION CONTROL PROCEDURES

No.	Title
201.	Change approval authorities
202.	Format and content of problem reports
203.	Processing of problem reports
204.	Format and content of preliminary ECPs
205.	Processing of preliminary ECPs
206.	Format and content of advance change study notices
207.	Processing of advance change study notices
208.	Format and content of notices of revisions
209.	Processing of notices of revisions
210.	Classification of changes
211.	Format and content of ECPs
212.	Processing of class I ECPs and VECPs
213.	Processing of class II ECPs
214.	Format and content of proposed specification change notices
215.	Processing of proposed specification change notices
216.	Format and content of proposed change pages
217.	Processing of proposed change pages
218.	Format and content of proposed software change packages
219.	Processing of proposed software change packages
220.	Format and content of requests for deviations
221.	Processing of requests for deviations
222.	Format and content of requests for waivers
223.	Processing of requests for waivers
224.	Format and content of approved specification change notices
225.	Processing of approved specification change notices
226.	Format and content of approved change pages
227.	Processing of approved change pages
228.	Format and content of configuration documentation revisions
229.	Processing of configuration documentation revisions
230.	Format and content of installation completion notices
231.	Processing of installation completion notices
232.	Format and content of approved revised source files
233.	Processing of approved revised source files
234.	Establishment of CCBs

TABLE 3-IV. CONFIGURATION STATUS ACCOUNTING PROCEDURES

No.	Title
301.	Format and content of CSA reports
302.	Processing of CSA reports
303.	CSA reporting frequency and distribution

TABLE 3-V. CONFIGURATION AUDIT PROCEDURES

No.	Title
401.	Preparation and conduct of in-process audits
402.	Preparation and conduct of functional configuration audits
403.	Preparation and conduct of physical configuration audits

TABLE 3-VI. METRICS PROCEDURES

No.	Title
501.	Format and content of CM metrics
502.	Preparation of CM metrics
503.	Format and content of project metrics
504.	Preparation of project metrics

3.5 EXERCISES

1. Provide a comparison of the four example CM plans in IEEE Std 1042 and contrast them with each other and the requirements in IEEE Std 828.

2. Estimate the effort required to produce the CM procedures identified in Table 3-II.

3. *Situational Problem:* You are the CM manager of an organization that is developing a variety of projects. Your manager calls you in and states that Project XYZ, a development project of 45 people engaged in developing a sensor control system, has just realized that they need CM. They are a year into a three-year development project and about to start

the detailed design of the hardware and the software. Various anomalies have arisen on the project which brought the need for CM to the Project Manager's attention: (1) there have been a series of changes in the system specification and no one knows how these relate to the current work, (2) the software used to date to develop the documentation will not load in the vendor's new version of the word-processor, and, (3) a series of uncoordinated changes have been approved for the software and hardware products and it now appears that they are incompatible. She has to attend a meeting with her manager in 45 minutes and would like to have your approach to correcting this problem on her desk in a half-hour.

REQUIREMENT: Provide a detailed creditable approach to resolving this problem.

4. *Situational Problem Continued:* Your manager has come back from the meeting with her manager. Your approach (provided for in Exercise 3) has been approved. Your manager now needs you to plan the costs and schedules (including personnel loadings) associated with your solution. They should be time-phased, keyed to the tasks that you proposed, and on her desk in the morning for her approval (and for forwarding to her manager).

   REQUIREMENT: Provide the detailed costs and schedules to implement your approach. The costs should be time-phased and keyed to the tasks previously identified.

5. Repeat Exercise 3 for a development project of seven people.

6. Repeat Exercise 4 based on the approach identified in Exercise 5.

4

CONFIGURATION IDENTIFICATION

The second step in managing a collection of items is to uniquely identify each one. As shown in Figure 1-2, the process of *configuration identification* is one of the five subprocesses of configuration management. As a process (or subprocess), configuration identification is the selection of the items and the documents that will comprise baselines for the system and for the configuration items involved, as well as the numbers to be affixed to the items and documents.

The purpose of the configuration identification subprocess is to incrementally establish and maintain a definitive basis for control and status accounting for configuration items throughout its life cycle. This subprocess flow is depicted in Figure 4-1. The numbers on the right-hand side of each box in Figure 4-1 identify the subsections where details on each of these subprocesses are provided. Subsequent chapters will cover topics associated with specific identification of hardware, software, firmware, and documentation.

4.1 ESTABLISH BASELINES AND DEVELOPMENTAL CONFIGURATIONS

The term *baseline* was originally used as an engineering surveying term. In that context, it was simply an established line whose direction and end points were fixed so that further extensions into unmapped areas could be made.

In the configuration management sense, a baseline is a document, or a set of documents, formally designated and fixed at a specific time during a CI's life cycle. However, the original concept still holds. Establishing baselines extends the orderly development of the system from specifications to design documentation, and then to the hardware and software items themselves.

In practice, a series of different baselines are established to permit an ordered flow of development work. Typically, as shown in Figure 4-2, four baselines are established in each project: functional, allocated, developmental configuration, and product. From a configuration identification viewpoint, the questions associated with each baseline are: what are the components of this baseline (documents or other products), and when are they established? The answers to each of these questions may vary from organization to organization and from project to project, but a typical set is shown in Table 4-I. Each one of these baselines is further discussed in the material that follows.

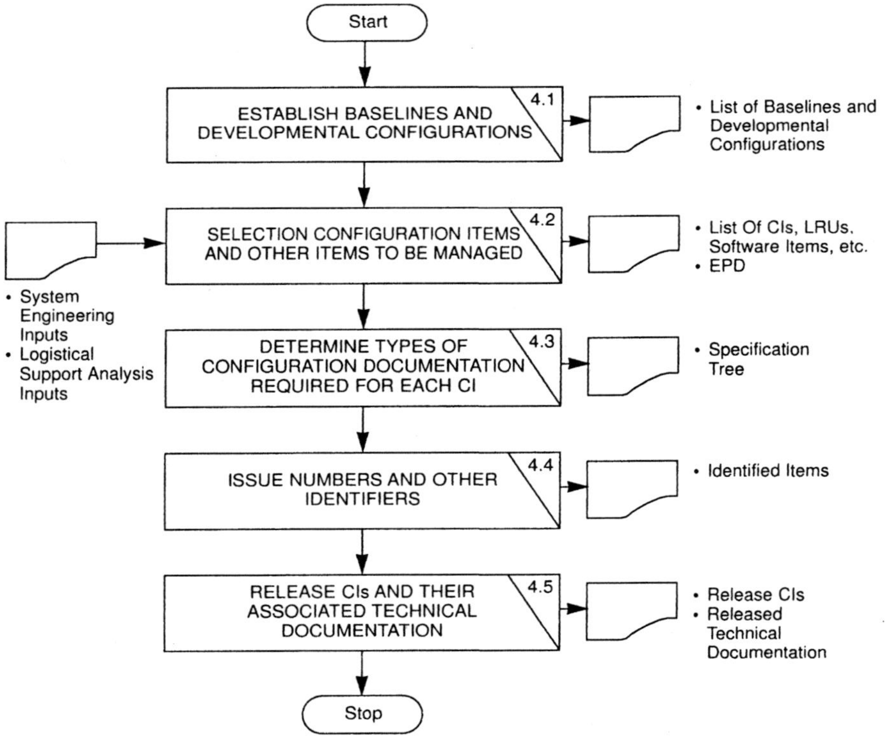

FIGURE 4-1. Configuration Identification Subprocess Flow Diagram.

4.1.1 Functional Baseline

The *functional baseline* is the initially approved documentation that describes a system's or an item's functional characteristics, and the verification required to demonstrate the achievement of those specified functional characteristics. This is the initial baseline to be established on a project and usually consists of the *system specification*, a document that establishes the technical characteristics of what the total collection of all the hardware and all the software is to do. (The term *functional baseline* is used because this baseline describes the functions that the system, acting as a whole, is to perform.)

The functional baseline is a part of the formal agreement between a customer (or user) and the developer. From this functional baseline, further efforts are to be made by the developer to partition the system into *hardware configuration items* (HWCIs) and *computer. software configuration items* (CSCIs).

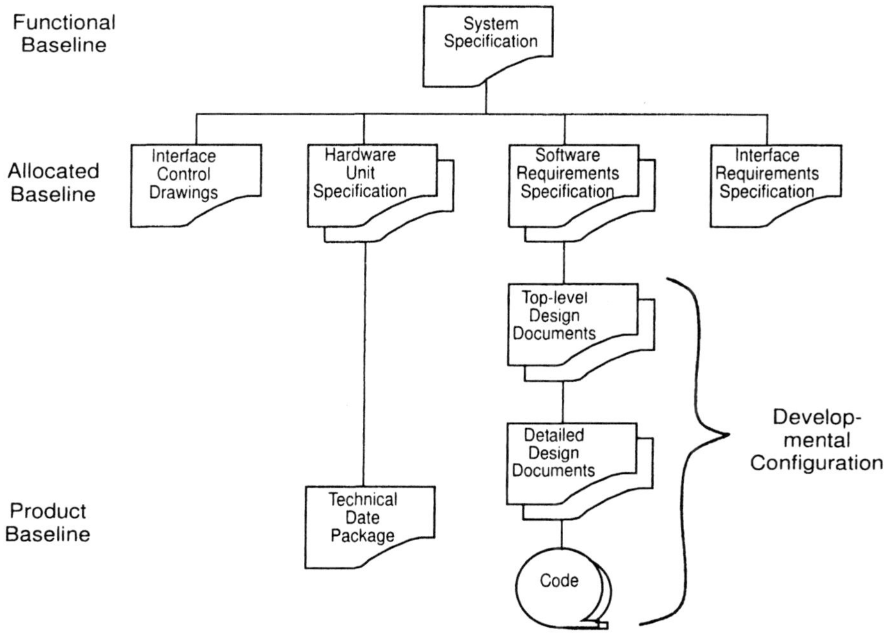

FIGURE 4-2. Typical Project Baselines.

The functional baseline is normally established at the time of contract award, although it can be established at a specified review after contract award.

4.1.2 Allocated Baseline

The *allocated baseline* is the initially approved documentation that describes: (1) an item's functional and interface characteristics that are allocated from a higher-level configuration item, (2) interface requirements with interfacing configuration items, (3) design constraints, and, (4) the verification required to demonstrate the achievement of those specified functional and interface characteristics.

Assuming that a system specification has been established, the total system requirements will normally be allocated to hardware and software items. These requirements are then collected into a series of documents

TABLE 4-I. ESTABLISHMENT OF TYPICAL PROJECT BASELINES

Baseline	Content	When Established
Functional	System specification	Contract award
Allocated	Unit specification	Negotiated, but not later than the critical design review
	Interface control drawings	
	Software requirements specification	Software requirements review
	Interface requirement specification	
Developmental configuration	Software top-level design documents	Preliminary design review
	Software detailed design documents	Critical design review
	Source, object, and executable code	Unit test
	Critical item product fabrication specifications	Critical design review
	Engineering drawings and associated lists	When released
Product baseline	Software design documents	Physical configuration audit
	Source, object, and executable code	
	Technical design package	

called the *allocated baseline* (as the requirements have been allocated to them from the system specification). The process by which this allocation is made, modeled, and verified is called *system engineering* and is beyond the scope of this book.

The allocated baseline consists of two types of documents:

(a) Specifications for the items themselves—For hardware, these are called *unit specifications* (or *critical item development specifications*); for software, these are known as the *software requirements specifications* (SRSs). These specifications describe each of the essential requirements (functions, performances, design constraints, and attributes) of each hardware and software configuration items, one specification per configuration item.

(b) Interface requirements documents—There are two types of these documents: *interface control drawings* (ICDs), and *interface requirements specifications* (IRSs). The interface control drawings identify the hardware interfaces between the hardware configuration items; the interface requirements specification identify the interfaces between the software configuration items. Collecting the interfaces into these documents avoids the duplication and confusion that would result if these interfaces were stated (and duplicated) in each of the unit specifications and software requirement specifications. There is normally one interface requirement specification and one set of interface control drawings per system.

Each of the unit specifications and software requirements specifications, together with the associated interfaces, is a formal agreement between specific management elements (for example, between a project manager and a software manager) stating the functional requirements that a particular configuration item will meet when completed. The individual elements of the allocated baseline are normally established on the successful conclusion of specific reviews covering those items (for software, this is sometimes called the *software specification review*). From a configuration management viewpoint it is not important that the reviews have particular names, or even that such reviews be held (although it is considered good practice); the important thing is that there are distinct events after which changes to specific documents will be made in a controlled and accountable manner.

4.1.3 Developmental Configuration

The *developmental configuration,* based on the contractor's software and associated technical documentation, defines the evolving configuration of a hardware or software configuration item under development. This is under the development contractor's configuration control and describes the configuration at any stage of the design, coding, and testing effort.

The developmental configuration applies to both hardware and software development. This is an internal baseline established to facilitate control of internal development activities. Current practice is to implement the developmental configuration in a phased manner as the individual components achieve specific values.

As shown in Table 4-I, the developmental configuration is established incrementally. Items of the developmental configuration are baselined when they are reviewed with others. The reasons for this are that substantial efforts have been made as part of these reviews, and the results reflect agreements reached with other parties. As such, some means of identifying the reviewed documents (and tracking their changes) is required, even though the documents remain under the control of the originating organization.

The developmental configuration is initially established with the top-level design documents at the time of the *preliminary design review* (PDR); the detailed design documents are processed in the same manner at the time of the *critical design review* (CDR), and the source, object, and executable code are added as their unit tests are completed.

There are many choices in how to document the design, and the specific choice is usually project-specific. The documents shown in Table 4-I should be considered only as representative design documents. The concept, however, is that as the software evolves inside the software development activity, portions of this software gain increasing value and should be stabilized and controlled in a reasonable manner.

4.1.4 Product Baseline

The *product baseline* addresses three issues: the initially approved documentation that describes all the necessary functional and physical characteristics of the configuration item; any required interoperability characteristics of a configuration item; and the selected functional and physical characteristics designated for production acceptance testing. For hardware, the product baseline typically consists of the technical data package (engineering drawings and associated lists, and all the rest of the items necessary to ensure that the hardware products can be fabricated by a third-party manufacturer). For software, the product baseline includes the software code on electronic media and the other items (for example, software tools and documentation) required to ensure that the code can be reproduced and maintained.

The product baseline is established on the completion of a formal acceptance testing of the system and on the completion of a *physical configuration audit* (PCA). (A PCA is a technical examination of a designated configuration item to verify that the configuration item, "as built," conforms to the technical documentation that defines the configuration item.) The product baseline replaces the other baselines, and is usually formally delivered to the customer.

4.1.5 Baseline Variations

There are a number of variations in baselines:

(a) On large projects, as shown in Figure 4-3, a system specification may be initially partitioned into subsystem specifications, which are then further allocated to configuration items. The subsystem specifications and their associated interface control documents and interface requirements specifications constitute a separate baseline. It should be noted that this results in two levels of interface documents. The first level establishes the interfaces between the subsystems. This allows each subsystem to be built by a separate group, independent of the construction of the other subsystems. The second level documents the interfaces that exist inside a specific subsystem.

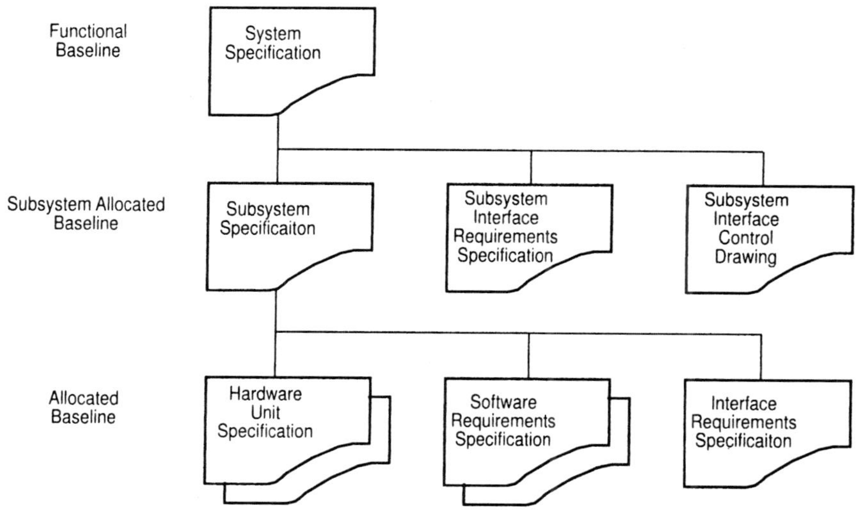

FIGURE 4-3. One Baseline Variation.

(b) On smaller projects, there may be no system specification. The agreement with the user may be to produce a software program or a specific hardware item. In this case, the requirement specification for that item becomes the functional baseline, and there will be no allocated baseline.

(c) As previously noted, requirements for the software portion of firmware are normally an allocation from a hardware unit specification. In such case, as shown in Figure 4-4, the firmware requirement specification can become a firmware allocated baseline.

Depending on the complexity of the effort, additional baselines may be established. For example: (1) a subsystem baseline may be established

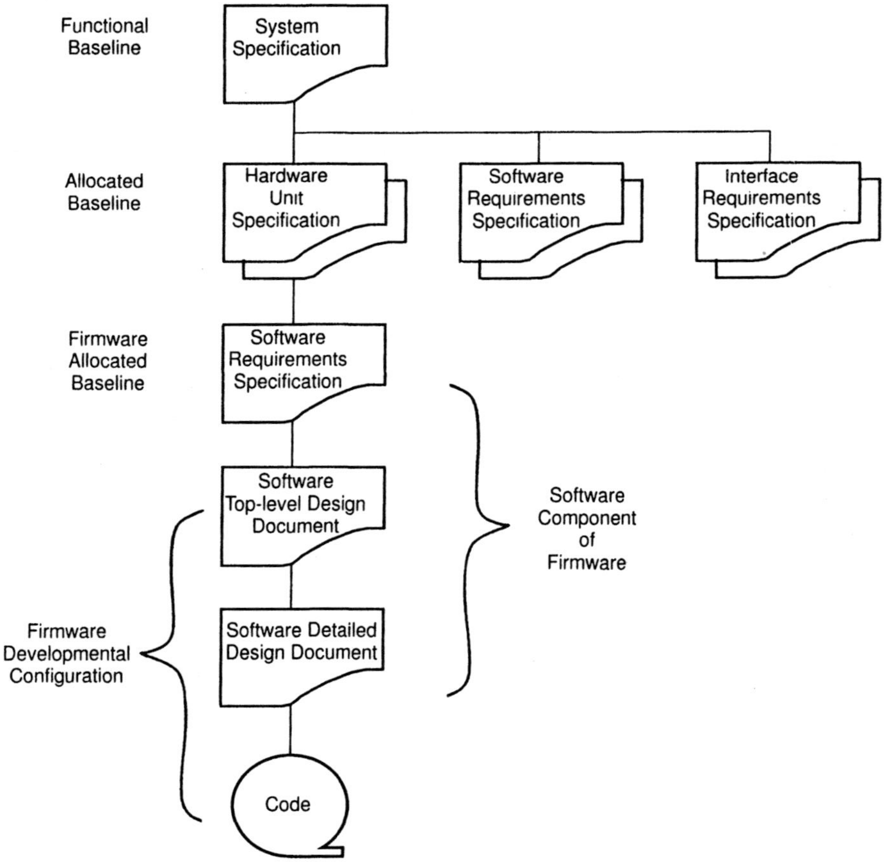

FIGURE 4-4. A Second Baseline Variation.

(between the functional baseline and the allocated baseline) to provide a controlled definition at the subsystem level, and/or, (2) a test baseline may be used when products are transferred across organizational boundaries.

4.2 SELECT CONFIGURATION ITEMS AND OTHER ITEMS TO BE MANAGED

This step bases its input on information taken from both the system engineering disciplines being applied to the project and the application of an integrated logistic support approach.

4.2.1 System Engineering Inputs

As part of the system engineering efforts, the system will be broken down into configuration items. Furthermore, the overall system engineering methodology to be used for this contract will dictate how the requirements for the configuration items will be stated and how the design is to be documented.

4.2.2 Integrated Logistics Support Inputs

Integrated logistics support is a term applied to the composite of all the support considerations necessary to ensure effective support of the items (system) throughout the life cycle. This includes such things as operator and maintenance manuals, spare parts and spare assemblies, provision for different levels of repair facilities, and so forth.

Two items from the integrated logistics support (ILS) efforts affect the configuration identification process: these are the item verification levels, and the associated definitions of the *line replaceable units* (LRUs). For example, depending on the integrated logistics system efforts, a particular hardware item (such as a radio), may be broken down into five line replaceable units. One line replaceable unit may be a power supply, which, if it fails, is replaced as a unit on a plug-in, plug-out basis. Each line replaceable unit will be assigned a unique serial number to permit unique identification of the line replaceable unit as it flows through the logistics system.

4.2.3 Process Outputs

The outputs of the process yields all of the configuration items in the form of a list and also in a form (Equipment Planning Diagram) that depicts their associated relationships.

4.2.3.1 Configuration Item List

The *configuration item list* is a list of the configuration items that will be controlled. These configuration items may be developed, purchased from a vendor, or provided by the customer for integration into the resulting system. The configuration items may be deliverable items under the contract or used to produce the deliverable items.

Table 4-II is an example of a configuration item list. In this table, the hardware configuration items are listed first, in alphabetical order, followed by the software configuration items. Acronyms and/or numbers may be used in documents and figures when the full names of the configuration items might be awkward.

4.2.3.2 Equipment Planning Diagram

An *equipment planning diagram* (EPD) is used to show the breakdown of a system into its software and hardware CIs, and deeper into its lower-level hardware components. The EPD is an engineering drawing prepared in a block diagram or an automated format which shows the assembly (top-down breakdown) in "family-tree" relationships of a system, set, group, unit, and so on, or a portion thereof. An EPD does not normally show the breakdown of software CIs for reasons that are discussed below.

An example of an equipment planning diagram is provided in Figure 4-5. This is usually an ancillary drawing prepared for management control and configuration management purposes and is produced in this example in a standard drawing format with a total of eight sheets, three of which are shown in the figure.

(a) Sheet 1 provides an explanation of the notations used on the other sheets. All of the terms are self-explanatory, except for the term *expanded work breakdown structure* (EWBS), which is an expanded form of the project work breakdown structure. (The expansion is made to take the work breakdown structure itself down to lower levels of identification.)

TABLE 4-II. STEAM POWER CONFIGURATION ITEMS

Name	Acronym	Number
Disk	DISK	7-10-4010
Processor	PROC	7-10-4020
Real-Time Control	RTC	7-10-5010
Support	SPT	7-10-5020

Work breakdown structures are an application of the same techniques used to decompose and specify functional requirements. The tasks are categorized into smaller tasks, which, in turn, are categorized into still smaller tasks until an appropriate level of granularity is reached. Concurrently, an alphanumeric identifier is assigned to each element and its subordinate elements. These identifiers provide an easy method of identifying tasks, and the funds allocated for and expended on each task. The *work breakdown structure identifiers* (often called *work breakdown structure numbers*, even though they can be alphabetic characters) are then used to provide a simple method of correlating schedule and cost information.

The equipment planning diagrams show only those portions of the work breakdown structure that refer to products. The work breakdown numbers are expanded in the equipment planning diagram to carry the identification of those items as belonging to a higher-order item already established.

Much more detail on work breakdown structures is available in MIL-STD-881, and that standard should be reviewed for an authoritative treatment.

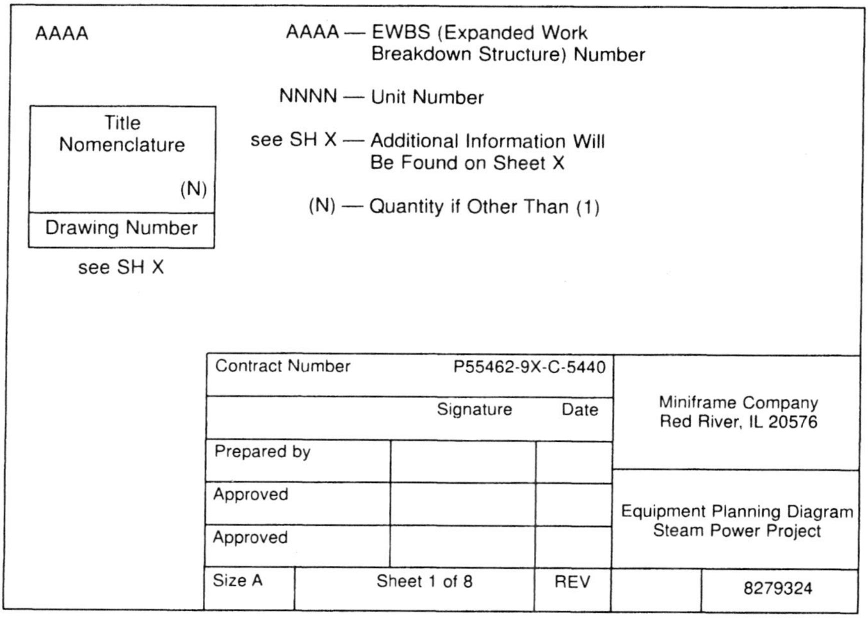

FIGURE 4-5. An Example Equipment Planning Diagram.

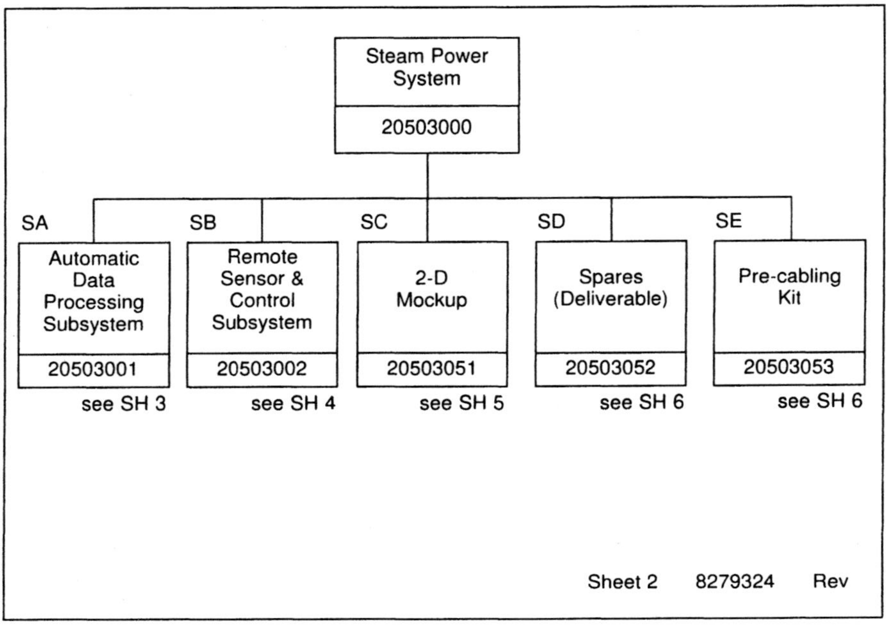

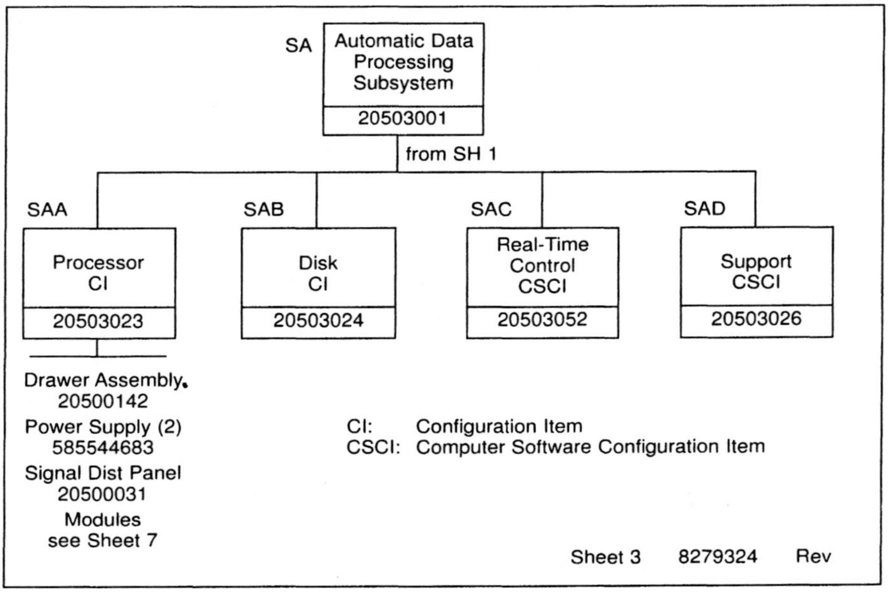

FIGURE 4-5. *(Continued)*

(b) Sheet 2 of Figure 4-5 shows an example system (the Steam Power System) at the first level of breakdown. Note that this does include items to be delivered (for example, spares), but does not include the data items identified in the contract data requirements list or the services to be provided (for example, maintenance services after delivery, or training). Note that this identifies both subsystems (such as the automatic data processing subsystem) and other items (for example, a pre-cabling kit).

(c) Sheet 3 identifies the breakdown of one subsystem into its configuration items. The components of the processor are further indicated on Sheet 3 while the disk, as an item to be purchased, is not further broken down. Two software configuration items are indicated as being part of the indicated subsystem.

Figure 4-6 shows the breakdown of hardware on a hierarchy basis and this breakdown would be reflected in the EPD as the design evolved. The

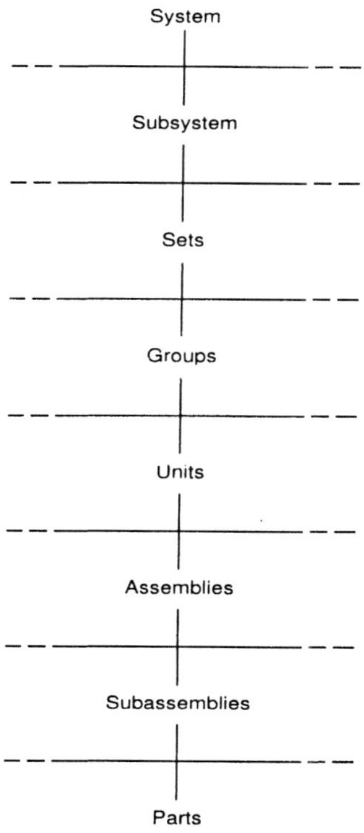

FIGURE 4-6. The Hardware Hierarchy.

correlation of a particular element of a hardware hierarchy to a configuration item (CI) is normally situation-dependent. Recognizing that a CI is defined as an aggregation of hardware or software that satisfies an end use function and is designated for separate configuration management, CIs could correspond to sets, subsystems, or systems, all three of which meet the criteria of satisfying an end use function.

CM of hardware shown in Figure 4-6, identifies and controls items at all the levels. This is not so for software. As noted above, an EPD does not normally show the breakdown of CSCIs because of the differences in views between the design hierarchy and the implementation hierarchy of CSCIs. Figure 4-7 depicts the following:

(a) In the CSCI design hierarchy, CSCIs consist of:

   (1) One or more computer system components (CSCs) in which a CSC is a distinct part of a CSCI. CSCs may be further broken down into other CSCs and computer software units.
   (2) Computer software units (CSUs) in which a CSU is an element specified in the design of a CSC that is separately testable.

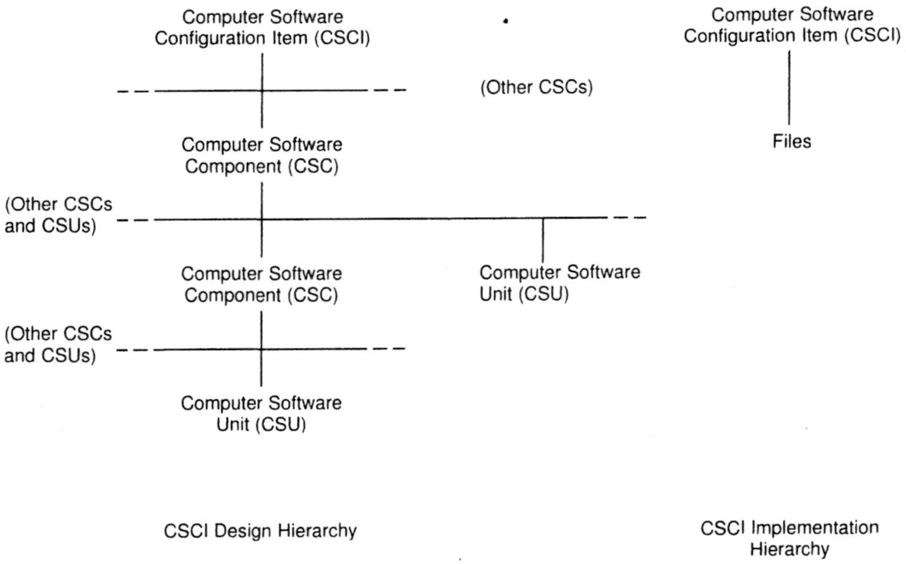

FIGURE 4-7. CSCI Hierarchies.

(b) In the CSCI implementation hierarchy, CSCIs consist of files at the lowest level at which that CM is implemented—the second level (files) is not recorded on the EPD.

The terms, CSCI, CSC, and CSU, are not universally used to indicate various levels of a design hierarchy. In some programming languages (such as Ada), terms are used that are unique to that language, whereas in at least one design methodology (Object-Oriented), different terms are used. The overall points, however, remain valid: (1) care must be used to avoid confusing software design hierarchies with software implementation hierarchies, (2) the level of CM control in the design hierarchy is normally limited to the CI (or CSCI) level, and, (3) CM control the implementation hierarchy goes down to the software file level.

There are many different ways to decompose a system, and this example should not be considered definitive. The important thing is to initiate the identification of the components early in the project in order to provide a controlled basis for changes and further categorization.

4.3 DETERMINE TYPES OF CONFIGURATION DOCUMENTATION REQUIRED FOR EACH CI

The types of configuration documentation required for each configuration item (CI) are normally determined by system engineering and are a function of the contract, the configuration baseline (for example, functional, allocated or product), the developmental configuration and other factors. Figure 4-8 provides an example overview of the items of interest.

(a) This figure shows that:

(1) The functional baseline consists of one document, the system specification.

(2) The allocated baseline consists of four different types of documents; two of which (the unit specifications—otherwise known as critical item development specifications—and the interface control drawings) detail the hardware CI requirements while the others (the software requirements specifications and the interface requirement specification) state the requirements for the software configuration items.

(3) For hardware, the developmental configuration consists of the critical item product fabrication specifications, the associated engineering drawings, and the software that flows down from the hardware specifications; (that is, the software component of

firmware). For software, the developmental configuration consists of the associated design documents and the software. Note that for the hardware, the developmental configuration also consists of the engineering drawings and associated lists that define the hardware products to be built.

(4) For hardware, the product baseline consists of the technical data package and the associated software. For the software, the product baseline consists of the product specification (normally, the design documentation) and the software.

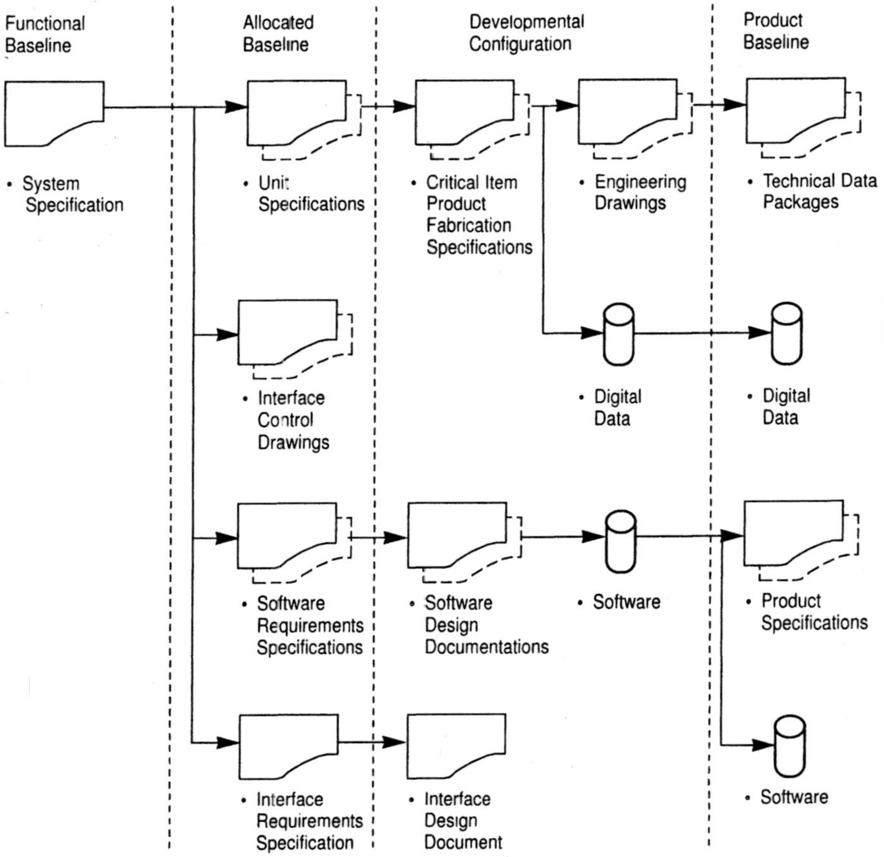

FIGURE 4-8. An Example Set of Configuration Documentation and Software.

(b) From the viewpoint of this section, two things should be noted:

(1) Software is normally a part of both the developmental configuration and the product baseline.

(2) Although not shown in Figure 4-8, any or all of the documents depicted in that figure may have been produced from software (for example, the system specification—Category VIII in Table 6-I), and that software also should be under configuration management.

4.3.1 Process Output—The Specification Tree

A *specification tree* (or document tree) is a reference diagram depicting the indentured relationships of the various specifications and other documents that define a configuration item or system. A typical example is shown in Figure 4-9. As shown therein, the system specification is the top-level document, and from that flows the specifications for the software and hardware. Below the top layer of the configuration item (software or hardware) requirements specifications may be design documents, followed by the code (for the software) and the technical data package (TDP) for the hardware.

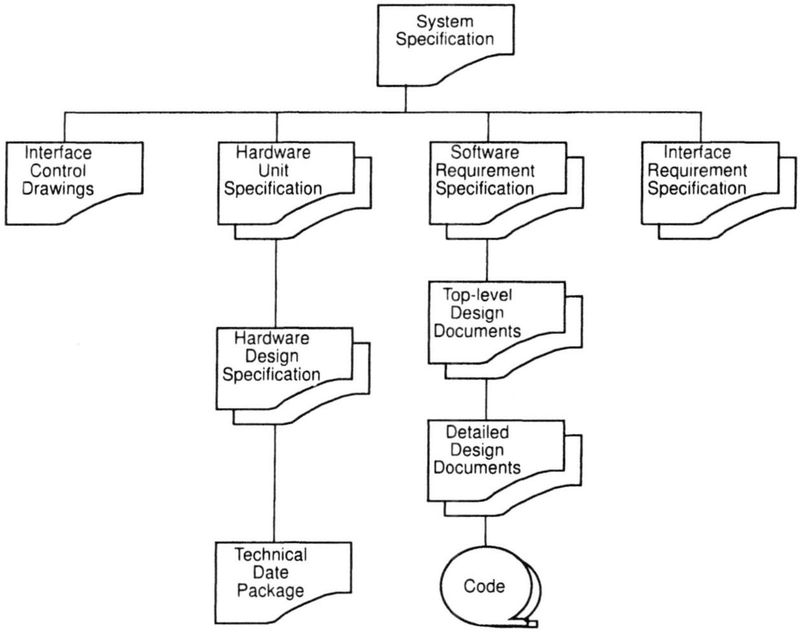

FIGURE 4-9. A Second Example Specification Tree.

4.4 ISSUE NUMBERS AND OTHER IDENTIFIERS

Five types of numbers and other identifiers are in general use:

(a) Engineering drawings and associated lists are normally identified in accordance with the requirements specified in Section 400 of MIL-STD-100E. See Section 8.1 for details.
(b) Documents other than engineering drawings and associated lists are normally marked in program-specific manners. These identifiers can be drawing numbers, CDRL numbers, unique combinations of alpha-numeric characters, or as specified by the customer. All of these identification methods are in general use. See Section 8.2 for details.
(c) Hardware items are normally identified with a *Part or Identifying Number* (PIN), in accordance with the requirements of Section 400 of MIL-STD-100E. Further marking and labeling instructions are found in MIL-STD-130G and MIL-STD-454. See Sections 5.1 and 5.2 for details.
(d) The identification of software is not as well established as hardware so a more detailed discussion is provided in Chapter 6.
(e) Firmware parts have been identified as hardware using the altered-item drawing numbers in accordance with MIL-STD-100E. As the state-of-the-art is extended into these items to allow remote programming of those parts, the situation has become more complex. See Chapter 7 for details.

4.5 RELEASE CIS AND THEIR ASSOCIATED TECHNICAL DOCUMENTATION

Engineering release is an action by which an item is officially made available for its intended use and becomes subject to configuration control procedures.

From a software viewpoint, releases are made into one or more controlled electronic or optical repositories from which controlled products are issued. To release configuration items and their associated technical documentation into a controlled electronic or optical repository requires execution of the four steps shown in Figure 4-10. This is the expansion of the fifth step in Figure 4-1 into its application of the release of software.

4.5.1 Establish The Engineering Release System For Software

Recognizing that there can be more than one intended use for an item, engineering releases are viewed as a series of actions in which a specific item might take part (for example, software could be released for a unit test, for an integration test, and for a formal qualification test). Establishing the release system for software could then require:

(a) Defining the levels at which each category of software (for example, as defined in Table 6-I) is to be released.
(b) Stating the criteria to be applied to each item to be accepted into a specific release level.

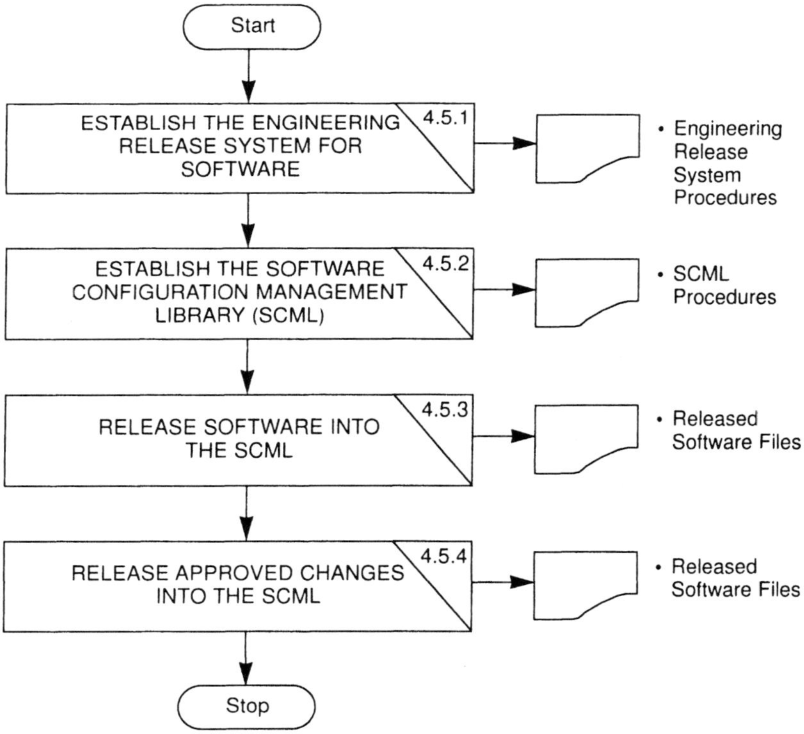

FIGURE 4-10. Configuration Identification—Release Software CIs and Their Associated Technical Documentation.

(c) Designating the persons who are authorized to release the software into specified levels.
(d) Designating the persons who are authorized to release changes to software that has been released to a specified level.
(e) Establishing the conditions under which the established procedures could be bypassed.

Table 4-III depicts an example set of release levels and authorities for one category of software, in this case, product software as defined in Table 6-I. (This is only an example and assumes a specific organization and a specific set of tests.) Table 4-III shows that:

(a) The initial release of the product software files is made by the responsible individual (RI). This release is, in essence, a judgment call on the part of the RI but will normally be based on the successful completion of a dry run of the unit test. These items are released into the software configuration management library (SCML) prior to the start of a unit test—the test by which the responsible individual demonstrates to the unit manager that the software meets its requirements. The change authority (the person who can authorize the release of changes to the software at that level) is the unit manager—it would be inappropriate to allow the RI, on a unilateral ba-

TABLE 4-III. AN EXAMPLE SET OF RELEASE LEVELS AND ASSOCIATED AUTHORITIES FOR PRODUCT SOFTWARE

Previous Release Level	Release Authority	Release Criteria	New Release Level	Configuration Change Control Authority
None	Responsible individual	None	Unit test	Unit manager
Unit test	Unit manager	Successful completion of unit test	Integration test	Integration manager
Integration test	Integration manager	Successful completion of integration test	Software acceptance test	Program manager
Software acceptance test	Program manager	Successful completion of software acceptance test	System acceptance test	Customer

sis, to change the software being tested while in the middle of the unit test. (Otherwise, people would always question the ability of the changed software to pass the previous tests—the ones that were passed by the unchanged software.)

(b) On the successful conclusion of the unit test, the software could be released by the unit manager to integration test; the integration manager would then become the person who could authorize changes to the integration test software.

(c) In a similar manner, releases are made to the software acceptance test level and then to the system acceptance test level.

The example of Table 4-III is associated with various release levels inside a developmental configuration. Eventually, this product software would be released to the product baseline.

There will be other actions that support release actions; for example, the use of configuration control boards at various release levels to recommend acceptance or rejection of changes. These other actions are part of the configuration change control process which is covered in Chapter 9.

4.5.2 Establish The Software Configuration Management Library (SCML)

Figure 4-11 provides two different views of CM libraries. One view is oriented to the products that the libraries provide (for example, documentation, drawings, and software). The second view is oriented towards the media on which the controlled items are placed. In the second view, the software configuration management library (SCML) provides controlled storage for all those items that originate from controlled software; as such, the scope of the SCML includes that portion of the software development library that is kept on electronic media and those portions of the documentation and drawing libraries whose contents originate from software.

From an operational viewpoint, SCMLs provide the ability to:

(a) Input new files. Figure 4-12 shows one way to do this that avoids the imposition of unnecessary change control procedures:

(1) The user initiates the process by placing the software and all of the associated script files that will produce its final representation (for example, engineering drawings), into a temporary controlled storage location in the SCML. The reason for using a temporary location is that should the software fail to gain ap-

proval to be released, the data can be erased from the temporary location or marked as rejected without excessive processing (for example, without producing and processing a change request).

(2) The CM group then transforms the software into its appropriate representation (for example, engineering drawings), using the script or command files (provided as a part of the software), and gives it to the user. The reason for the CM group to perform this transformation is to ensure that the product can be objectively produced by a specified process—and that the product under control is the product that is being approved.

(3) If the product (for example, the engineering drawings) does not meet the approval criteria, then the user can request the previously provided data be purged. The data would then be purged directly without rigorous record-keeping.

(4) If the product is approved for release, the CM group would move the software into permanent controlled storage. Any further changes in the software would require more formal change control actions.

(b) Restrict access and usage of specific files. Typically, this includes the capability to allow/disallow individual users to:

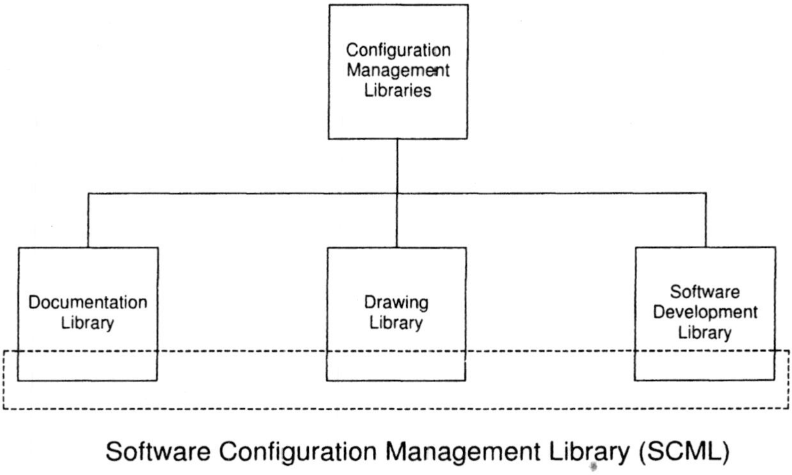

FIGURE 4-11. Categories of Configuration Management Libraries.

(1) Copy a file from the SCML to a location outside of the SCML. Unless the information is classified from a security viewpoint, this type of access is normally provided to all users.
(2) Copy a file from the SCML to a location outside of the SCML, modify the file, and place the modified file in the SCML. Placing the modified file back into the SCML is normally a function of who the change control authority is, and how much formality is required for the approval. There are a number of schemes associated with the implementation of this capability, including the use of a TRANSFER facility previously discussed, establishment of hierarchies of directories depending on usage, and the implementation of a check-out/check-in facility. Details are provided in Section 11.2.
(3) Copy a file into the SCML. This is an extension of the material covered above.

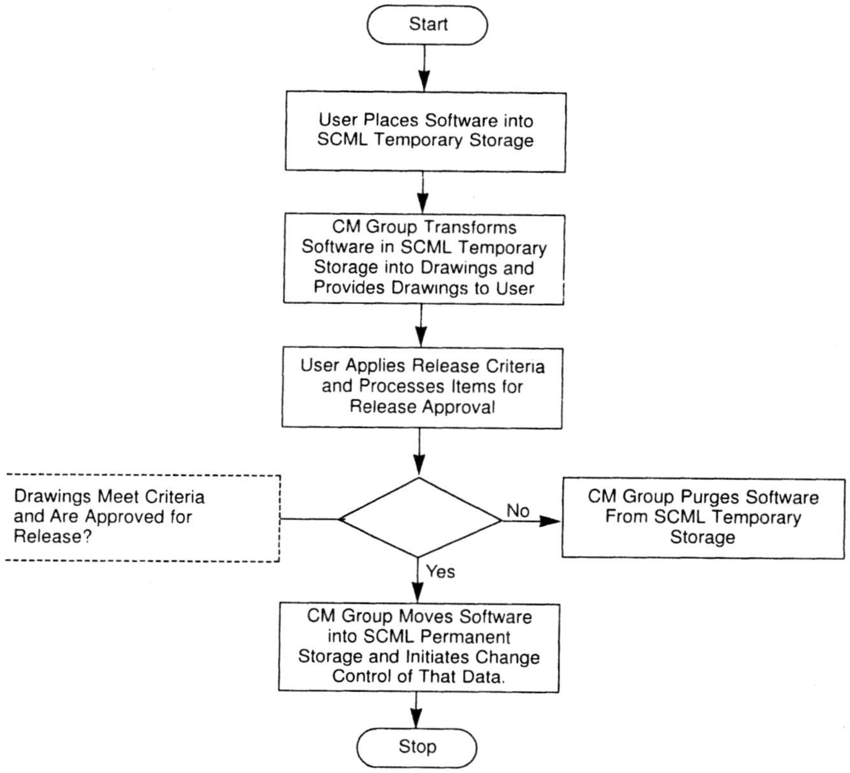

FIGURE 4-12. An Example Process for Entry of New Material into the SCML.

(4) Execute a file inside the SCML. This execution inside the SCML (using a script or command file) may be restricted to the CM group. Users who want to compile files and produce products will usually copy the files and compile outside the SCML. Copies for formal use (for example, to be used in the conduct of a formal acceptance test) will be provided by the CM group.
(5) Delete a file inside the SCML. This is usually restricted to the CM group.

(c) Designate specified files as part of a larger collection (for example, to be used as source files for a specific build). This can be done in a number of ways (for example, by tagging specific files for specific purposes, by a promotion system where files go through a hierarchy of usage, and so on).
(d) Use the support software and script files under controlled conditions to transform source and/or intermediate files into final files. This is usually termed a *MAKE* facility from the name of the associated UNIX utility.
(e) Support the reporting of problems. There are two different views of problem-reporting systems. The first view is that problem reporting is not part of a CM system. In this view, CM (the change control process) is initiated when the cause of the problem has been determined and a solution that changes an item under configuration control is proposed.

The second view is that the CM system includes problem reporting. This view is becoming more and more accepted in the area of CM of software partially because of convenience:

(1) Problem-reporting systems are usually more efficient when they are automated.
(2) It is usually considered highly desirable to provide traceability between problems and their solutions. (Of particular interest, for example, is the change that when implemented, will resolve a particular problem.)
(3) CM systems that manage software also provide tools and facilities to automate an associated problem-reporting system.

From an overall view, it is not particularly important if a problem-reporting system is part of a CM system, per se. It is important that an automated problem-reporting system be available and be integrated with the CM system. The view in this document is that CM of software includes the establishment and operation of an appropriate problem-reporting system and these aspects are covered in Chapter 9.

(f) Provide both periodic preformatted reports and on-line inquiries on the status of items in the CM library. This is in support of the configuration status accounting subprocess and is covered in Chapter 13.

4.5.3 Release The Software Into The SCML

This is performed in a manner similar to that shown in Figure 4-12.

4.5.4 Release Approved Changes Into The SCML

Changes to software already in the SCML are normally provided as revised files and are processed in a manner similar to that shown in Figure 4-12.

4.6 SUMMARY

Configuration identification is initiated with the identification of the baselines to be utilized on the specific project, and then the identification of the specific items within each baseline. Functional, allocated, developmental configuration, and product baselines are usually established, although these may be expanded to include other baselines (such as a subsystem allocated baseline), or contracted (for example, concatenated to only functional and product baselines), depending on the needs of specific projects.

Identification of the items inside each baseline requires input from other project elements; the two major disciplines identified herein are system engineering and integrated logistics.

Application of configuration identification to hardware, software, firmware, and documentation is provided in the chapters that follow.

4.7 EXERCISES

1. Identify the complete set of specification types and state the use of each. (Hint: use MIL-S-83490A).

2. Provide an example specification tree which shows at least one of each type of specifications identified in Exercise 1.

3. Prepare a flow chart depicting the functions that the UNIX MAKE utility provides.

4. Repeat Exercise 3 but for a VAX Alpha MAKE utility.

5. *Situational Problem:* You are engaged in the initial planning efforts for a development project. The project manager has just informed you that vendor-provided software is to be specified, purchased, and used on the project. The project manager asks you: (1) how the vendor-provided documentation is to be specified, (2) what baseline(s) will include these specifications, and, (3) what baseline(s) will include the vendor-provided documentation (such as technical manuals)?

   REQUIREMENT: Answer the questions and defend your choices.

6. *Situational Problem Continued*: The hardware development manager informs you that they are developing six consoles which are identical except for variations in the individual console keyboards. They do not want to designate these as separate CIs because of the cost and complexity of dealing with six different sets of configuration documentation (specifications, design documents, test plans, and so on). They want to make the situation simpler and more cost-effective and are asking for your help.

   REQUIREMENT: Provide a cost-effective solution to resolve the console documentation problem.

5

HARDWARE IDENTIFICATION

The theory of configuration identification is straightforward. Applying the theory is not always as easy as it appears. The overall goal, that of maintaining the integrity of the product, is clear; achieving that goal in the most cost-efficient manner takes thought, using different approaches in different situations. This chapter discusses the application of initial and additional identifiers to hardware, and the concerns and considerations associated with the identification of parts. Subsequent chapters will cover software, firmware, and documentation.

5.1 INITIAL IDENTIFIERS

Wander into any hardware store and you can usually buy any tool by referring to it by name. This is good and sufficient for the casual buyer, but those who restock the store's inventory will usually refer to the tool by the name of the supplier and the item number assigned by the supplier. The reason for the use of numbers rather than names is to permit precise identification and further processing by computers.

In a similar manner, pick up any catalogue and you can buy any item listed therein by the manufacturer's code and item number. However, you will encounter difficulties if you want to get the best price for a particular item from a variety of manufacturers. In that case, you will have to know all the manufacturers who make that item as well as the item number used by each manufacturer to designate that item.

In much the same way, you can buy microchips from a distributor's catalogue very easily. This requires a greater degree of knowledge of each manufacturer's product than you might really like to know, so perhaps a better approach is to use a generic item number (for example, a 68000 microchip). Unfortunately, unless each manufacturer is building the item to a controlled specification (for example, MIL-R-55182E, "Resistors, Fixed Film, Established Reliability, General Specification For," January 26, 1990), two items with the identical generic item number may have different characteristics. For instance, consider two programmable logic arrays, item number PAL16L8. The programming voltages, wave form timings, slew rates, and other parameters may vary from manufacturer to manufacturer.

To ensure that items identified by the same number have common characteristics, the government has established a series of controlled standards and specifications for items. Buying an item that meets a controlled standard or specification can be done by specifying the standard or specification number in place of the manufacturer's item number, and by buying that item (using that specification or standard number) from a qualified manufacturer.

Thus, identifying the items that we want to buy can be done, in the worst case, by using the manufacturer's code and manufacturer's item number and, in the best case, by using only the part or identifying number (usually abbreviated as PIN) that refers to the controlled standard or specification.

5.2 ADDITIONAL IDENTIFIERS

When the item is manufactured, it can start to accumulate other item identifiers. These include the identification of the manufacturer, the name of the item, the lot number, the date of manufacture, and a serial number. Each of these is discussed below.

If only the PIN has been specified (for example, the item is being procured using a standard or specification number), then the manufacturer's code will normally be inscribed. For government usage, manufacturer identifications (codes) are specified by a five-position alphanumeric *commercial and government entity* (CAGE) code and a *NATO supply code for manufacturers* (NSCM) (for example, 94117). Manufacturers' codes are also considered part of the identification number. To preclude two manufacturers having the same number for different parts, all manufacturers' codes are contained in a government handbook, *H-4*, and all manufacturers must register in order to obtain a code.

If the name has not been previously assigned (because, say, the item is new and being developed as part of a higher-level item), a name will be assigned at this time. In government usage, the name will be the same as the title of the drawing that describes the item.

Manufacturers normally produce items in *lots*; specifically, the manufacturer will produce a quantity of item 111, and then reconfigure the assembly line to produce item 112. A lot, then, is a collection of identically manufactured items that have been treated as a unique entity. If, because of some anomaly in the manufacturing process, items from a particular lot start exhibiting rapid failures, the manufacturer will want to be able to identify items that came from that lot and advise those using parts from that lot about problems. For this reason, items are usually marked with the manufacturer's lot number and date of manufacture.

Items that are repairable are usually assigned serial numbers. These provide a unique notation to identify a single unit of a family of like units, and are normally assigned sequentially. This enables unique identification of replaceable assemblies and allows each of them to be tracked through a logistics system. In this context, a *replaceable assembly* is an item which upon failure, is designed to be removed or replaced from a higher-level item. Some of these categories include *line replaceable units* (LRUs), *quick replaceable assemblies* (QRAs), *shop replaceable assemblies* (SRAs), and *bench replaceable assemblies* (BRAs).

Those engaged in government work should refer to MIL-STD-130G, "Identification Marking of U.S. Military Property," for detailed requirements and how they apply to the various levels of hardware. Recognizing that such standards change, the best course of action is to refer directly to that standard for detailed government requirements.

5.3 THE "WHERE-USED" PROBLEM

For most applications, complete identification may only be of cursory interest. For critical applications, however, if the purchased part (or purchased subassembly or assembly) is being used in which failure could affect safety or cause serious social or financial losses, complete marking could be of distinct interest.

Consider the case of an aircraft engine that fails and causes the aircraft to land in an Iowa corn field. There is an intense interest in finding out what caused the problem and taking all necessary action to ensure that the problem does not happen again. After scouring the cornfield and picking up all the available pieces, it may be determined that the engine failed due to the disintegration of a turbine. Engineering analysis indicates that the overall turbine design is sound, but that this particular turbine failed due to a flaw in the manufacturing process. The question that immediately occurs is, "Where else in that series of engines (and in other types of aircraft engines) are turbines in use that were manufactured using that flawed manufacturing process?" Identifying all the turbines that were manufactured using the defective process, and the current status of each of those turbines, can usually only be done if that configuration identification capability has already been implemented in the configuration management system.

The problem identified in the previous paragraph is a generic one, and is called the *where-used* problem. For some products, the where-used question does not apply. For others (for example, automobiles where a safety component may fail), the question applies and can lead, if nothing else, to product recalls in which potentially defective items (such as brake cylinders) will be replaced.

The where-used problem clearly reveals the need to provide additional information on the "as-built" drawings including the manufacturer's code (if not already supplied), lot number, and date of manufacture; these additional capabilities then need to be implemented in the configuration management system.

It should be noted that the where-used problem also applies to software. For example, given that a bug has been identified in a specific version of a particular source file of code, it may be necessary to provide a list of all the software products that incorporated that particular source file and their location.

The where-used problem currently poses difficulties, but consider how interesting it will become as software reuse grows. For example, consider what happens when: (1) a vendor of a group of mathematical algorithms discovers that under certain conditions, a particular release of that product produces incorrect results; (2) hardware manufacturers have purchased and incorporated those algorithms in their products as either firmware or support software; and (3) those products have been used to compute the stress loads on the wings of commercial or government aircraft. Prompt corrective action is required, and the first step is to determine which manufacturing or engineering process used that particular release, and which products were manufactured based on it.

Thus, the more detailed the identification, the easier it is to trace the product.

5.4 PARTS IDENTIFICATION

There are a number of substantial concerns associated with parts identification, and some of these are addressed in the material that follows. In reading this material, the reader should be careful to distinguish between the terms used. In other contexts, the terms may be used interchangeably; to do so in the context of the configuration management discipline will result in confusion.

5.4.1 Use of Exchangeable Items

This is an era of rapid change. As changes occur, parts and subassemblies that were being built and available for purchase at one time may suddenly become obsolete and are no longer available for purchase. Alternately, when the purchaser places orders for items on a bill of materials, it may be found that certain items, although not obsolete, are not readily available at the time desired, because, for example, the supplier's long lead-time requirements for fabrication.

To resolve these problems and to keep the production lines flowing, three types of exchangeable items in the order of the preference of their use, have been defined: interchangeable items, substitute items, and replacement items.

5.4.1.1 Interchangeable Items

When an order comes into a factory to fabricate a major assembly that the factory produced five years ago, it may be found that certain items on the bill of materials are no longer available. They are obsolete, their manufacture has been discontinued, and they are no longer available on the open market for purchase. These obsolete items have in fact been superseded by other items, which are equivalent in form, fit, and function, but are different and bear different identifiers.

When an item has been declared obsolete by the government, another item will normally be identified as the superseding item, and the superseding item is interchangeable with the obsolete item. In this context, an *interchangeable item* is one that:

(a) Possesses such functional and physical characteristics as to be equivalent in performance, reliability, and maintainability to another item of similar or identical purposes; and,
(b) Is capable of being exchanged for the other item:

(1) Without selection for fit or performance, and,
(2) Without alteration of the items themselves or adjoining items, except for adjustment.

The effect of this superseded item declaration, in the government world, is to allow free usage of the superseding item without any further requirement for government approval. This is significant in the government world, since substantial work has been expended to ensure that a particular manufacturing process using specified parts will result in a product having defined characteristics (see Chapter 15 on the functional and physical configuration audits). Changing either the approved process or the approved parts would require a revalidation to ensure that the characteristics of the final product had not changed.

5.4.1.2 Substitute Items

When a vendor cannot supply sufficient parts to meet factory deadlines, it may be necessary to substitute one part for another. For example, the vendor may not have a sufficient number of "screws, pan-head, cadmium-plated" to fill the order; therefore, a substitute part, "screws, pan-head, stainless steel" may be ordered to fill the need. The substitute part will probably cost more, but the cost of delaying production of the system outweighs the additional incremental cost of the substitute part.

In this context, a *substitute item* is an item that possesses such functional and physical characteristics such that it can be exchanged for another item only under specified conditions or in particular applications, and without alterations of the items themselves or the adjoining items.

This situation is similar to the case of superseded parts, except that substitute parts acceptable in one application may not be acceptable for use in another application. Cadmium-plated screws, for example, may not be acceptable as a substitute part in a space environment. To take a more mundane example, in an indoor application, if galvanized-iron nails are not immediately available, aluminum nails can be used as an substitute. The aluminum nails are more costly, but the consequences of stopping the job until the cheaper nails are available might be even more costly. On the other hand, galvanized iron nails, if used as a substitute for aluminum nails in an outdoor environment, will rust long before the aluminum nails do, and thus may be an unsatisfactory alternative.

The allowance for the use of substitute parts is thus job-specific and must be in accordance with the application for which the substitute part is to be used.

5.4.1.3 Replacement Items

A *replacement item* is an item that is interchangeable with another item but differs physically from the original item in that the installation of the replacement item requires operations such as drilling, reaming, cutting, filing, or shimming, in addition to the normal methods of attachment. Use of replacement items, in the context of requiring operations such as drilling to attach, is normally done only on a case-by-case basis.

5.4.2 Cost-Effectiveness Considerations

The challenge in establishing an exchangeable item capability is in its cost-effectiveness. The bill of materials, parts lists, and engineering drawings for the system, assembly, subassembly, and so on, must accurately reflect the composition of the item being built; this includes all of the part and subassembly identification marks. If parts or subassemblies change, then a revised bill of materials (revised drawing) is required, and these revisions can then ripple all the way through the entire drawing package (back into the next higher subassembly and assembly, and eventually into the system drawing). These changes, in turn, affect the supporting drawings for the installation of the assemblies—and the case then becomes incredibly complicated and very costly.

At the millennium, all drawings will be on electronic media, and automated systems will produce revised drawing packages with no further intervention. At this time, the current state-of-the-art in automated drawing control and production systems is not quite at that point at all locations. Attempting to reflect the current state of exchangeable parts can be substantial in terms of cost-effectiveness, since the cost of preparing and implementing change notices (see Section 12.2.1 for details of change notices) is considerable. The costs can further escalate over a number of years for large systems in sustained production.

5.4.2.1 Use of a Superseded Parts List

As noted above, when the government identifies an obsolete part, a superseding part is also identified. The total of these superseded parts can make quite an impressive list (about a one-inch-thick pile of computer paper). This illustrates the need to have both an efficient procedure to handle these changes and an efficient process to tell the factory what specific parts are to be used in a specific assembly. Otherwise, processing change notices will be required for every bill of materials.

Different situations may require different solutions, but one solution to this problem is to use a superseded parts list as a referenced drawing. The top-level drawing contains a standard statement which initiates a superseded parts list as a controlled drawing (a part of the drawing package). The superseded parts lists provides a "from-to" listing of obsolete parts and their replacements. As more parts become obsolete, the superseded parts list is revised under formal change control in the same manner as any other controlled drawing. Any parts on lower-level drawings, bills of materials, and so forth are automatically replaced by the indicated superseding part.

This type of scheme is normally instituted on a company-wide basis so that the cost of maintaining a current accurate list of obsolete parts and the associated superseding parts will not be duplicated in various locations inside the same company.

5.4.2.2 Identification of Substitute Parts

As noted above, if changes are going to be made to a bill of materials and/or the associated drawings, parts list, or technical data package, it can be expensive.

One approach to reducing the associated cost and schedule impact is to provide for the use of substitute parts on the bill of materials itself. This can be done, for example, by placing the substitute part identifier directly below the desired part, and placing the code "SUB" in the "quantities required" column. This indicates that no quantities are to be ordered unless the desired part is unavailable. If the desired part is not available, the bill of materials will be altered at the factory to change the SUB code to reflect the procurement of the substituted part. This change of the bill of materials can be done most efficiently if it is done as part of an integrated factory procurement system; it can also be done as one global change notice that requires only limited approvals. In particular, the changes do not have to be processed through the design activity, because the design activity has already concurred with the change. In effect, the appearance of the SUB designation on the bill of materials delegates the authority to make the change to the procurement function without further approvals being required.

5.4.3 Identification of Screened Parts

Parts or subassemblies are normally purchased in bulk and tested for compliance to specifications using statistical testing techniques. In that implementation, a number of samples are chosen from a lot and the results used to determine the acceptability of the entire lot for the desired purpose.

In certain critical applications, the customer may have a requirement for all the parts to be screened (for example, requesting an inspection be performed in which each item of product is inspected for designated characteristics, and removing those items which are defective). Difficulties can then arise about how to distinguish the items that have been screened from those that have not been screened.

It should be noted that the application of the screening process is not a selection of the unscreened parts. These parts are not required to meet further restrictions of the item for fit, tolerance, performance, or reliability within the range or limits prescribed for that item. In this instance, the use of a selected item drawing does not apply. (If it did, then the requirement would be to identify the selected items using the selected item drawing number, and the discussion would be moot.)

Identification of screened parts can involve several aspects. In an operation that uses only screened parts, identification is a shipping and warehousing problem and can be easily solved. Parts that arrive from a vendor are automatically shipped to a testing site (either in-house or to a subcontractor). When the testing site returns the screened parts to the factory, they are placed in inventory and handled in the usual manner.

In a factory that makes many different items, some of which require screened parts and some of which do not, identification problems can arise (for example, how to distinguish on the factory floor and throughout the process between screened and unscreened parts). Solutions to this problem are situation-dependent:

(a) One solution is to make a deliberate decision, based on cost, to use only screened parts throughout the entire factory. This has the advantage of eliminating the possibility of mixing screened and unscreened parts, and the costs associated with tracking two different items. The disadvantage of this approach is the additional costs of the screening process itself. Furthermore, this solution would not work in an environment in which different customers require different screening tests on some base part.

(b) A second solution is to reidentify the parts. This implies removing the vendor's markings that were placed on the unscreened part when it was manufactured and placing another identifier on the part, indicating that it passed an additional qualifier, the screening process. The disadvantage of this is the cost of the reidentification process, but (even more significant) the process of removing the vendor's identifiers may result in injury to the part itself. Also, this might not be allowed by some customers.

(c) A third approach is to add a dab of paint by the vendor's identification number to indicate that the part has passed a screening inspection. This is relatively inexpensive and provides quick identification on the factory floor as to whether or not a part has been screened. The difficulty is that the dab of paint is not a data element that can be entered in an automated inventory system, and the use of two identifiers, one on the part itself and a second in the data processing system, can easily lead to confusion.

(d) A fourth approach is the addition of a parenthetical marking on the parts list (not on the part itself) after the part identifier to indicate that the part has passed a screening inspection. In certain cases, this appears to be the most practical.

5.4.4 Identification of Vendor "Better-Than" Parts

In government procurements, if vendors supplying government contractors are unable to fill orders for a specific item, the vendors can, on specified parts and on their own initiative, supply an item that meets the form, fit, and function of the original item, as long as that vendor-substituted part is "better than or equal to" the item that was ordered. For example, the vendor could supply a part that is more reliable or meets better tolerances than the originally specified part. No changes in the original drawings are required, and the "better-than-or-equal" parts can be used interchangeably with the originally specified parts.

As an example, consider paragraphs 3.30.4 and 3.30.5 of MIL-R-55182F, covering fixed film resistors. This allows the vendor to substitute "better-than" parts. If a manufacturer orders parts from a vendor using that specification, "better-than" parts may show up on the receiving dock. This may occur because the supplier may have the resistor manufacturing line running at reliability level "S," and all his parts are being made to that level. The supplier is then authorized by the terms of the specification to ship level "S" parts to satisfy orders for parts with reliability levels "M," "P" or "R."

This situation can be confusing with regard to the qualification aspects. For example, if an item is to be subjected to a reliability test, and the item includes "better-than" parts (of higher reliability than those specified in the drawings), then the reliability test will not be representative of the other items to be fabricated. As a result, the use of "better-than" parts is not allowed for items that are to undergo equipment qualification and reliability demonstration testing.

One solution to this situation is to have the contractor program manager notify the factory in which items for equipment qualification and reliability demonstration testing are being built. This alerts the factory that "better-than" parts cannot be used in the fabrication of those models. This may create some difficulties at the factory if the originally specified parts cannot be obtained from any vendor.

A more serious difficulty is encountered in the batch production of many items. Normally, samples are taken from the lot and subjected to confirmatory testing to ensure that the items' quality has not varied from the specified limits. However, in a production environment it would be very difficult to segregate and identify the items that did not contain any vendor substituted parts at all, particularly as the items become larger and more complex and may include assemblies fabricated by subcontractors. Thus, the items chosen for normal production qualification testing (confirmatory testing) may contain "better-than" parts as production rolls on.

Several arguments can be made in favor of doing nothing. The first is that the contribution of "better-than" parts is inconsequential, and the overall change to the system reliability caused by complete use of "better-than" parts becomes increasingly insignificant when assessed against the reliability influences of other components (for example, microcircuits). A second argument is that if the samples are chosen in a random manner, this is just another random variable to be cranked into the overall assessment.

On the other side of the fence is the concern that a contractor could make the items to be tested completely from "better-than" (and more expensive) parts, pass the reliability and other tests with those more expensive items, and then reduce the production costs by using the originally specified, lower-quality (and less expensive) parts.

The most straightforward way to resolve the impasse is to submit a request for deviation (see Section 12.2.6) at the start of the program, delineating the restrictions in the use of "better-than" parts. This is best done at the start of the program, in the early stages of the development cycle, so that the matter can be thoroughly aired, completely discussed, and resolved before time becomes a critical factor. This would normally result in a change to the contract.

5.5 SUMMARY

Hardware parts identification is usually provided by either a manufacturer's identification and manufacturer's part number, or a PIN that reflects a standard or specification number. When complete traceability is required, the manufacturer's lot and date are added as additional identifiers. Complications can ensue with the use of interchangeable and substitute parts; the cost-effective identification of these items (which includes identification and the use of screened and "better-than" parts) places increasing requirements on automated configuration management systems.

5.6 EXERCISES

1. Provide a copy of a mechanical schematic drawing of a lawn mower (or equivalent device) that identifies all the parts of the lawn mower and their relationships to each other. With this provide a copy of the associated list that provides complete identification of each of the parts on the drawing.

2. Provide the complete identification of any three items in the current J.C. Penny's catalogue.

3. Provide an analysis and include a flow chart of the "better-than" parts substitution policy expressed in MIL-STD-973.

4. Determine the mean-time-to-failure specified in MIL-R-55182F for each of the failure-rate designation levels of "M," "P," "R," and "S."

5. *Situation Problem:* You are the production manager for a manufacturer of office safes. These safes are sold throughout the entire world, weigh a minimum of one ton, and thousands of the current model have been sold. In the course of a break-in in Abu Dia, a large pipe wrench was applied to the handle of the safe and the lock failed, thus permitting the safe to be opened. An investigation discovers that the failure of the safe was directly traceable to the fractures of seven bolts that failed to meet specifications for tensile strength. Further investigation has determined that these seven bolts were all from the same manufacturer and were all part of one lot. 700 of these bolts were purchased and installed in safes that have since been delivered. Your records do not show the specific safes in which these defective bolts were installed. The Chief Executive Officer of the firm has told you that he wants your solution to this problem on his desk in the morning, and that such a solution should be: (1) creditable (the good name of the firm is in disrepute), and, (2) cost-effective.

   REQUIREMENT: Prepare a cost-effective solution to this problem and compare it to the cost of sending technicians to all the safes of this type currently in the field. As part of your solution, identify: (1) the tasks to be performed, (2) the schedules for the completions of the tasks, (3) associated milestones, and, (4) the costs associated with each task.

6

SOFTWARE IDENTIFICATION

Applying configuration identification to software is in some ways easier, and in other ways more difficult than the corresponding application to hardware. Whereas hardware can be seen and felt, software is an abstraction, and configuration identification techniques can only be applied to software's physical manifestations.

This chapter covers: (1) software identification of computer programs and their associated files, (2) categories of software and how the designation of categories influences overall identification, (3) specific file identification schemes, and, (4) the identification of the electronic medium that contains the software. The emphasis in this chapter is on the application to software of two subprocesses: selecting the software items to be managed, and issuing numbers and other identifiers.

6.1 SELECT SOFTWARE ITEMS TO BE MANAGED

Figure 6-1 shows the expansion of the second step in Figure 4-1 into its application to software to determine what files are to be placed under configuration management. Each of the steps depicted in Figure 6-1 is covered in the following subsections.

6.1.1 Identify And Define The Categories Of Software To Be Managed

Different types of software will have different identification (and control) requirements: therefore, one of the steps in the configuration identification process should include the definition of software categories. This allows statements to be made on a policy basis concerning how the software in each category is to be identified (and later controlled). Items in each category can then be separately identified, deleted, added, and so on, without causing extensive administrative problems.

This step generates a detailed table that identifies and defines all the categories of software that fall under the purview of configuration management. These categories may include software that is:

(a) A deliverable end item (for example, a computer software configuration item).
(b) Part of a deliverable end item (for example, the software component of a firmware device that is part of a hardware configuration item).
(c) Used to produce a deliverable end item (for example, software used to operate numerically-controlled machine tools).

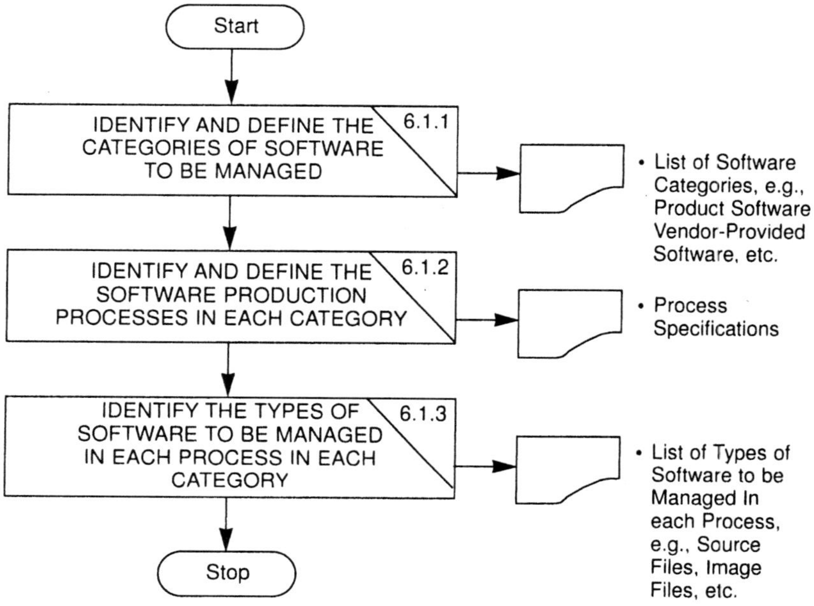

FIGURE 6-1. Configuration Identification—Select Software Items to be Managed.

(d) Used to determine if a deliverable end-product meets its requirements (for example, test vectors).
(e) Used as input to a production process that produces a deliverable item (for example, when a deliverable hard copy document is produced from one or more software source files).
(f) Used as input to a development process that maintains or enhances a deliverable product (for example, a system simulation).

A typical set of categories is depicted in Table 6-I. This identifies nine categories of software as follows:

(a) Category I: *Product software*—This is software to be developed as an end product or as part of an end product. Figure 6-2 provides a typical example of software being developed as a part of an end product. In this example, the various software computer programs are part of the automatic data processing subsystem of the Steam Power System. For some organizations, this is where the process stops. For other organizations, however, the product software is just the tip of the iceberg, and further categories require definition.

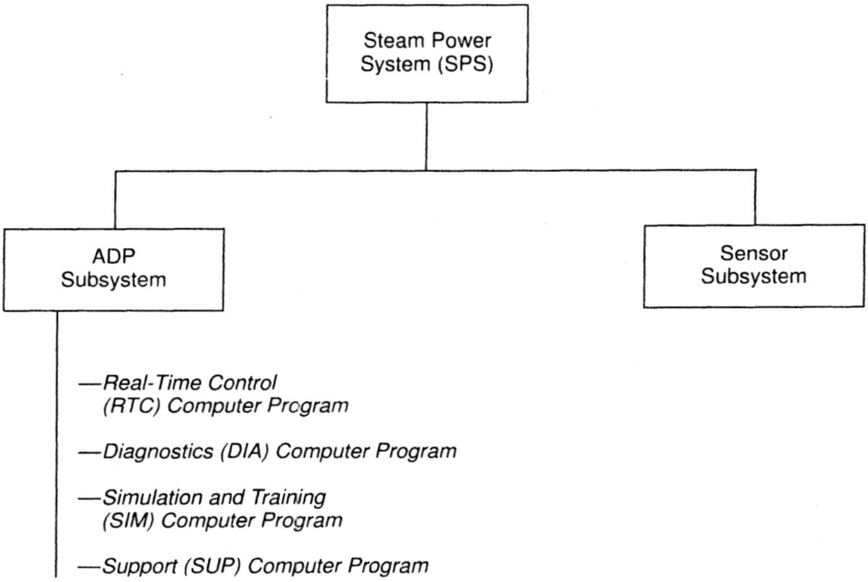

FIGURE 6-2. Steam Power System Structure.

(b) Category II: *The software component of product firmware*—This is software that is to be developed and embedded in a firmware end product. Several discussions can ensue at this point. One view is that this software should be treated in exactly the same manner as any other product software. Another view is that the software to be embedded in firmware is different because it is to be embedded in a hardware device. Both views can be strongly defended. To avoid the confusion that can accompany this process, it is recommended that the software to be embedded in product firmware be explicitly

TABLE 6-I. AN EXAMPLE SET OF SOFTWARE CATEGORIES

Category	Title	Definition
I	Product software	Software developed as a part of a deliverable CSCI.
II	The software component of product firmware	Software developed as part of a deliverable HWCI.
III	Vendor-provided software	Software that already exists as a vendor-provided product and is provided and maintained by a vendor.
IV	Test software	Software that is developed to support the formal acceptance test of category I, II, and III software.
V	Product support software	Software that is developed to support the formal process of producing software but which is not formally identified as a deliverable product.
VI	Electronically-formatted engineering design data	Data (software) that is developed or used by the design activity and that is required to support the manufacture, test, or modification of deliverable hardware items.
VII	Manufacturing support software	Other software used in the manufacturing process.
VIII	Documentation	Software used to produce configuration documentation other than engineering drawings and associated lists.
IX	Other software	All other software not otherwise defined. this includes software developed to support informal tests.

named as a category; how to manage the configuration of that category is then a separate discussion.

(c) Category III: *Vendor-provided software*—This is software that already exists and is provided by and maintained by a vendor. This category should include vendor-provided operating systems, relational database management systems, configuration management tools, and so on; that is, all the software that is used to support the development and operation of the other software categories. The key here is that the vendor will continue to maintain this software; otherwise, there may be a need for the developer to provide maintenance (and operation and maintenance documentation) for this software. Furthermore, as the vendors release new versions of the software, special arrangements for their implementation into the support of the developing products will be required.

(d) Category IV: *Test software*—This is software that is developed to support the formal acceptance testing of Category I, II, and III software. This includes the test drivers, test data, and test collection software that surround the execution of the formal acceptance test as well as the analysis programs used by the test team to reduce test data to meaningful results. In many cases, there is no perceived need to formally test Category III software. This may be because the software is tested by the vendor prior to release and/or the developer's support organization prior to operational use. However, if, for example, the developer runs benchmarks and regression tests on vendor-provided software to determine its fitness for use on a project, then the software used for benchmark and regression testing should be included as part of this category.

(e) Category V: *Product-support software*—This is software that is developed to support the formal process of producing Category I, II, IV, and VI software, but it is not formally identified as a product. Software in this category would include standards-checking tools used by the configuration management organization to make sure that source files of code, and the command files used to compile, link, and load the executable versions of Category I and II software, and so on, comply with contract requirements.

(f) Category VI: *Electronically-formatted engineering design data*—This includes the CAD/CAE/CAM software files used to produce engineering drawings and associated lists. This also includes software used to control numerically controlled machinery as well as the software used to execute factory tests on the hardware (if that software was developed by the design activity as part of a CAD/CAE/CAM activity).

(g) Category VII: *Manufacturing-support software*—This is the software used by the manufacturing organization to support hardware production. Software in this category would include the software that controls numerically controlled machinery as well as that software used to execute factory tests on the hardware.

(h) Category VIII: *Documentation software*—This would include, for example, the source files of the requirements documents. This does not include the vendor-provided software that supports the production of the documentation; that is covered as a part of Category III. It also would not include the vendor-provided word-processors.

(i) Category IX: *Other software*—This would include the software developed to support informal tests.

The identification of a software category may or may not imply that the software in that category will be identified and controlled by some outside group. Details on that will be provided as part of the implementation. The benefit of identifying the software categories is that it ensures that certain software is not being overlooked. For good reason, some categories of software may be explicitly declared to be completely outside the scope of formal configuration management. Both the identification of that software and the reflection of the associated policy statements should be a part of the basic configuration management plan.

There are other nuances associated with categorization, such as how to manage reusable software (software developed for another project and projected to be transferred to this and other projects). Each of these categories requires identification, thought, and agreement on how to handle them.

6.1.2 Identify And Define The Software Production Processes In Each Category

This step generates a process specification for each of the production processes that are associated with the categories of software previously identified.

Figure 6-3 illustrates a generic software production process:

(a) The input can be source files of code, backplane geometry files, or any other type of software that is to be electronically processed which will provide a stated output.

(1) The software to be input into the production process is not entered via the keyboard. Keyboard entries should be:

(a) Limited to the commands necessary to initiate the production process; further commands should be provided by a command or script file.
(b) Completely specified as part of a standard written procedure that can be objectively executed by a person who is not familiar with the overall process.

(2) The preparation of the input through the use of a software tool that accepts direct subjective input from an operator or engineer (for example, a text editor), is not part of the production process itself.

(b) The software production environment includes the software tools that are used to transform the inputs into the outputs. This is not only vendor-supplied tools but also any special-purpose tools that have been developed by the using organization and required to support the generation process.
(c) The output of the production process can be software on electronic or optical media (for example, tooling files, a print file to produce a document, or a raster file for an engineering drawing), a hard copy of the documents themselves, or both.

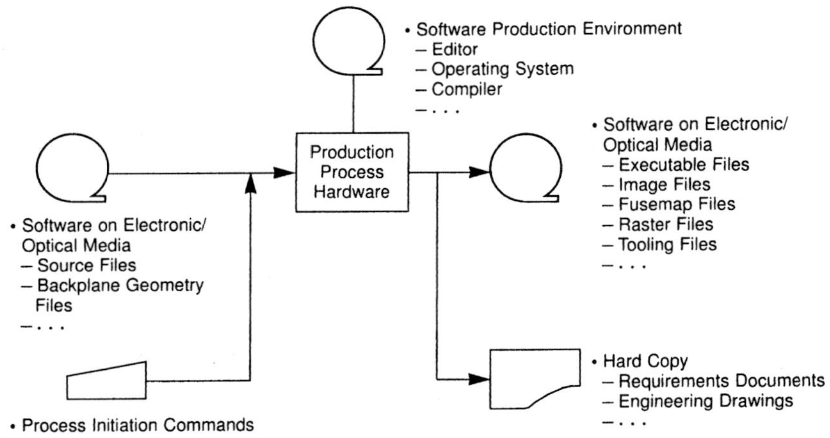

FIGURE 6-3. A Generic Software Production Process.

6.1.3 Identify The Types Of Software To Be Managed In Each Process In Each Category

To illustrate the types of software to be managed in each category, two different example processes have been depicted: (1) an example firmware production process, and, (2) an example computer-aided wire-wrap design process. Delineation of the actual processes in the previous step enables choices to be made to determine the minimum amount of software required to be placed under configuration control.

6.1.3.1 An Example Firmware Production Process

This step identifies the types of software to be managed. The decisions that need to be made are illustrated in Figure 6-4, an example firmware production process. As shown therein, this consists of four subprocesses:

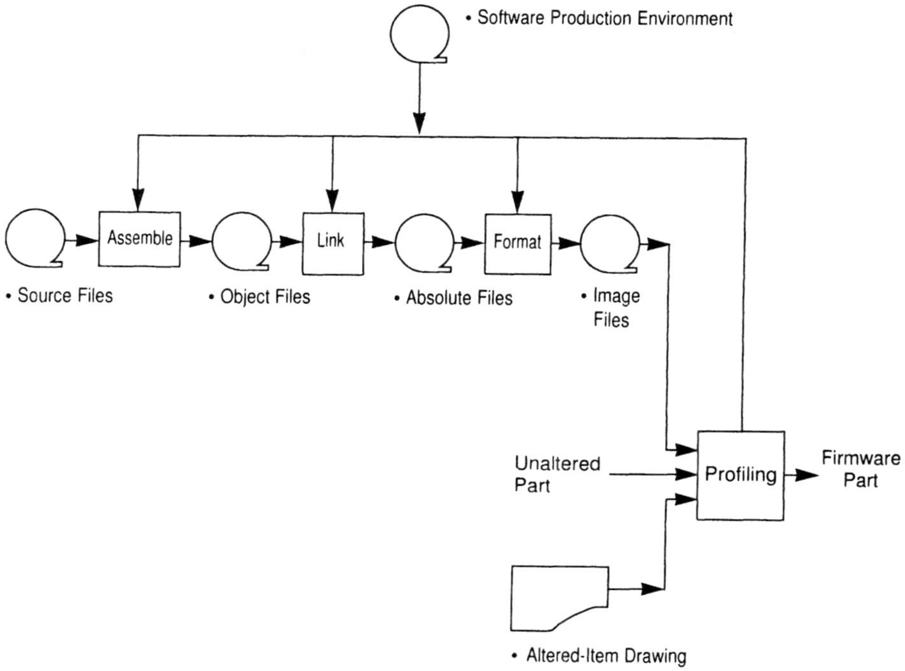

FIGURE 6-4. An Example Firmware Production Process.

(a) The source files are assembled into object files
(b) The object files are linked to form absolute files (also known as *executable files*).
(c) The absolute files are formatted into image files
(d) The image files are embedded into the firmware part by the profiling process (also known as *programming*).

Table 6-II provides an example of the choices to be made for the firmware production process example which is shown in Figure 6-4.

(a) In some firmware production processes, all the changes are made at the source file level only, and all the source files (changed and unchanged) are reassembled (recompiled), linked, and used directly in the profiling subprocess. In this case, the intermediate products (object, absolute, and image files) have no retentive value and are discarded after their first use in the next subprocess. As a result, the only software items requiring configuration management are the source files and the software production environment.
(b) In most firmware production processes, the overall firmware production process is divided into two parts. The first part starts with using the sources files as the input and ends with the production of the image files. The image files themselves are then used as the input for the second part of the firmware production process (as a part of the hardware manufacturing process) at another location. In this case, the image files themselves are kept under configuration control.
(c) In the production of some firmware, the amount of firmware is so large that reassembling all the source files to implement a few mi-

TABLE 6-II. AN EXAMPLE DECISION MATRIX ON THE CONTROL OF THE SOFTWARE ITEMS IN ONE FIRMWARE PRODUCTION PROCESS

Types of Software to be Used in the Production Process		Types of Software to be Controlled: Source Files	Software Production Environment	Object Files	Absolute Files	Image Files
Unchanged object files	No	Yes	Yes	No	—	—
	Yes	Yes	Yes	Yes	—	—
Unchanged absolute files	No	Yes	Yes	—	No	—
	Yes	Yes	Yes	—	Yes	—
Unchanged image files	No	Yes	Yes	—	—	No
	Yes	Yes	Yes	—	—	Yes

nor changes is not considered cost-effective. In that environment, the unchanged source files are not reassembled and their associated unchanged object files are used directly. In this case, configuration management of the object files is also required.

(d) Other possibilities exist (for example, the use of unchanged absolute files, as well as combinations of the above). In each case, however, the types of software to be reused need to be identified and controlled.

6.1.3.2 An Example Computer-Aided Wire-Wrap Process

Figures 6-5 and 6-6 depict a more complicated case, the use of computer-aided design (CAD) tools to produce backplane wire-wrap manufacturing data. Figure 6-5 shows the interactive development of the mechanical and the electrical design. From a configuration management viewpoint, the items of interest are:

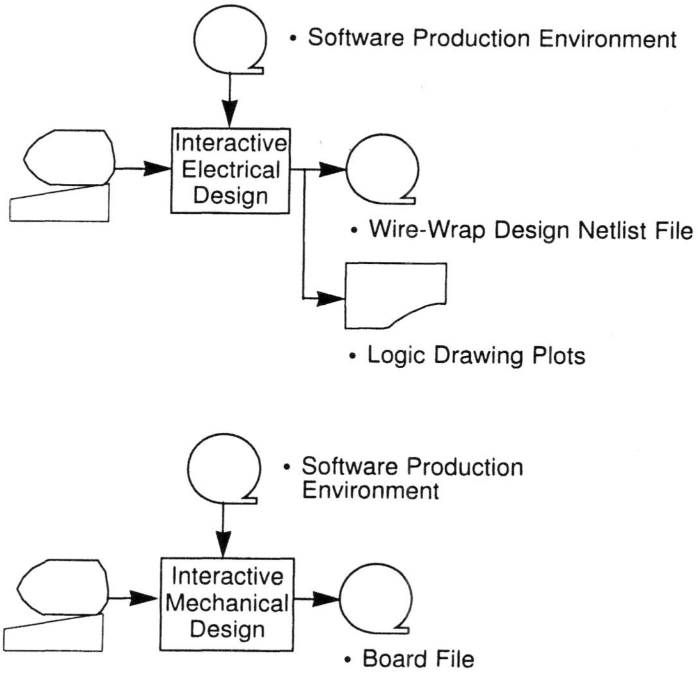

FIGURE 6-5. Example Interactive Subprocesses of Computer Aided Backplane Wire-Wrap Design.

(a) The items that comprise the software production environment. (For the purpose of this example, the items that comprise the software production environment are treated collectively. Not all items are used in all the processes in Figures 6-5 and 6-6.)
(b) The outputs, which in this case are the wire-wrap design netlist file and the board file. These would be placed under configuration management as they constitute inputs to the production process shown in Figure 6-6.

Figure 6-6 shows an example production process for backplane wire-wrap design and identifies the three processing steps (wire-wrap netlist processing, routing, and tooling) and the associated inputs, outputs, and intermediate products. (The same process is used to develop the initial end products; these are intermediate reports that provide diagnostics to the development efforts.)

The same questions associated with firmware production (which intermediate products should be placed under configuration management) also

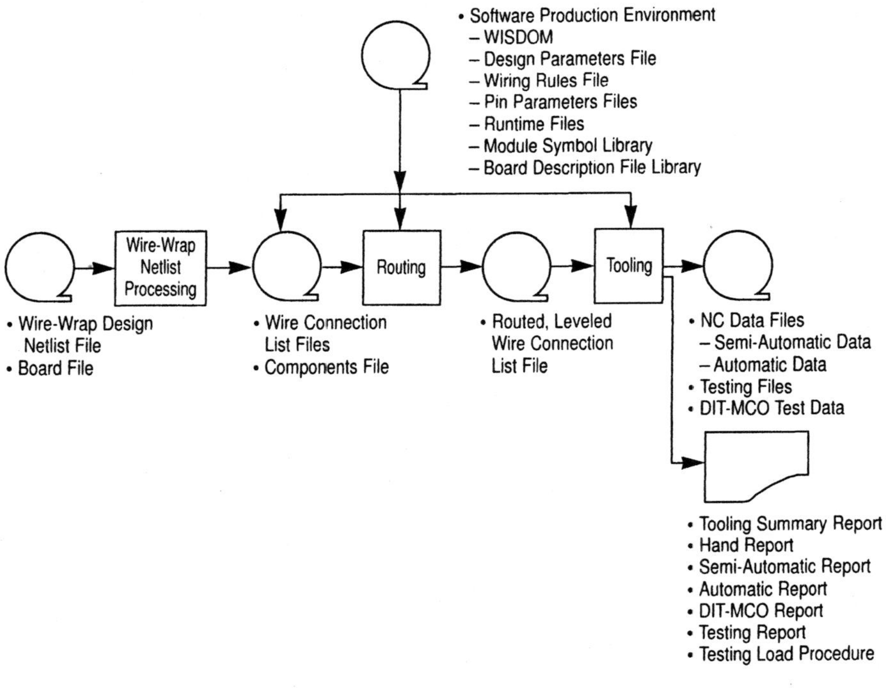

FIGURE 6-6. An Example Computer Aided Backplane Wire-Wrap Design Production Process.

arise in this production process; there is, however, an additional complication, that of a defined maintenance process.

Figure 6-7 shows an example maintenance process which has two options. Option 1 is the production of the engineering change notice report, the wireman's report, and so on, by the use of interactive inputs. From a configuration management viewpoint, interactive maintenance is not a preferred implementation since it does not lead to the production of the required outputs by an objective repeatable process.

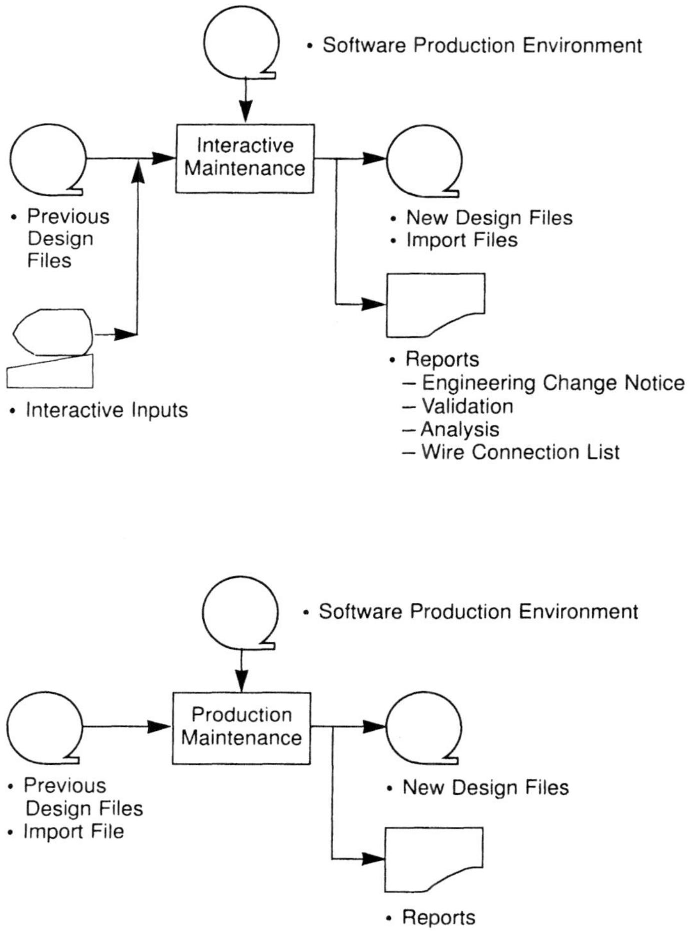

FIGURE 6-7. Two Different Options for Maintenance of Computer Aided Backplane Wire-Wrap Design.

From the viewpoint of having a controlled repeatable process used to produce changes to a backplane wire-wrap design, a preferred method is to use the interactive maintenance process to produce an input file (shown as one of the outputs in the interactive maintenance process in Figure 6-7) which would then be placed under configuration management and used to produce the final products. This would require the previous design files (those that are used as an input to this process) to be completely identified and placed under configuration control.

6.2 ISSUE NUMBERS AND OTHER IDENTIFIERS

Figure 6-8 expands the fourth step in Figure 4-1 in its application to software. Note that the last subprocess, **Determine The Marking And Labeling To Be Used For Hardware In Which Software Is Embedded,** is a part of firmware identification, and is discussed in Section 7.4.

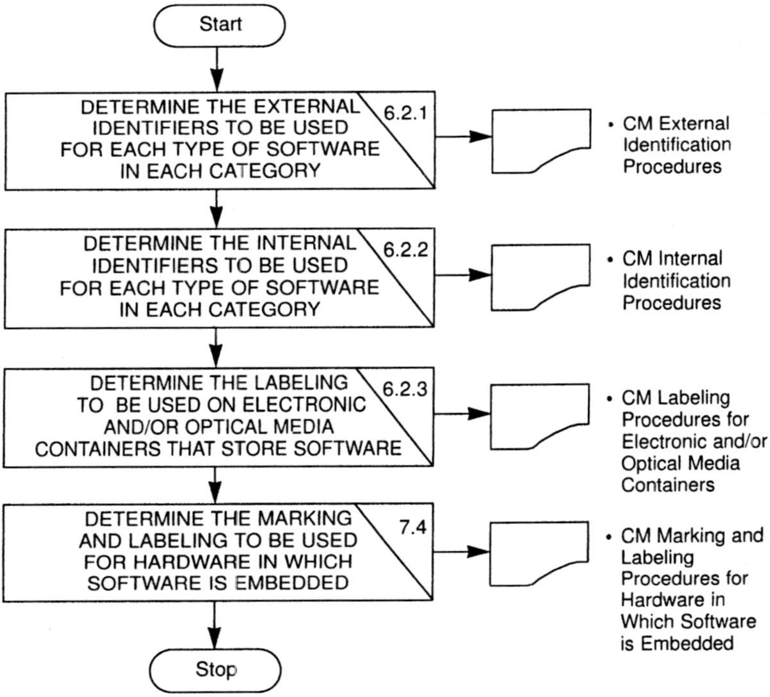

FIGURE 6-8. Configuration Identification—Issue Numbers and Other Identifiers for Software.

6.2.1 Determine The External Identifiers To Be Used For Each Type Of Software In Each Category

External identifiers for software are the identifiers which refer to the software files. The naming conventions for files can take several forms and vary depending on:

(a) The type of file
(b) The process which generated the file, and
(c) The software production environment, in particular, the operating system

Hardware is identified at the configuration item level and also at many other levels (for example, part, subassembly, and so on). As discussed in Section 4.2.3.2, software is identified at two levels, the configuration item (computer program) level and the file level. Table 6-III shows the typical identifiers at the computer program level; each program has a name, an acronym, and a number. In government usage, the number is called a *computer software configuration item* (CSCI) identification number. These identifiers provide a common identification for the collection of items that make up the computer program, and serve as an address for all actions and documentation applicable to that computer program.

6.2.1.1 Software File Identification

Code is usually identified (and controlled) at the individual file level, and, as shown in Figure 6-3, there are a number of different types of software files to be identified (source, object, executable, image, and so on). The reason to control the code at the individual file level is that to control the entire collection of source code for one computer program as one item is unworkable. For example, one computer program may consist of 40,000 lines of source code. With an average size of 100 lines of source code per file, this

TABLE 6-III. STEAM POWER COMPUTER PROGRAMS

Name	Acronym	Number
Diagnostics	DIA	7-10-5005
Real-time control	RTC	7-10-5010
Simulation	SIM	7-10-5015
Support	SPT	7-10-5020

implies about 400 source files contained in one computer program. During the integration and test activity, each of these source files will probably change at least once, and some as many as ten times. If identification is only at the computer program level, then at least 400 issues of the complete computer program would be required (although some may be grouped) to accurately track all the changes to the individual source files. This would be an impossible task.

Thus, this requires that each file be identified as an entity, which will be uniquely identified and separately controlled. (The term *file* is used here, rather than *module, procedure, unit, routine*, or *subroutine*, to avoid confusion. The other terms have different meanings in different programming languages, whereas the term *file* is unambiguous. The reader should be aware that certain government standards, such as DOD-STD-2167A, speak of controlling *units*; however, unless *units* are equated with *source files*, the term *unit* is ambiguous and at variance with the reality that physical collections of code are grouped into files.)

6.2.1.1.1 File Identifier Fields

Software is identified at the file level, and each file identifier can have three fields that can be used: the file name, the file type, and the version number (or date).

A typical file identifier is depicted in Figure 6-9. As shown therein:

(a) The file name is "RTC_101." The usual conventions for file names determine that the first set of alphanumeric characters identify the computer program. In this case, *RTC* is the acronym identifying the Real-Time Control computer program. The second set of characters is separated from the computer program acronym by an underscore, "_," and provides a meaningful name. In this case, 101 refers to an input/output function.

(b) The file type of *FOR* is separated from the file name by a period, as in this case wherein Digital Equipment Corporation (DEC) conventions are used. FOR is the file type referring to a FORTRAN source code file, which is a source file containing FORTRAN source statements.

RTC_101.FOR;5

FIGURE 6-9. An Example File Identifier.

(c) The version number, "5," is separated from the file type by a semicolon.

The UNIX operating system does not use file version numbers but rather assigns a date/time at the time of file creation. The lack of a file version number necessitates the mandatory use of a software tool for configuration control. In this case, the UNIX operating system provides such a tool, SCCS, while many more powerful tools are commercially available.

As a second example, Table 6-IV delineates the manner in which the INTERLEAF program identifies its files. As shown in Table 6-IV, the INTERLEAF file extensions can be grouped into four categories: (1) icon name (file name, for example, ***filename***), (2) icon type (file type—for example, ***doc***), (3) copy extension (such as, ***#1***), and, (4) version (or summary) extension (for example, ***3***). The point being made here is that different processes may use different naming schemes and that to control the files, the naming schemes and the associated processes must also be known.

The result of all of this is that one major emphasis in establishing CM external identification procedures for software is to establish file naming conventions; a number of different approaches are available:

(a) Use drawing numbers. While this ensures that each file name is unique, it does have some drawbacks:

TABLE 6-IV. INTERLEAF FILE IDENTIFIERS

Filename Extension	Meaning
filename.doc	The document (the file that appears as an icon on the desktop).
filename.doc,1	The backup version of the document.
filename.doc#1	The second document with the same name in the same directory.
filename.doc#1,1	The backup version of the second document.
filename.doc,2	The checkpoint version of the document.
filename.doc,3	The crash version of the document.
filename.doc,4	The work-in-progress version of the document.
filename.doc,5	Lisp methods associated with the document.
filename.doc,6	Persistent lisp data associated with the document.
filename.doc,8	An autonumbering and autoreferencing file for the document.
filename.doc,9	An indexing summary file for the document.

(1) The numbers provide no additional information (for example, the function that the file performs).
(2) There is a greater opportunity for confusion and errors if the person keyboarding in the drawing number makes a keyboard entry error (for example, transposes two numbers).

(b) Assign meaningful names. This could be based on the function that the file is to perform (for example, IOCPP1, could be the Input/Output Controller with PP1 being assigned by the originator).

Sections 5.3.6.5 and 5.3.6.7 of MIL-STD-973 specify requirements which may be invoked on a government contract.

6.2.1.1.2 Source File Identification

Source files are the input to the code generation process and can be uniquely identified by using the file name, file type, and version number.

The source file name and file type are assigned at the creation of the file by the originator and are continued through the remainder of the code creation process. The file name and file type can be changed by an operator command, but this is not usual practice.

Reasonable practice is to distinguish between successive revisions of a specific source file by the version number; for example, the revision of RTC_101.FOR;5, would be identified as RTC_101.FOR;6. However, this introduces a complication. Usually, the version number of a source file is automatically incremented when the file is edited. Because a file may be edited a number of times before all entries have been satisfactorily completed, the next complete revision of RTC_101.FOR;5 may be RTC_101.FOR;10. To resolve this, the version number is reset to the next higher number (in this case, "6"), prior to the revised file being formally entered into the configuration management library. This can be done by using, for example, the RENAME command.

As an additional precaution, the file identifier to include the version number should be placed as a comment on the first line of the source file. This practice is similar to writing a name on the inside collar of a shirt before it is sent to the laundry. If the slip is lost, the shirt can still be identified as belonging to a particular person. This does imply additional processing, or the use of a tool, to ensure that the file identifier recorded on the comment line is identical to the external file identifier. The cost of the additional processing is an insurance cost, and should be paid depending on the risk of the file identifier (in particular, the version number) being changed inadvertently and the likely consequences should that change take place.

6.2.1.1.3 Object File Identification

Object files result from passing the source code through a compiler or assembler, which changes the statements of the source code to machine language. In this transformation:

(a) The file name remains the same as the source file name.
(b) The file type is changed, as an example, from FOR (for FORTRAN—a programming language) to OBJ (for object code). This is done automatically as part of the compilation process.
(c) The version number is changed to be the next higher number from the highest version number of the existing object file with the same file name and the same file type. This, too, is done automatically as part of the compilation process.

Whether or not object files are controlled is a function of the code generation process. If all the source files are recompiled every time a revised executable file is required, then the object files are not required for long term recovery. In this case, keeping track of object-file version numbers is unnecessary.

If, on the other hand, revised executable files are prepared using the changed source files, and the object files are prepared from the unchanged source files, then the object files must be under the same control as the source files. In this case, control of object-file version numbers is usually required. In particular, if the compilation time of a large number of source files is significant (for example, four hours to two days), then there is a substantial advantage to controlling and using object files, as this would substantially shorten the processing time.

6.2.1.1.4 Executable File Identification

One executable file results from the linking of a number of object files and is identified by file name, file type (for example, *EXE* for executable), and version number in a manner similar to source file identification.

Recognizing that many object files are being combined to yield one executable file, there is usually a default naming convention applied automatically by the code generation process. To preclude surprises, it is considered best to specify the executable file name at the time of generation. This is usually a name meaningful in the computer program's context.

6.2.1.2 Patch Identification

The use of *patches* (binary code inserted into executable files) is not considered acceptable software engineering practice for a number of reasons (for example, the lack of visibility of the changes); however, there are circumstances in which there is no other choice. If patches are to be used, an identification scheme is required. Patches are identified as executable files, and the identification fields include the file name, the file type, and the version number. As a specific example, a particular patch can be completely identified as "MAKEPATCH.EXE;3."

6.2.1.3 File Identification Responsibilities

File names can be assigned in a number of ways, and the details of these assignments are normally a function of the category. For cost-effectiveness, the authority to assign file names should be delegated to the lowest possible management level. In the best of all possible worlds, these assignments would be made by the individual developers, but that is not always feasible.

One set of assignments for file naming is as follows:

(a) Category I software names are assigned by a formal project office configuration management instruction. The requirement for this level of responsibility is consistency across the project. In this case, the project instruction will establish the naming scheme and probably specify the first portion of the name, leaving the rest to the originators.
(b) Categories II, VI, and VIII software names are assigned in a similar manner as are Category I names.
(c) Category III software names use the vendors' identification (for example, VMS Version 5.01).
(d) Category IV, V, and VII software names are usually assigned by the software development group.
(e) Category IX software names are usually assigned by the originator of the software.

6.2.1.4 Determine The Internal Identifiers To Be Used For Each Type Of Software In Each Category

Internal identifiers are placed inside the software files (for example, as comments) when the software files permit that type of usage. Source files of software code permit that usage as do some formats for image files. When the identifier is composed of the filename, the file type, and the file version number, the complete identifier can be placed inside the file as a comment (and, if necessary, the external file identifier can be renamed to correspond to the internal file identifier).

The situation becomes more complex under UNIX since the date/time is used as the means of externally distinguishing between two files that have the same file name and the same file type. Attempting to keep the date/time portion of the file identifier consistent between the external and internal identifiers leads to complications. There are a number of approaches to this problem, one approach is to reserve the last two characters in the file name for an incremented number which would then provide the basis for distinguishing between two files (this may cause further complications if the files call other files ...). As a result, it may not be practical to have the complete UNIX file identifier located inside the code.

See Section 5.3.6.7.1.A of MIL-STD-973 for specific government requirements which may be invoked on a contract.

6.2.2 Determine The Labeling To Be Used For Electronic And/Or Optical Media Containers That Store Software

Software is normally placed on electronic or optical media for transmission, archiving, or long-term storage. The media (magnetic tapes, disks, and so on) must be labeled so that the contents of the media can be ascertained without it being necessary to physically read the media. The label both identifies the media so that reference to it can be made on a unique basis and provides immediate information about the package. The label should also provide a complete reference to the *version description document* (VDD) where complete information about the software stored on the media is available.

Figure 6-10 shows an example label for a magnetic tape. As shown therein the elements of information are:

(a) The date when the copy was made. In identifying dates, there are various notations that can be adopted. For clarity, it is recommended that the month be provided in alphabetic characters rather than by a number, and that the year be indicated with all four numbers (rather than just the last two).
(b) Details associated with the media itself. In this case this is a 9-track tape with a recording density of 1600 bits per inch (BPI). This is provided to avoid difficulties in attempting to read the tape.

(c) The short name or number of the CSCI and the build number. CSCIs are normally built in a succession of increasing capabilities. This would be the second issue of Build 5 (the first was 5.0).
(d) The copy number. Normally, several copies of a particular master tape are made. Providing the copy number assists in distinguishing between the various copies.
(e) The label identifier. This is normally a unique number and in this example, contains a meaningful prefix.
(f) The VDD number. Details of the contents of the VDD are provided in Section 6.3.1.
(g) The name, organizational address, and the telephone number of the person who made the copy. This is provided to allow direct contact with the preparer should a misunderstanding or an anomaly arise that could be quickly resolved by discussion.

Other information could be added (for example, the contract number). See Section 5.3.6.7.1 and .2 of MIL-STD-973 for requirements that might be invoked on a military contract.

6.3 ASSOCIATED TOPICS

The nature of software requires that it be stored on electronic media. This requires that the media itself be identified (and controlled) and that there be some means of identifying the contents of the media.

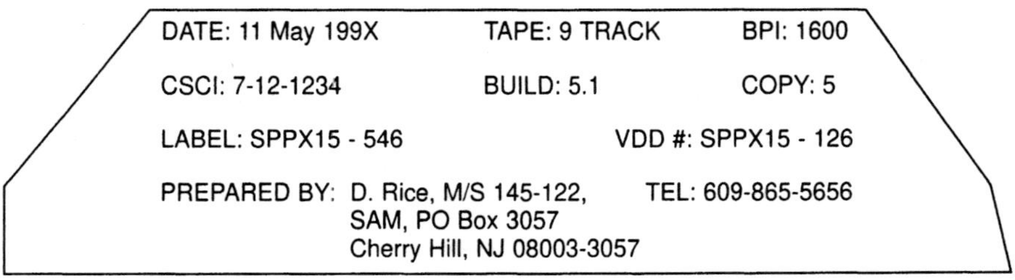

FIGURE 6-10. An Example Magnetic Tape Label.

6.3.1 Version Description Documents

Version description documents are usually used to document the contents of all magnetic media except vendor software and daily, weekly, and monthly backup tapes. One copy of the version description document (VDD) (with an attached listing identifying all the files on the magnetic media) should accompany the master and each copy of a released tape or disk.

The VDD is like the bill of lading on a truck; it provides the reader with information on the detailed contents of what is in the truck—otherwise the reader would have to open the truck and inventory the contents. As part of this, the VDD should:

(a) List the files contained on the magnetic or optical media. This should include file name, file type and file version number (if a version number exists), or other data sufficient to make the identification unique (such as the date).

(b) Identify the specific versions/releases of vendor-provided software required to develop and maintain the software on the media.

(c) State all changes incorporated in the software since the previous issue.

(d) Describe the operational effect of each change identified in the VDD.

(e) Identify any known problems or known errors with this issue of the software.

(f) Identify all operational and support documents that are required to load or regenerate the software.

(g) List in one location in the VDD all the documents referenced in the VDD; also, identify the sources of these documents and where they can be obtained.

See Data Item Description (DID) DI-MCCR-80031A for requirements that might be invoked on a military contract.

An example is shown in Figure 6-11. As shown therein, the version description documents identifies what is contained on the media, where copies are stored, how the software was prepared, what changes were made, and the known problems.

6.3.2 Database Concerns

In some organizations, there are collections of software tools that operate on databases to produce specific products. For example, computer-aided software engineering (CASE) tools can be used to develop a database that can

1.0 Scope
This VDD describes increment Build 5 Version 1.04 of the Real Time Control (RTC) Computer Program (5010) of the Steam Power System. See attached listing for details.

2.0 Copies
These are stored at the indicated locations:
 a. Master copy: Magnetic Tape Number 0421 (Archive)
 b. Copy 1: Magnetic Tape Number 0423 (148-209)

4.0 Preparation
This version was compiled using the VAX Ada Compiler Version 1.0 operating under VAX/VMS Version 4.18.

5.0 Changes Installed
The following changes have been installed since the previous version.
 a. ECP-CSS-055, 15 Dec 19xx, with SCN 05, 11 Dec. 19xx.
This added a light pen capability.

6.0 Interface Compatibility
No other computer programs are affected by this release.

7.0 Reference Documents
 a. SRS: 5010-SRS-04
 b. IRS: IRS-04
 c. SDD: 5010-SDD-04

8.0 Installation Instructions
Use Qualification Test 501 to verify this version.

9.0 Possible Problems and Known Errors
 SPR CSS-41 is not closed.

D. Rice

One Attachment (as stated)

FIGURE 6-11. An Example Version Description Document.

be further processed to provide documents and even code. Both the documents and the code must be controlled, and for ease of maintenance, it may be projected that the database produced by the CASE tool should also be a controlled item. The next issue to be addressed is how far back in the development chain one should reasonably go to capture and control the data.

Practical difficulties with sole reliance on identification of the database as an entity occur with the identification of the changes that have been made to the controlled database. Unfortunately, although differences between the previous and projected databases can be identified by a DIFFERENCES program, the output of the DIFFERENCES program, run on the data itself, will probably not be produced in any form that is recognizable to the human eye. Attempting to run DIFFERENCES on the print file may be equally nonproductive, particularly when the print file contains graphics implementations. So, while DIFFERENCES can be run, that approach is not always effective in a database application. Thus, caution is advised before making a projection that code and/or documents will be controlled at the CASE-tool database level.

In this context, the issue is not if the CASE-tool database itself can be identified (and controlled), but rather, on a practical level, whether or not the effect on the product of entering changes at the database level can be easily determined at the output (document or code) level. While visualizations have been made of tools that would provide overlays of old and new graphics, those visualizations have not yet been reduced to engineering practice. As a result, current methods for making this determination are not satisfactory.

6.4 SUMMARY

Configuration identification of software begins at the computer program level. The manner and the extent to which various identification schemes are used is a function of the category in which a specific computer program is placed (for example, vendor-provided software), and specific examples of categories have been identified and discussed.

The next level of detail of software identification is the software files that make up the computer programs. Software files are usually identified by file name, file type, and file version number.

Complete identification of software includes identification of the electronic media on which the software resides. This is normally performed through the use of labels placed on the media and documents that record the details of the software on that media.

6.5 EXERCISES

1. Define the software production processes associated with: (1) Category IV, Test Software, (2) Category VIII, Documentation, and, (3) Reusable Software. Include the appropriate verification steps.

2. Prepare a software file naming procedure for the Steam Power System CSCIs in Table 6-III, one which includes source, object, and executable code.

3. Review and provide comments on the file identification requirements contained in Sections 5.3.6.5, 5.3.6.7.1, and 5.3.6.7.2 of MIL-STD-973. Change the wording for those sections to implement your comments.

4. *Situation Problem:* You have just returned from a project meeting with your manager. Because of previous excellent work, the scope of the Diagnostics (DIA) Computer Program is to be increased to include performance monitoring, fault detection, and fault isolation of the entire Steam Power System (including the furnace and the electrical distribution lines). You estimate that this will raise the size of DIA to 100,000 lines of source code (1,000 source files of code) which may affect your approach for CM and its corresponding support of tests and integration. It now appears that the previous approach, that of performing a complete recompilation of all the source code when corrections are being implemented, has to be reconsidered. Your manager wants to meet with you this afternoon to hear if you plan to go to partial recompilations and maintain control of the object files.

   REQUIREMENT: Diagram the steps associated with performing partial recompilations and using previously-compiled object files of unchanged code to produce new executable files. Provide a list of the advantages and disadvantages of each course of action (complete compiles versus partial compiles). Identify any unknowns that affect your decisions and make reasonable assumptions concerning any unknowns. Provide your decision and document the reasons that led you to make that decision.

7

FIRMWARE IDENTIFICATION

In most organizations, firmware is a funny animal, neither fish nor fowl. Looking at it, firmware is actually the combination of a hardware device and computer instructions, or computer data, which reside as read-only software on the hardware device where the software cannot be readily modified under program control. Both the software and the hardware components need to be identified, as does the resulting firmware product itself.

This chapter focuses on the unique aspects of firmware: what additional items require identification, how the type of firmware item affects the manner in which identification is made, and the associated documentation considerations.

Four items require consideration:

(a) The basic hardware item; that is, the unprogrammed part, on which the software is to be embedded. This hardware is identified, as is any other hardware item, with the manufacturer's code and part number. Hardware identification is covered in detail in Chapter 5, hence it will not be repeated here.

(b) The software to be embedded in the hardware—Figure 2-6 provides an overview of the merging of the hardware item and the software image file, while Chapter 6 discusses the identification of source files, object files, and executable files. In the production of the software to be embedded in a hardware part, one more software step is necessary: the production of an image file from the previously produced executable file.

(c) The firmware itself; that is, the basic hardware part that has had the software added to it.

(d) The equipment that contains the firmware.

7.1 IMAGE FILE CONSIDERATIONS

An *image file* is a structured collection of executable (absolute) files, formatted in accordance with the requirements of the device that places the image file in the hardware item. The formats for image files can vary widely, but there are two items that require configuration management attention:

(a) The format is a manufacturing interface and must be stated explicitly. Once established, the code generation process used by the configuration management organization must include the software to produce the image file in that format.

(b) There are advantages to some formats in terms of being able to add *headers* (non-executable code), which would include the image file identifier. The use of a software header provides additional insurance in case the external markings on the hardware part itself are obscured. Therefore, all else being equal, the preferred format choice should be the format that allows the file identifier to be a part of the image file itself.

7.2 FIRMWARE TYPES

There are many different classifications of firmware devices and some of the major ones (ROMs, PROMs, EPROMs, and EEPROMs) have been mentioned previously. The technology, however, is becoming more sophisticated, and new devices (with new names) are continuously surfacing. Furthermore, recognizing the emotional baggage that the term *firmware* sometimes carries the preferred, and less confusing, term to use is *programmable parts*.

From a configuration management viewpoint, there are five types of solid-state programmable parts.

7.2.1 Type 1 Programmable Parts

These parts are programmed at the time of manufacture and cannot be reprogrammed. The most common type in use today is ROMs, although there are others; for example, *PALs* (programmed array logic).

Type 1 programmable parts acquired from suppliers with embedded commercial software (provided by the suppliers) should be identified by using the suppliers' part numbers. In this case, the commercial software is a product developed and maintained by the supplier.

Type 1 programmable parts acquired as part of a higher-level assembly from suppliers should be acquired together with the appropriate supplier documentation that provides complete identification of the embedded software. Caution should be exercised at this point. The term complete identification means the software is uniquely identified. It should not be construed to mean that the supplier will provide the source code.

Custom software to be placed on Type 1 programmable parts being manufactured by suppliers should be identified as part of a *vendor item drawing* (formerly specification control drawing) or a source control drawing. In this case, the supplier has a unique manufacturing process which is not specified on either of the two drawings.

Custom software to be placed on Type 1 programmable parts being manufactured by the developing organization should be identified as part of a software drawing (see MIL-STD-100E and ASME Y14.24M-1989). This identification is then made a part of an overall "build-to" set of drawings that provides a complete description of how to build the part while incorporating the specified software.

7.2.2 Type 2 Programmable Parts

These parts are programmed after the time of manufacture and cannot be reprogrammed. They typically include PROMs and other devices.

The custom software to be placed on the device is identified on *an altered-item drawing*. The altered item itself (the programmed part) is identified by using the altered-item drawing number.

7.2.3 Type 3 Programmable Parts

These parts are programmed after the time of manufacture and can be reprogrammed only by removing the individual devices from the next higher assembly. They typically include EPROMs, although not all EPROMs fall into this type. For example, installations where EPROMs, mounted on the next higher assembly, can be erased in bulk while mounted on that next higher assembly do not fall into this category. Furthermore, this category can include EEPROMs, which, because of the wiring on the printed circuit board to which they are attached, cannot be reprogrammed while mounted on that board.

These parts are handled in the same manner as Type 2 parts; that is, the custom software to be placed on the device is identified on an altered-item drawing, and the altered item itself (the programmed part) is identified by using the altered-item drawing number.

7.2.4 Type 4 Programmable Parts

These parts are programmed after the time of manufacture and are programmed and reprogrammed only while mounted in the next higher assembly.

Software to be placed on these parts should be identified by using a software drawing and the software drawing itself should be a referenced drawing to the next higher assembly. Additional lower-level drawings (to identify the software on each chip) should not be required.

Type 4 parts are becoming more common as solid-state devices begin to replace hard disk and floppy disk drives. The trend is to avoid the use of altered-item drawings (which would require remarking the devices), and instead identify the software by using a software drawing at the appropriate higher-level assembly (for example, board, rack, equipment, and so on).

7.2.5 Type 5 Programmable Parts

Type 5 parts are programmed after the time of manufacture, are initially programmed as individual parts, and are reprogrammed only while mounted on the next higher assembly.

This type is used when a part must be programmed as a separate part and then mounted on a board to provide the board with the capability to load other software. For example, one chip may be required to hold a bootstrap loader software program, which, in turn, will be used to load application software onto other (unprogrammed) chips mounted on the same board. The original software on the Type 5 part may be replaced as a part of loading application software onto the board.

The programmed part must be handled as an altered item during the assembly of the board; otherwise, the programmed part will be indistinguishable from the unprogrammed part. As such, it should be identified by using an altered-item drawing.

The software to be loaded when the parts are mounted on the board should be identified by using a software drawing in a manner similar to that for Type 4 parts. In addition, the software drawing should state whether or not the software on the Type 5 part is being replaced.

7.3 DRAWING REQUIREMENTS

The purpose of identifying software on drawings is to enable the firmware to be controlled and reproduced. To do this the data on the drawing should include:

(a) The location at which the software has been archived.
(b) The electronic media label number of the media that contains that software.
(c) The date on which the media was archived.
(d) The number of the version description document that describes the contents of the electronic media (see Section 6.3.1).
(e) The file name, file type, and version number of the image file.

In this context, the software part of the firmware is treated as software for archiving purposes, and the altered-item drawing should provide sufficient information to permit recovery and further modification of the software.

Caution, in terms of the contents of software drawings, should be used in following the requirements of Section 11.10 of ASME Y14.24M-1989. This standard requires that the source code and/or object code be replicated on the drawing itself. Unfortunately, this requirement serves no apparent useful purpose as the code itself can not be usefully recovered from a hardcopy listing. (Consider having to recover 1000 lines of source code from hard copy and place them on electronic media ...) A preferred approach is to archive the source, object, executable, and/or image files on electronic media in a secure location, and then provide a reference on the software drawing to that archived copy.

7.4 DETERMINE THE MARKING AND LABELING TO BE USED FOR HARDWARE IN WHICH SOFTWARE IS EMBEDDED

This is the fourth step of the process identified in Figure 6-8. There are several scenarios that can occur and several considerations that should be made:

(a) Figure 7-1 (an abbreviated form of Figure 6-4) shows the scenario when piece parts (for example, ROMs and PROMs) are formed individually from unprogrammed parts. The resulting firmware part (the altered-item) is identified and marked with the design activity's CAGE code and PIN (when the PIN is the drawing number of the altered-item drawing).

(b) Figure 7-2 extends Figure 7-1 to show the process in which the software, previously placed on a part, is erased (for example, by placing the EPROM in a specific tool and exposing it to ultraviolet light). The part is then reprogrammed, placing different software in the part. Next, the part is reidentified and remarked, using, for example, an adhesive label.

(c) Figure 7-3 shows the scenarios when parts have been programmed and mounted on a printed circuit (PC) board. The software is then erased in bulk while on the PC board and reprogrammed. This raises cost-effectiveness issues that may require resolution on a individual project basis. There are two schools of thought associated with this action:

(1) The first is that such erasure and reprogramming requires an altered-item drawing for each reprogrammed EPROM, and that each reprogrammed EPROM should be reidentified. This is a

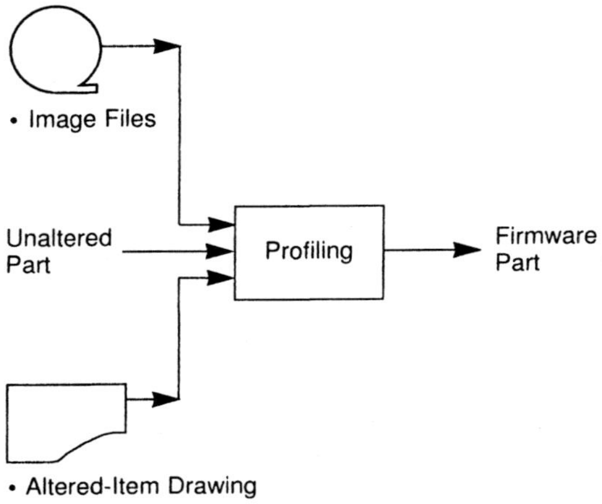

FIGURE 7-1. An Example PROM Production Process.

hardware approach and is consistent with the requirements in MIL-STD-100E and MIL-STD-130G.

(2) The second is that the assembly (printed circuit card) should be treated as one item. The revised assembly drawing should require that the original EPROMs on the PC board be relabeled as generic EPROM parts and that the revised assembly drawing should identify the software that is to be placed on each EPROM. This is a software approach and treats the EPROMs as bulk storage memory.

The differences between these two approaches can be ascertained from a review of Table 7-I. This assumes that the PC board contains 8 EPROMs, each of which contains different software.

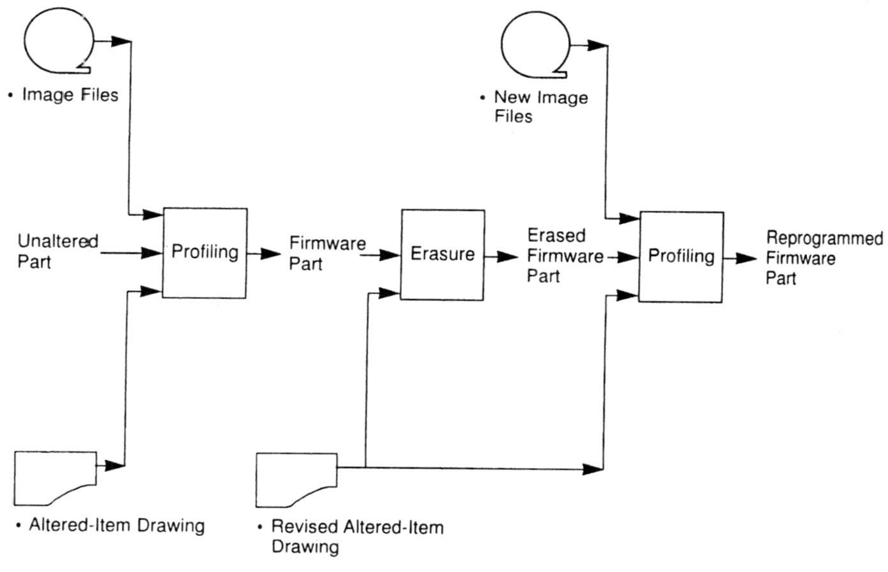

FIGURE 7-2. An Example EPROM Production and Reprogramming Process.

TABLE 7-I. DRAWING REQUIREMENTS FOR THE PROCESS IDENTIFIED IN FIGURE 7-3

Drawing Requirements	Software Approach	Hardware Approach
Assembly drawings	2	2
Altered-item drawings	8	16
Total drawings required	10	18

(d) Figure 7-4 shows the case where unprogrammed parts are mounted on a PC board and are then programmed directly. Similar considerations apply as discussed in the previous scenario.

(e) Figure 7-5 extends the situation to equipment that contains programmable parts that can be reprogrammed through communications lines (for example, EEPROMs). It is perhaps at this point that an approach of reidentifying and remarking all the individual programmable parts in an equipment begins to become untenable. It does not seem reasonable, for example, to require a person at a re-

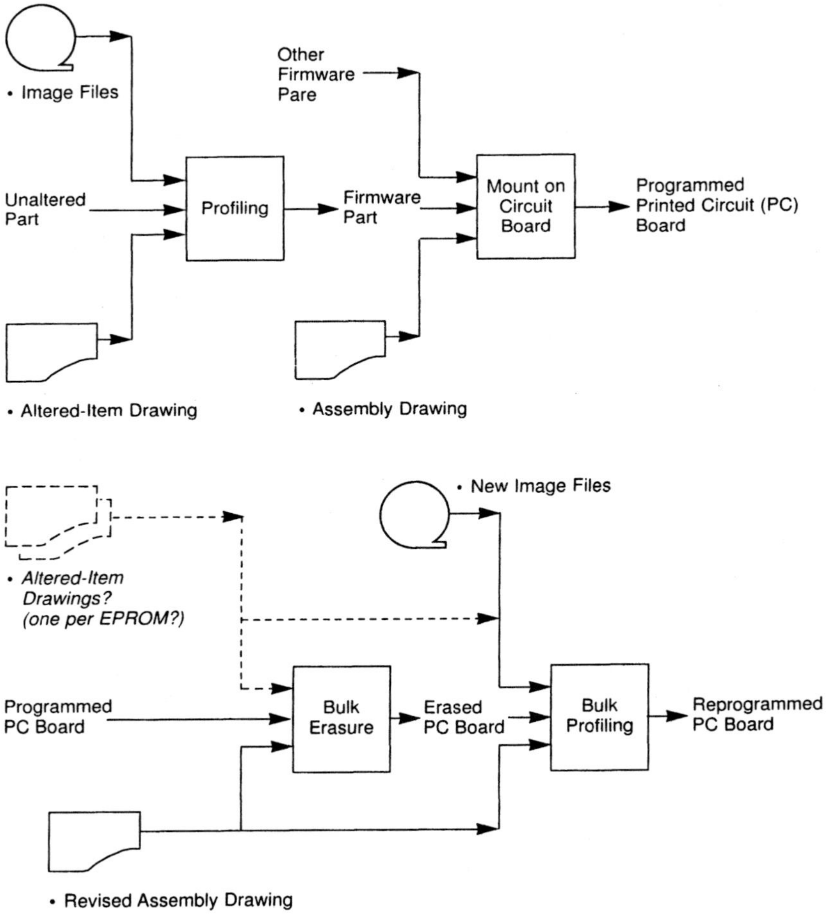

FIGURE 7-3. An Example EPROM Production and Bulk Reprogramming Process.

mote site to open up equipment, pull circuit boards, and paste adhesive labels on EEPROMs when the software has been placed on the equipment from another location. The situation becomes even more pronounced when the equipment at an unattended site has been remotely reprogrammed. The value of requiring a person to go to that remote site, open up equipment, pull circuit boards, and paste adhesive labels on EEPROMs does not appear reasonable.

Section 4.14 of Requirement 67 of MIL-STD-454 provides a method for identifying equipment that contains software through the use of a local or remote display. That still does not resolve the individual piece-part or circuit board identification and marking issues on a generic basis. Pending revision of MIL-STD-973 and MIL-STD-100E, those identification and marking issues will need to be resolved on a project-specific basis. Whichever approach is taken should be expressed in the CM plan, and if MIL-STD-100E and/or MIL-STD-130G are contractually required, then a request for deviation should be submitted to the contracting officer.

Determining the marking and labeling to be used for hardware in which software is embedded requires careful consideration. It is not clear that un-

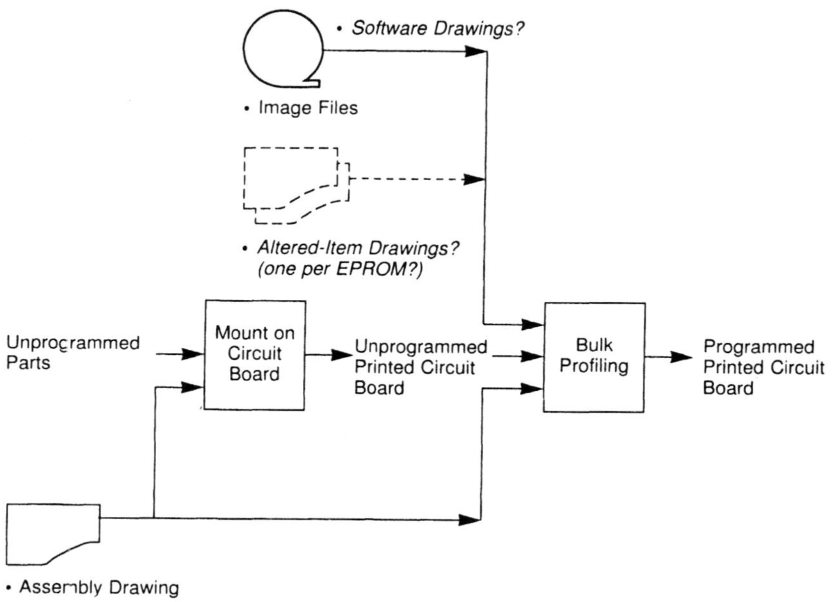

FIGURE 7-4. An Example EEPROM Circuit Board Production Process.

questioning adherence to the military standards provides cost-effective solutions in all cases. Resolution of these concerns at the present time are project-specific and may require the initiation of requests for deviations on specific contracts.

7.5 SUMMARY

Firmware is a unique commodity, a mixture of hardware and software—and both aspects require consideration for proper identification. As the demand for firmware devices increases, and the technology advances, a classification of firmware is needed that reflects the need to identify and control those devices in a cost-effective manner. Pending such action, local procedures will be required to avoid unnecessary costs.

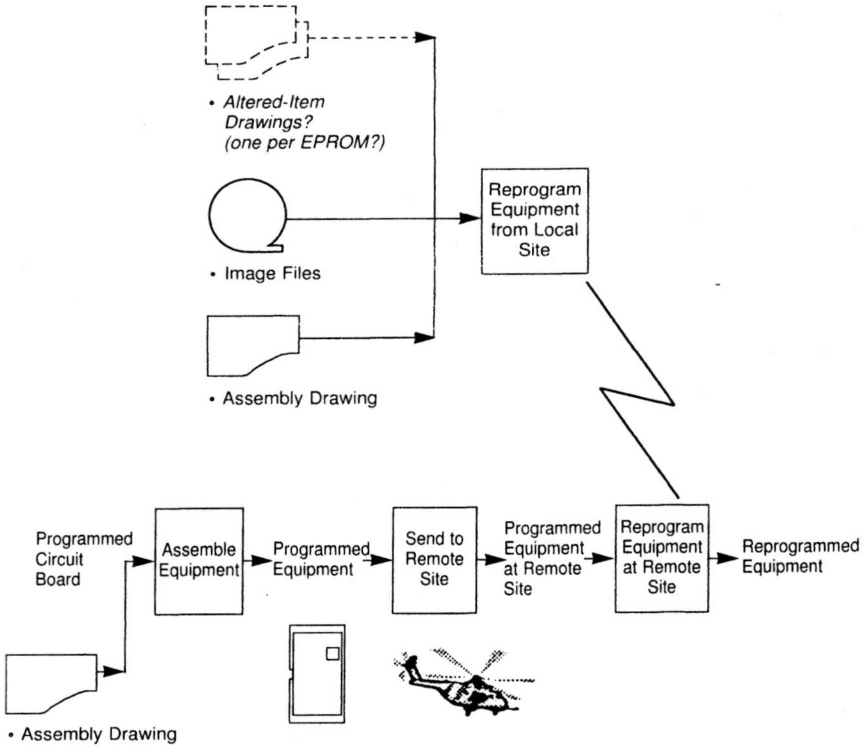

FIGURE 7-5. An Example EEPROM Circuit Board Remote Reprogramming Process.

7.6 EXERCISES

1. Provide a list of the engineering drawings required by MIL-STD-100E and ASME YN14.24M-1989 which defines a circuit card containing four PROMs that were programmed prior to being mounted on the card. Identify the information provided on each type of drawing and relate each type of drawing to the other drawings in the circuit card drawing package.

2. Estimate the cost associated with retrieving the bit patterns from a software drawing per ASME Y14.24M-1929 as a function of: (1) the size of the program, (2) the accuracy of the data retrieval and entry, (3) the bit size of the computer, and, (4) the cost of correcting errors in the executable code. Illustrate this by using the following data: (1) 2,000 lines of source code, (2) 99% accuracy of data retrieval and entry, (3) 32 bits per computer instruction, and, (4) two man-days of effort to find and correct each error at a cost of $40,000 per man-year of engineering time.

3. Compose a bit pattern per Sheet 2, page 31 of ASME Y14.24M-1989 and print the resulting pattern. Use a flat-bed scanner to scan the resulting printout to recover the bit map and place it on electronic media. Perform a DIFFERENCE operation to identify all the differences between the original bit pattern as printed on the paper and the bit pattern as recovered by the use of the scanner.

4. Provide a table comparing the uses and contents of the following Y14.24M-1989 drawings: (1) Procurement Control, (2) Vendor Item, (3) Source Control, and, (4) Design Control.

5. Add an additional column to the table developed in Exercise 4 and use it to identify the differences between the requirements of Y14.24M-1989 and MIL-STD-100E for control drawings.

8

IDENTIFICATION OF DRAWINGS AND OTHER DOCUMENTS

Having identified the hardware, software, and firmware, the remaining categories of items to be identified are drawings (together with their associated lists) and other documents.

8.1 DRAWINGS AND ASSOCIATED LISTS

A *drawing* (or an engineering drawing, to use the full term) is an engineering document that discloses (directly or by reference), through the means of pictorial or textual presentations or a combination of both, the physical and functional end-product requirements of an item. Drawings come in many sizes and flavors, but usually share the following characteristics:

(a) A drawing consists of a sheet of drafting material displaying the basic format features, such as title block, general tolerance blocks, and margins.
(b) Drawings are produced to specified formats, including the arrangement and organization of information within a drawing. This includes such features as the size and arrangement of blocks, notes, lists, revision information, and the use of optional or supplemental blocks.

Drawings are normally augmented by associated lists, which provide a tabulation of pertinent engineering information depicted on an engineering drawing or a set of engineering drawings (for example, a parts list).

Drawings and associated lists are normally collected and put into engineering drawing packages; these are collections of engineering drawings, associated lists, documents, manufacturer specifications and standards, and other information relating to the design and manufacture of an item or system.

Details on drawings, per se, are specified in MIL-STD-100E (for those in government work) and also in ASME Standard Y14.24M-1989, "Types And Applications Of Engineering Drawings."

8.1.1 Identification

Drawings are identified by a drawing number, which consists of a unique set of letters, numbers, or a combination of letters and numbers, which may or may not be separated by dashes. The number is assigned to a particular drawing (or list) for identification purposes by the design activity. The drawing number assigned by the design activity is normally augmented by the manufacturer's identification when the drawing is to be used outside of the organization that assigned the drawing number. (In government work, the manufacturer is normally assigned a Commercial and Government Entity (CAGE) Code or an NATO Supply Code for Manufacturers (NSCM) code as an agreed-to manufacturer's designation.)

In a similar manner, each drawing has a drawing title. This is the same title by which the part or item is known and consists of a basic name, a type designator (if a government drawing), and sufficient modifiers to differentiate like items in the same major assembly.

Identification of associated lists is done by using the drawing number of the drawing with which the list is associated, and combining it with a prefix that specifies the type of list (for example, PL for parts list). The list title reflects the basic noun or noun phrase of the item to which the list applies (for example, wiring harness).

8.1.2 Drawing Classification

Drawings are classified according to their projected usage. The former usage, in DOD-D-1000B, was to provide this classification by the use of levels and descriptive titles. The current usage, in MIL-T-31000, is to classify drawings using the descriptive titles without the use of level numbers. The usage of level numbers has been so widespread that they should be part of the configuration management vocabulary; hence, they are provided herein.

(a) Level 1, *conceptual and developmental design drawings*, as a minimum disclose sufficient engineering design information to evaluate an engineering concept, and usually provide information sufficient to fabricate developmental hardware.
(b) Level 2, *production prototype and limited production drawings* are used to disclose a design approach suitable to support the manufacture of a production prototype and limited production model.
(c) Level 3, *production drawings*, provide engineering definitions sufficiently complete to enable a competent manufacturer to produce, and maintain quality control of item(s) to the degree that physical and performance characteristics interchangeable with those of the original design are obtainable without resorting to additional product design effort, additional design data, or recourse to the original design activity.

There are two consequences of the drawing classification. The first consequence is on the configuration change control authority; Level 1 drawings are controlled less formally than Level 2 drawings, while a change in a Level 3 drawing may require customer approval.

The second consequence is the additional requirement that the production drawings be sufficiently complete to enable a competent manufacturer to produce equivalent items. Manufacturing processes can be quite involved and there can be a great deal of difficulty encountered in taking production drawings from one manufacturer and making them the basis of soliciting bids from other manufacturers to build the same item. Long-term experience is that the production drawings are not always complete and that there is no viable way to judge the completeness of the production drawings without physically building the desired items using those drawings. At least one third-party manufacturer has made a very comfortable living bidding very low prices to manufacture radios for the US using government-supplied production drawings. Inevitably, a year into the production, the government contracting officer would get a call from this manufacturer saying that: (1) the radios were built exactly according to the drawings, (2) they did not work, (3) the manufacturer had determined what was wrong with the drawings and, consequently, what had to be changed in the radios, and, (4) the cost for these changes (to make the radios work) would greatly exceed the original bid price.

8.1.3 Drawing Types

Table 8-I provides one set of engineering drawing categories as defined in DOD-STD-100C, while ASME Y14.24M-1989 provides another set. DOD-STD-100C has since been replaced with MIL-STD-100E, which in turn provides a reference to ASME Y14.24M-1989. ASME Y14.24M-1989 does provide a cross-reference to DOD-STD-100C drawing categories, and would usually be preferred. The definitions of the drawing categories identified in Table 8-I are provided in Appendix A.

TABLE 8-I. ENGINEERING DRAWING CATEGORIES

Category	Subcategory
Assembly	Arrangement
	Detail
	Exploded
	Inseparable
	Installation
	Matched parts
	Photo
	Tabulated
Construction	Erection
	Plan
	Plot (plat)
	Vicinity plan or site
Control	Altered-item
	Envelope
	Installation
	Interface control
	Selected item
	Source
	Specification
	Standardized military
Diagrammatic	Connection or wiring
	Interconnection
	Logic
	Mechanical schematic
	Piping
	Schematic
	Single-line or one-line

TABLE 8-I. (Continued)

Category	Subcategory
Detail	Monodetail
	Multidetail
	Tabulated detail
	Tube bend
Elevation	
Installation	
Layout	
Special-purpose	Book-form
	Wiring list
	Cable assembly
	Certification data sheet
	Combinations of adopted items
	Contour definition
	Correlation
	Formulation
	Kit drawing
	Modification
	Numerical control
	Printed wiring master (Stable base artwork) pattern
	Printed wiring master
	Ship equipment (marine item)
	Undimensioned
	Wiring Harness

8.1.4 Caution

Care and judgment should be used prior to accepting and implementing the use of a new drawing category. For example, ASME Y14.24M-1989 introduces a new drawing category of a computer program/software drawing. As stated and shown in Section 11.10 and Figure 51 of this standard, such a computer program/software drawing would include a listing of the code, a load map, and so forth. The difficulty with such a drawing is in its usage.

The purpose of an engineering drawing is to enable the described item to be built from the description contained within the engineering drawing. Unfortunately, for a reasonable-size computer program (10,000 lines of source code), it is usually not reasonable to expect that the computer program can be regenerated from the source code listing. Attempting to have a typist enter the program from a keyboard will produce the usual complement of errors, which for software might prove to be very interesting. Consider, for example, the line of FORTRAN source code in Figure 8-1. This is a perfectly valid FORTRAN expression and is the start of a DO loop. What this says is that the sequence of instructions down to the instruction identified with the label "5" should be executed for the values of the variable I = 1, 2, 3, 4, 5, 6, and 7.

In a similar manner, Figure 8-2 is also a valid FORTRAN expression. In reading it, however, it should be recognized that FORTRAN will concatenate blanks. What this states is that the value of the variable DO5I is set equal to 1.7.

The only difference between the two FORTRAN statements is the substitution of a period, for a comma, both of which are difficult to distinguish in a computer program listing. This is a trivial error that could easily be made by a typist (or a scanner), but it is exactly this type of error that once caused a spacecraft to fail after being launched.

The preferred way to reproduce the code is to keep the code on electronic media and change it under process control. If the code will be kept on electronic media under controlled conditions, the cost-effectiveness of keeping a printed listing of the code as a controlled drawing should be evaluated before initiating such an endeavor.

8.2 DOCUMENTS

The term *documents*, in the context of this book, includes specifications, standards, pamphlets, reports, and printed, typewritten, or other information relating to the design, procurement, manufacture, test, or inspection of items or services under a contract. To preclude confusion, the usage of the term *document* in this book does not include drawings (engineering drawings) or associated lists. Care is recommended in the use of the terms *drawing* and *document*, as in some contexts the terms may overlap and cause confusion.

```
DO 5 I = 1, 7
```

FIGURE 8-1. A FORTRAN Statement Example.

```
DO 5 I = 1.7
```

FIGURE 8-2. Another FORTRAN Statement Example.

8.2.1 Document Identification

Each document has a *document identification number* (DIN), which consists of numbers or combinations of letters, numbers, and dashes. In addition to the title, this number is assigned to a document for identification purposes.

Drawing numbers can be used as documentation identification numbers but this usage is not always preferred for the following reasons: the use of drawing numbers requires a central office of issue and record, and a drawing number provides no additional information. For these reasons, other schemes are used in order to include sequential project numbers, contract data requirement list numbers, and document type numbers.

Sequential project numbers combine a fixed project identifier of, typically, five alphanumeric characters that identify the project, followed by a unique number. The number is initialized at 1 and incremented for every new document. Revision letters are used to indicate when a revision of the document has been issued. A typical documentation identification number is shown in Figure 8-3. As shown therein, the project identifier is 714F and is fixed for that project. The number that follows, separated from the project identifier by a dash, indicates that this is the 101st document issued on the project, and that this is the second revision.

If the document is being provided as part of a contract, the contract requirements for all the documentation to be provided as part of the contract may be expressed in a *contract data requirements list* (CDRL). In this instance, the unique CDRL number used to identify the requirements for that particular document can be used as part of the identifier. In this case, as shown in Figure 8-4, the CDRL number is used. In this scheme, some method is required to ensure that CDRLs from one project are not mistaken for CDRLs from another project. To avoid this, a project identifier is pro-

714F–101B

FIGURE 8-3. A Documentation Identification Number Example.

714F
CDRL C005

FIGURE 8-4. An Example of a Documentation Identification Number Using a CDRL Number.

vided in the prior line. This can present difficulties if more than one document is being provided as part of that CDRL (for example, if as part of one CDRL requirement, 14 different specifications are being delivered for 14 different computer programs). Further combinations of sequential numbers (1 through 14) and revision letters can be assigned, but the information content defining the document is not as great as it could be (for example, identifying the specific computer program to which it applies).

A better usage is shown in Figure 8-5. As shown therein, the documentation identification number starts with the project identifier (714F). The first documentation identification number employs a field that identifies the computer program by using the computer program acronym (in this case, RTC for Real-Time Control). In both cases, the next field is the document acronym (SRS for software requirements specification, and MTEP for master test and evaluation plan). Each ends with the revision letter (A or B). This not only provides a unique numbering scheme but also identifies the type of document. For a document cover this information is not needed, as the cover will contain the name of the document, the computer program to which it applies, the project of which it is a part, and so forth. However, in cross-referencing (for example, in a configuration status accounting report), the ability to tell what the document is without further effort becomes quite valuable.

In the long run, it is not extraordinarily important what document identification scheme is used; it is important that such a scheme be established early in the life of the project and followed consistently thereafter.

8.2.2 Document Source File Names

The preferred method of handling documentation is to store and maintain it on electronic media. This requires that the source files of the documents themselves be named in some manner to facilitate unique identification. Furthermore, although the documents themselves are under configuration control as complete items, the sizes of the documents usually require that a total document be maintained in more than one file, usually broken up into chapters. Figure 8-6 shows a typical procedure for naming documentation source files. As shown therein: (1) each source file that is part of a particu-

714F–RTC–SRS–B

714F–MTEP–A

FIGURE 8-5. Informational Documentation Identification Number Examples.

lar document has a file name, which provides complete identification of the document itself and the particular revision of which this file is a part; and, (2) the command procedure, which uses the source files to produce the finished document, has a meaningful name itself. The purpose for all of this is to provide meaningful information to those who use these files and preclude operator errors. (The term *SDML* in Figure 8-6 refers to a particular file type.)

8.2.3 Document Formats

One task sometimes undertaken by the configuration management organization, as a matter of enlightened self-interest, is the development and production of documentation templates. MIL-STD-100E and ASME Y14.24M-1989 already provide detailed information and examples regarding the for mat and content of engineering drawings and associated lists; however, current technology for specifications, for example, is not as well developed.

SPP-CM-114

To: Distribution A

SUBJECT: Document File Naming Conventions

Effective this date, the structure and naming conventions for all deliverable software documentation on this project shall conform to the following:

File Name	File Content
XXXX_YYYY_ZZZZ_FRONT.SDML	Title Page and Preface
XXXX_YYYY_ZZZZ_CH_1.SDML	Chapter 1
. . .	
XXXX_YYYY_ZZZZ_APP_A.SDML	Appendix A
. . .	
XXXX_YYYY_ZZZZ_CMD.SDML	Command Procedure
. . .	

Notes:
1. XXXX is the computer program short name; e.g., RCDC.
2. YYYY is the Document Type CI abbreviation; e.g., "SRS."
3. ZZZZ is the Document Revision Indicator; e.g., "A."

D. Boss

FIGURE 8-6. An Example Document File Naming Convention.

The average engineer, when told to write a requirements specification, will immediately need to determine the content of such a document and what format is to be used. In various levels of detail, that data exists in associated documents; for example, Data Item Description DI-MCCR-80025A covers software requirements specifications, as does IEEE Std 830-1994. Neither of these provide sufficient information in order to state precisely what a particular organization's requirement specifications should contain and how they should be formatted.

One way to solve this problem is for the organization to go through a series of iterations on the requirements specifications until there is common agreement on one specification as an example of good practice. The rest are then required to use that approved requirement specification as an example for the remaining specifications. This is both expensive and time-consuming. The configuration management organization shares this pain as the configuration management library churns with repetitive entries and duplications.

Another way to solve this problem, or at least to reduce its intensity, is for the configuration management organization (in coordination with the software manager) to produce appropriate documentation templates, complete with examples and advice. The configuration management organization is suggested for this task because it is a disinterested party with no particular bias towards any one specialty area. This lack of bias serves to reduce the configuration management workload associated with the processing of multiple issues of the same document; because of this, the configuration management organization will be viewed as directly contributing to the success of the project.

Producing the templates means planning the efforts, writing the first drafts, coordinating the results, implementing the comments, and so forth. It should not be construed that the configuration management organization would produce the final templates and then attempt to force them on the developers.

8.3 SUMMARY

The fourth category of material which needs identification includes drawings and documents. The identification and formats of drawings and their associated lists is specified in both government and consensus standards. Identification and formats of documents are currently not so rigidly specified. Various schemes exist for document identification; one should be chosen early in the project and used consistently thereafter. Finally, as an expansion of the configuration management task, it is recommended that the configuration management organization develop, publish, and gain a consensus on specific document templates.

8.4 EXERCISES

1. Define the types of associated lists and state the purpose for each. (Hint, see ASME Standard Y14.34M)

2. Define the relationships among: (1) Altered-Item Drawings per Y14.24.M, (2) Process Charts per ANSI Y14.3M-1979, and, (3) Process Specifications, MIL-STD-490A. State the relationships and show how each is referenced by the others.

3. Prepare a convention to identify documents using the specification tree in Figure 4-9 and the Steam Power System structure shown in Figure 6-2. As part of this, extend the Steam Power System Structure to include three hardware CIs.

9

CONFIGURATION CONTROL

The third step in managing a collection of items is to control the changes made to these items; this process, *configuration control*, is the third major process identified in Figure 1-2. As a process (or subprocess), configuration control is the systematic proposal, justification, evaluation, coordination, approval or disapproval, and implementation of all approved changes in the configuration of an item after formal establishment of its configuration documentation. This subprocess flow is depicted in Figure 9-1. The numbers on the right-hand side of each box in Figure 9-1 identify the subsections where details on each of these subprocesses. (It should be noted that this view of the process flow includes the identification of the problem. This larger view of the configuration control process is taken because the actions involving problem reports affect the maintenance of the integrity of the product.)

9.1 IDENTIFY THE PROBLEM

The failure of an item to conform to specified requirements is one of the items that initiate the configuration control process. The others (shown in Figure 9-1), are concerned with enhancements or directed changes.

9.1.1 Document The Occurrence

The first step in resolving a problem is to formally record the failure on a *problem report* (PR); this should be done at the time it occurs. There are many good reasons for not formally recording a failure immediately; however, if a failure is not recorded at the time it occurs it is normally unrecoverable. Also, the failure will reoccur—probably at a less opportune time.

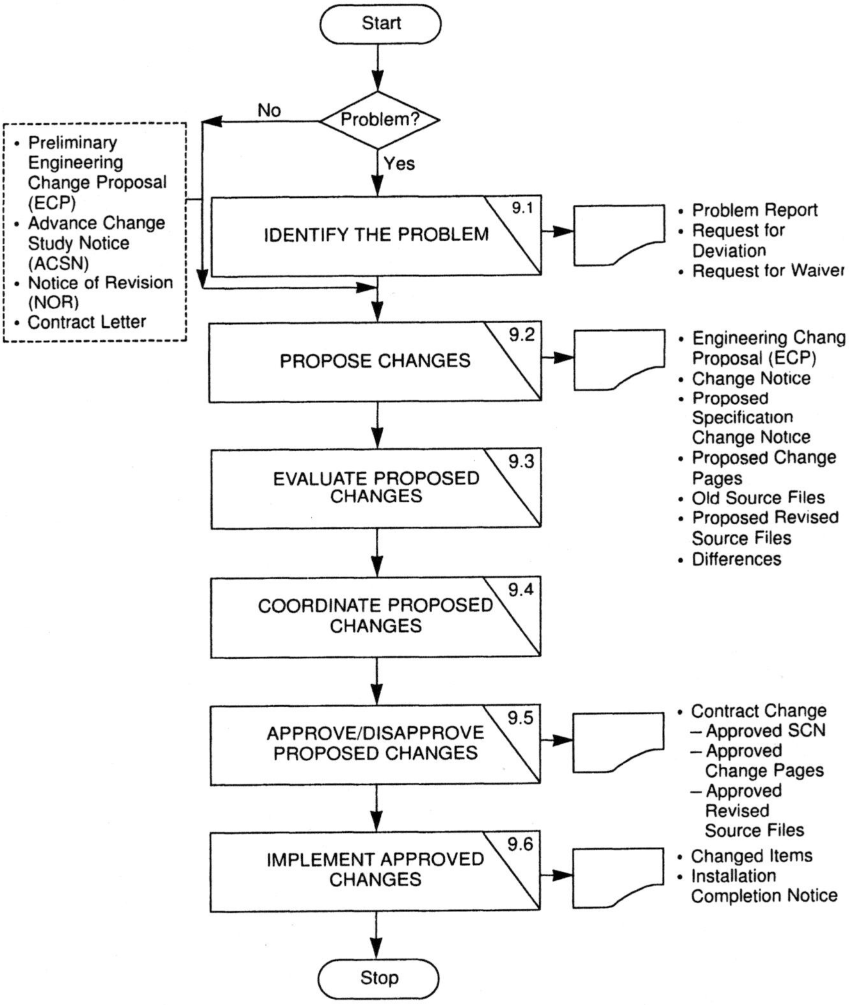

FIGURE 9-1. Configuration Control Subprocess Flow Diagram.

Problem reports are made on any item that is part of an internal or external baseline. The degree of formality is a function of the project size, but there are usually several characteristics:

(a) The problem must be formally documented by the originator on either paper or electronic media. In the latter case, a form is provided on the screen and the data fields to be entered are highlighted. Commercial products that provide all the problem reporting functions are unknown to the author, probably because a specific organization's requirements need a high degree of tailoring.

    There are many products that support the development of a problem reporting system; for example, forms management systems are commonplace and many of the data base management systems have an associated forms development capability. In contemplating these usages, consideration should also be made of how the information from the problem report will be processed. Automatic transferral of data from a problem report into an electronic database is the next logical step in improving the overall development process. This is because the problem report data can be processed in a number of ways to provide management insight into means of improving the overall development processes. However, the integration of the problem reporting system may present major interface difficulties, unless this capability is considered at the time when the problem reporting system is being established.

(b) The problem report should indicate the essential elements of information to be recorded. These should include the date, time, and location of the problem occurrence and the environment in which it happened. For example, if this took place in the middle of a formal acceptance test of the hardware, items of interest would include the hardware configuration, the software that was being run on the machine, and the exact item of the procedure (step number) at which the screen went blank. (See Section 12.2.5 for more details on information elements of problem reports.)

At the time the event occurs, it will probably not be possible to identify the fault, that is, the physical condition that caused the item to fail to perform in a required manner (for example, a short circuit or a broken wire). At the time the failure occurs, it is important to not spend an undue amount of time trying to determine the cause of the failure. Attempting to determine the cause of a failure on the spur of the moment is normally unproductive.

When a problem occurs, it is very difficult to state exactly what caused the problem. For example, in one complex computer-controlled communications system, the system became nonfunctional three days after the test was initiated. Restarting the test resulted in another failure of exactly the same type in a similar period. Both the hardware and software had previously passed all their acceptance tests, but the system was failing (this occurs more often than not). It took a period of approximately four weeks to determine the precise cause of the failure. The source of the problem was that the computer had eight hardware-initiated interrupts. Only six were used in the design of the software. The other two hardware-initiated interrupts could be externally initiated, and lines for that purpose were wired to connectors in the computer. After three days of steady operation, static built up on the connectors, eventually causing one of the two interrupts to be initiated. This switched control of the program to a location specified in a specific hardware register. This problem could be construed as having two causes: the hardware, because the terminator cards for the interrupt connectors were not installed, (thus allowing the interrupt to be initiated); and the software because the contents of the last two registers were not specified as part of the design. The bottom line is that a preconceived notion that it was either a hardware or a software problem would have precluded applying both hardware and software skills in finding a solution to this problem.

There are many different circumstances in which a problem report could be written, for example:

(a) During a technical review of design documentation
(b) In the test facility during hardware/software integration
(c) During the conduct of a formal acceptance test
(d) In the factory when an item of product exceeds the allowable limits
(e) During operation of the item in the field

Each will normally have different requirements for information; as a result there may be different problem report forms for different situations. The important thing is to identify what the item's life cycle is, decide what information is needed during each phase of the life cycle, and establish the required forms before they are to be used.

9.1.2 Review the Problem Report

The second step in resolving the problem is to have one or more management reviews of the problem. An initial review is made to ensure that the statement of the problem is clear, that all essential elements of information that were available have been recorded, and that the problem as stated is a valid failure. Following that determination, a priority of action is assigned, and resources are allocated to determine the cause of the failure.

Depending on the circumstances, these decisions can be made directly by an integration director at the time of the failure, or, for a very large system already in the field at various locations, the problem report may be reviewed by a problem report board for disposition.

9.1.3 Determine the Cause of the Failure

The majority of this task is outside the scope of configuration management, per se, but the data gathered during this subprocess is extremely valuable. In this process, then, configuration management acts in a wider context to support the gathering of metric data for project improvement actions. Problem reports contain data that, when the problem is solved, would assist the project and the company to improve the development and production process. When processed, these categories can provide valuable insights into the process and the indicators of where additional effort could best be expended. However, caution should be used in applying data from the problem report (for example, an entry indicating the cost or time used to fix the problem). That data is notoriously inaccurate and will probably be different from the data in the cost accounting system. Reconciling this data with the cost accounting system data is a thankless task, done after the fact and accompanied by much anguish and pain.

9.1.4 Determine the Corrective Action

After determining the fault, several different courses of action can be pursued. Some of these are indicated below:

(a) If a hardware item has been tested in the factory as part of a production run, and it has been determined that the item has failed to conform to specified requirements, then the action is processed as a nonconformance (see Section 10.1).

(b) If the item is found to depart from the specified requirements, but nevertheless is considered suitable either for "use as is" or after repair by an approved method, then a request for waiver will be initiated (see Section 12.2.7). A *request for waiver* is a request to have an item accepted which, after manufacture, has been found to depart from specified requirements. As an example, a request for waiver might be initiated if it were found that source files did not comply with a contractual requirement that each source file was to contain not more than 100 executable statements.

(c) If, prior to manufacture, departure from a particular performance or design requirement of a specification, drawing, or other document is desired for a specific number of units or a specific period of time, then a request for a deviation will be initiated. The request for deviation does not contemplate revision of the applicable specification or drawing (see Section 12.2.6). A request for deviation might be submitted, for example, to permit a particular component of a computer software configuration item to be coded in the FORTRAN programming language when the contract called for all software to be coded in Ada.

For the majority of the actions, the problem report is used to initiate the PROPOSE CHANGES subprocess.

9.2 PROPOSE CHANGES

9.2.1 Inputs

There are a number of different documents that can be used to begin the change process and, as shown in Table 9-I, each of these can be used to initiate another document in that group.

(a) The most common item that initiates a change is a problem report, the report documenting the occurrence of a failure—an event in which the item was unable to perform its required function. In turn, depending on the circumstances surrounding the problem report,

TABLE 9-I: THE ITERATIVE NATURE OF INITIATING DOCUMENTATION

Originating Document	Resulting Document			
	Preliminary Engineering Change Proposal	Advance Change Study Notice	Notice of Revision	Contract Letter
Problem report	Yes	Yes	Yes	Yes
Preliminary engineering change proposal	—	—	Yes	Yes
Advance change Study notice	—	—	—	Yes
Notice of revision	Yes	Yes	—	Yes
Contract letter	Yes	Yes	Yes	Yes

the problem report itself may cause any one of the other four types of change-process initiating documents to be initiated.

(b) *Preliminary engineering change proposals* (ECPs) and *advance change study notices* (ACSNs) are documents used to obtain customer concurrence to proceed with an ECP classified as routine (which of the two documents is to be used is normally specified by contract). The reason for the submittal of these documents is that there can be substantial costs associated with the preparation of an ECP. The contractor would prefer that these costs be allowable charges under the contract; the customer, on the other hand, would want to have a voice in the decision to expend any substantial amounts of money that will be charged against the contract. Both the preliminary ECP and the ACSN provide an opportunity for customer review of a change proposal concept in its early stages.

(c) A *notice of revision* (NOR) is a document originated by one contractor that proposes changes to an item not under the design activity control of that contractor. As such, if approved, it may result in the further preliminary documents identified in Table 9-I.

(d) Finally, the configuration control subprocess may be initiated by a contract letter proposing that some change be made. In turn, a contract letter may lead to further documents as shown.

9.2.2 Processing

Figure 9-2 shows an example process by which proposed changes are processed:

(a) On receipt of a problem report (PR), notice of revision (NOR), or a contract letter, the document goes through a review and approval cycle. If not approved, the originator is notified and the process is terminated.

(b) Further work may be required to propose a solution to the problem, to complete the change proposed in the notice of revision, or to respond to the contract letter. (In this context, the response to the problem may be to request a waiver or a deviation from the terms of the contract.)

   (1) If additional substantial effort is not required to define what is to be done, then a change package will be prepared, terminating the PROPOSE CHANGES step.

   (2) If additional substantial effort is required to define what is to be done, then either a preliminary engineering change proposal or an advance change study notice (depending on the terms of the contract) will be prepared.

(c) As shown on Figure 9-2, a preliminary engineering change proposal or an advance change study notice may result from a problem report, and so on, or may be initiated independently. Regardless of the origin, the documents go through a contractor internal review and approval cycle and are then sent to the customer for approval to proceed.

9.2.3 Outputs

The output of this PROPOSE CHANGES step is a *change package*, a set of documents that completely describes and justifies changes to configuration documentation, software, and/or engineering drawings.

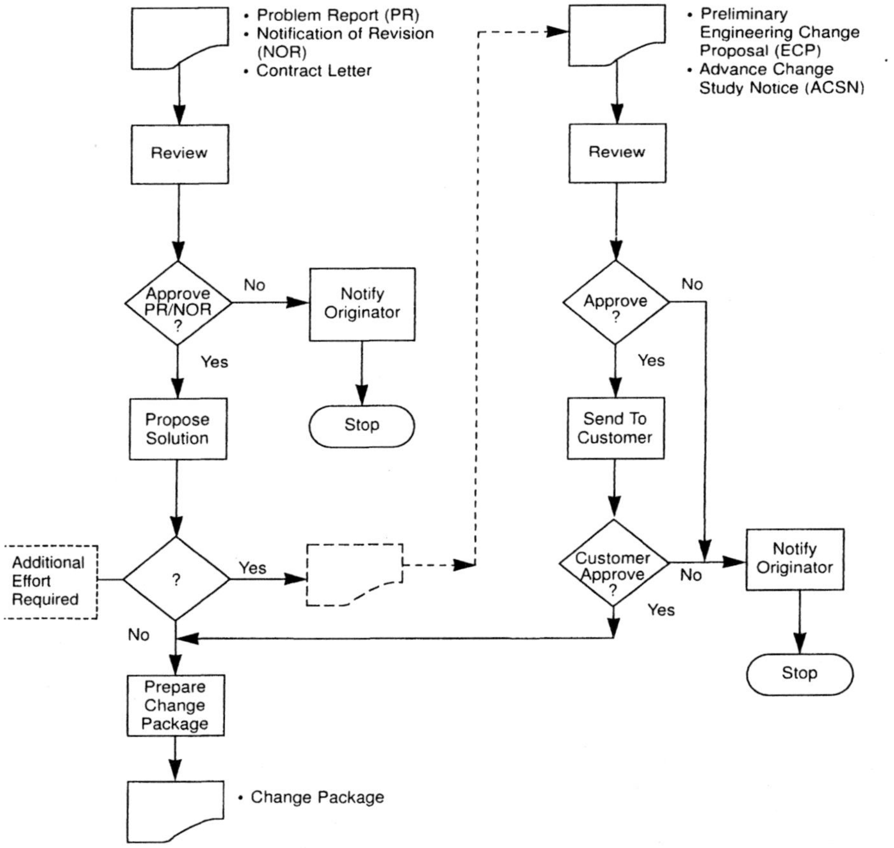

FIGURE 9-2. An Example PROPOSE CHANGES Process Flow.

9.2.3.1 Baseline Change Packages

Items that are part of a change package for baselined items (for example, items that are part of a functional, allocated, or product baseline) are identified in Table 9-II.

(a) The engineering change proposal is the most common item and, for government contracts, is usually highly stylized. Some of the determinations to be made in preparing an engineering change proposal are shown in Figure 9-3. Detailed definitions of the items identified in Figure 9-3 are provided in Section 5.4.2 of MIL-STD-973.

(b) *Change notices* (CN) [otherwise known as *engineering change notices* (ECNs), or *design change notices* (DCNs)] are used for changes to engineering drawings and associated lists; they detail the changes to be made to drawings and provide a transmittal form. For Class II changes, a further transmittal form is not used. For Class I changes, the change notice is attached to the engineering change proposal.

Justification	Type	Classification	Priority
B — Interface	Preliminary	Class I	Routine
C — Compatibility	Final	Class II	Urgent
D — Deficiency			Emergency
O — Operational or Logistic Support			
P — Production Stoppage			
R — Cost Reduction			
S — Safety			
V — Value Engineering			

FIGURE 9-3. Some Determinations to be Made in Completing an Engineering Change Proposal.

TABLE 9-II. EXAMPLE CHANGE PACKAGE COMPOSITION FOR A BASELINED ITEM

Change Package Components	Baselined Item to be Changed					
	Configuration Documentation		Software		Engineering Drawing	
	Class I	Class II	Class I	Class II	Class I	Class II
Engineering change proposal (ECP)	Yes	Yes	Yes	Yes	Yes	—
Change notice (CN)	—	—	—	—	Yes	Yes
Specification change notice (SCN)	Yes	Yes	Yes	Yes	—	—
Change pages	Yes	Yes	—	—	—	—
Old source files	—	—	Yes	Yes	—	—
Revised source files	—	—	Yes	Yes	—	—
Differences	—	—	Yes	Yes	—	—

Change notices are also of interest to the software community because: (1) the body of the drawing may refer to software (for example, an altered-item drawing for a programmable part), and/or, (2) the change notice itself may be produced from software.

(c) *Specification change notices* (SCNs) are used to identify changes in controlled documents (excluding engineering drawings and associated lists), and one specification change notice per document to be changed. In software usage, specification change notices are also used to identify the source files in a computer software configuration item that are to be revised. Details applicable to government usage are provided in Appendix F of MIL-STD-973.

(d) Identification of changes to be made to documents can be done in a number of ways; using change pages is the most common. Change pages can take many forms; for example, the changes may be indicated in hand-written form on a copy of the old page being changed, or the actual change in a particular paragraph itself may be indicated in a "from-to" manner. Alternately, when the revisions become so voluminous that change pages are inappropriate, then a complete revision may be issued.

The change pages for a specific document are normally attached to the specification change notice which addresses that document.

Figure 9-4 provides an example change package for baselined documents. As shown therein, the two specifications change notices (SCNs) (one per document to be changed) are attached to the engineering change proposal. In turn, attached to each specification change notice are change pages for those pages in the documents that are to be changed.

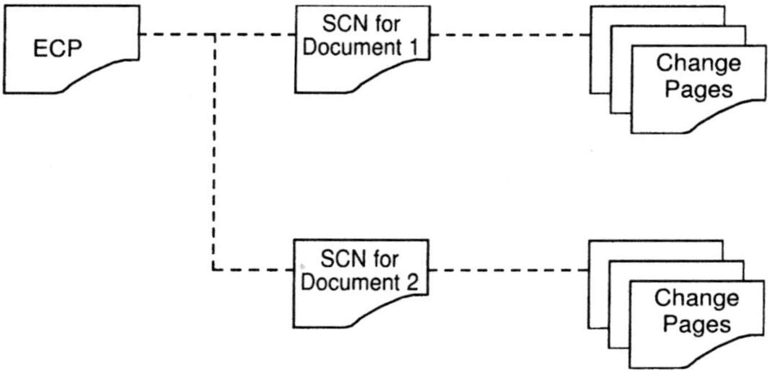

FIGURE 9-4. Example Change Package for Baselined Documents.

Figure 9-5 shows an example change package for software files where the ECP provides management data, the SCNs list (for each CSCI) the files that are proposed to be changed, and the changes themselves are identified by a listing of the old source files, a listing of the revised source files, and a listing of their differences. The listing of the differences is the result of running a DIFFERENCES program against the two sets of files—the DIFFERENCES program compares the two files and prints a list of the differences.

Methods used to identify the changes to software differ and can take several forms:

(a) Figure 9-5 shows the source files being provided as part of the change package. In this case, the output is a product whose changes cannot be readily inspected by a reviewer (for example, an executable file that consists of "1s" and "0s"). As a result, an assessment of the validity of changes to an executable file should include a review and assessment of the original source file(s), the changed source file(s), and the DIFFERENCE files.

(b) Alternately, if the input software is not readable by a reviewer, then the printed output is usually used to highlight the changes made to the previous version. As an example, consider the source file for a what-you-see-is-what-you-get (WYSIWYG) document; it is readable when displayed under program control on the face of a CRT but the printed source file itself may be difficult to analyze.

The use of inputs or outputs and/or differences may not provide a complete solution to the problem of identifying what changes have made and assessing the effect of these changes to documents. Some tools (for example, computer-aided software engineering (CASE) tools) have a ripple

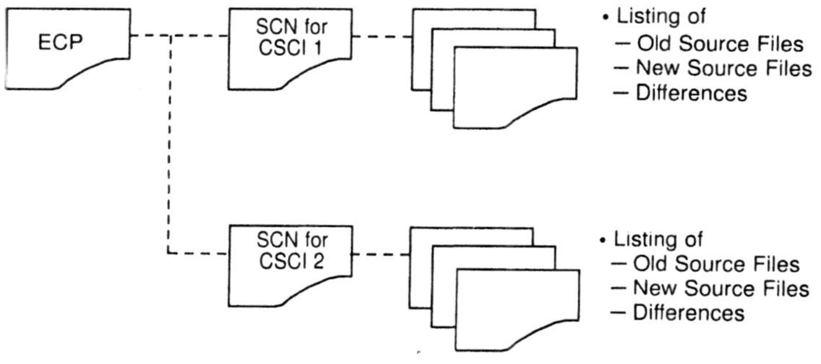

FIGURE 9-5. An Example Change Package for Software.

effect on their outputs (one change in one input line may cascade into many changes in the output), and the current state of DIFFERENCES tools do not operate on graphics.

9.2.3.2 Developmental Configuration Change Packages

Table 9-III extends the material discussed in Table 9-II to developmental configuration items. The major differences between the two tables are that:

(a) There is no delineation between Class I and Class II as all items in the developmental configuration are under the change control of the developing organization.
(b) Although engineering change proposals are used, the highly-stylized format associated with the government forms is usually not used. Rather, local forms are used and these may, depending on the developing organization's needs, just be a cover memorandum.

9.3 EVALUATE PROPOSED CHANGES

Prior to coordinating a proposed change package, an evaluation of the proposed change package is required to avoid coordination of an incomplete or unsuitable change package.

TABLE 9-III. EXAMPLE CHANGE PACKAGE COMPOSITION FOR A DEVELOPMENTAL CONFIGURATION ITEM

Change Package Components	Developmental Configuration Item to be Changed		
	Configuration Documentation	Software	Engineering Drawing
Engineering change proposal (ECP)	See accompanying text	See accompanying text	—
Change notice (CN)	—	—	Yes
Specification change notice (SCN)	Yes	Yes	—
Change pages	Yes	—	—
Old source files	—	Yes	—
Revised source files	—	Yes	—
Differences	—	Yes	—

Evaluating a proposed change package involves an assessment of the package against established criteria. Some of these criteria are identified in Table 9-IV, and are expressed in the form of questions. These are example criteria only; a more detailed set can be derived from Department Of Defense Form DD 1692, Engineering Change Proposal.

Evaluating the changes prior to approval normally requires that the end product (for example, an executable file, an image file, a document, an engineering drawing, and so on) be provided for that evaluation. Software end products are usually produced in the following manner:

(a) The inputs are in a storage area controlled by the CM organization (for example, a designated temporary holding area in the SCML).
(b) When produced, the software end products (for example, a print file for an engineering drawing) are also in the same controlled storage area.
(c) The transformation of the inputs into the end products is a controlled objective process executed by the configuration management organization.

The benefit of this approach is that, after the end product has been evaluated and approved, the source files, intermediate files (as appropriate), and the software end products can be transferred to the appropriate baseline or developmental configuration directory in the SCML without concern about the reproducibility of the results. Otherwise, the situation may arise where the proposed changes were approved but the resulting source files cannot be compiled (this is only one example).

TABLE 9-IV. EXAMPLE CRITERIA AGAINST WHICH TO EVALUATE PROPOSED CHANGE PACKAGES

No.	Question
1.	Is the change package clear; for example, can the solution be implemented in an objective manner by a person who does not have a detailed knowledge of the system?
2.	Is the solution consistent; for example, does this solution conflict with other items either already approved or in the approval process?
3.	Does the change package provide a reasonable degree of assurance that the solution, if implemented, will resolve the concern?
4.	Is the solution complete; for example, does the solution include all the changes that will be required to resolve the concern?
5.	Does the change package identify the costs and the schedule to implement the solution?

For hardware, things may not be so easy. For changes being made in a production line or for items in the field, prototypes and extensive testing may be required before directions are issued for a change. These become situation-specific.

9.4 COORDINATE PROPOSED CHANGES

Coordination is usually accomplished in two steps. The first step is the widespread distribution of the change package throughout the organization for preliminary review. This can be done by electronic mail, but in the case of more bulky packages, it is usually done by duplication and distribution of printed copies. Two factors appear to inhibit paperless transaction at this time: (1) the packages usually require referencing from one section to another. This is more easily done with paper than by changing views on a terminal, and, (2) force of habit. People are used to dealing with paper and are more comfortable with it. Both of these are subject to change and, at this time, at least the smaller packages should be transmitted by electronic mail.

The second step in coordination of change packages takes place in some organizations at one or more configuration control board (CCB) meetings during which the individual packages are discussed and any questions resolved. Normally, subordinate CCBs are established to take care of specialized areas. CCBs come in many varieties and flavors, and yet the basic purpose of all of them is the same: to provide a central point for the coordination of changes to baselined items within the scope of their authority. Figure 9-6 shows an example set of configuration control boards for a large project:

(a) The *project configuration control board* (CCB) provides the top-level review of all engineering change proposals, requests for deviations, requests for waivers, and notices of revisions. Within the scope of those actions not requiring customer approval, the chair of the CCB usually delegates the authority to approve specified classes of actions to the chairs of lower-level boards.

(b) Acting as subordinate boards to the project configuration control board are a *software configuration control board* (SCCB) and a *hardware configuration control board* (HCCB). Each of these has a separate sphere of activity and, acting under the scope of their delegated authority, advises the software manager or hardware manager on the disposition of proposed changes. Those changes that require the project manager's approval are normally processed by the subordinate (hardware or software) configuration control board and are then forwarded to the project configuration control board with appropriate recommendations.

(c) The *engineering change notice board* (ECNRB) reviews all proposed changes to any drawing prepared by the program. The board is usually the final approval/disapproval authority for all Class II drawing changes. All proposed changes that the ECNRB deems to be Class I candidates would be forwarded to the project CCB for further evaluation.

(d) The *problem report board* (PRB) provides an initial assessment of problems while assigning priorities and resources for resolutions. Then, after the cause of the problem has been determined, it reviews the proposed corrective action. Depending on the volume of problems to be handled, the problem report board may be split into a software problem report board and a hardware problem report board.

(e) The *material review board* (MRB) covers hardware nonconformances arising on the production line, and is covered in Section 10.1.

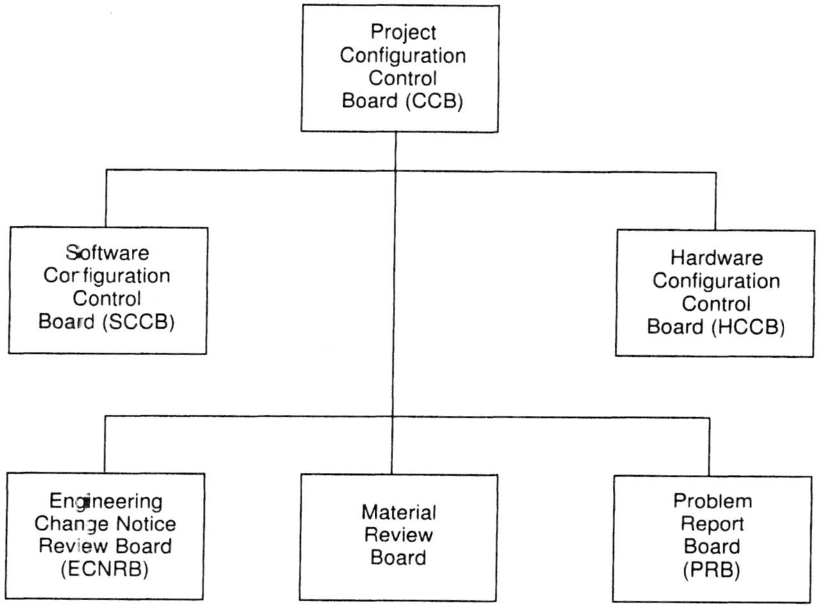

FIGURE 9-6. An Example Set of Configuration Control Boards.

The purpose of establishing these various boards is to reduce the number of people who must come together to discuss any one group of actions. For example, all the software managers will be interested in software changes, but very few will be interested in discussing a proposed change in the type of conductor to be used on a printed circuit card. Therefore, the boards are partitioned along communities of interest.

Although there are good motives for establishing various configuration control boards, one caution must be observed: more time can be wasted in configuration control board meetings than in any other activity. Configuration control boards can become a sink into which the management talent of the company can easily be poured. Running such boards efficiently requires the following actions:

(a) A written, published project instruction that establishes each board, states the scope of the boards' activities, and identifies the members.

(b) Regularly scheduled meetings. Anyone can make it to any meeting, as long as it is scheduled long enough in advance. Therefore, the goal is to schedule the meetings once a month (or once a week) for a fixed time, place, and date.

(c) An agenda. This should be published well in advance of the meeting, with all the items (for example, engineering change proposals) to be covered at that meeting. The goal is to enable the individuals involved to review the material in depth prior to the meeting, giving them the opportunity to raise their concerns. In the best of all possible worlds, at least 90% of the items to be discussed will have been settled prior to the meeting. The meeting, then, focuses on confirming the agreed-to resolutions; this type of meeting takes little time.

    Providing the material well in advance will not always be possible, for example, when dealing with changes that the software configuration control board must approve in order to keep a formal test program on schedule. But it is the goal.

(d) A secretary and chair. These are the two key jobs. Without good people in these jobs, far too much time will be wasted.

    The secretary ensures that the paperwork is distributed in a timely manner, including the agendas, minutes of the previous meeting, and the material to be considered as part of the next meeting.

    The chair should be the person responsible for making the decisions. In the case of the project configuration control board, the project manager should be the chair and run the meeting. If the chair requires that the agenda be followed and closes off extraneous discussion, meetings will proceed efficiently. If the chair allows the members to wander and engage in other discussions, meetings will take an inordinate amount of time.

There are other ways to coordinate proposed changes. One of the more common ways is to place the proposed changed package in a designated reading room for a one-week or two-week period. People can come by at their convenience, read the document, and initial that they concur (or alternately, schedule a further discussion for resolution of items of difference). A second way is for the proponent to hand-carry the change proposal to the people concerned, discuss it with them, and obtain concurrence at those times.

There are many different ways to coordinate change packages and CCBs (or change proposal reviews, or change review meetings) have been heavily used for that purpose. Which way is used is really a function of what works most expeditiously and what costs the least.

9.5 APPROVE/DISAPPROVE PROPOSED CHANGES

For configuration control to be effective, there are three fundamental questions to be answered: (1) what is to be controlled, (2) who is the configuration change control authority, and, (3) how are the products to be controlled. The first question regarding what needs to be controlled has previously been identified and answered in Section 4.1. These are the baselines, and are part of the configuration identification process.

9.5.1 Baseline Change Control

The answers to the second and third questions are complex, and part of the answer is provided in Table 9-V. This table identifies an example set of configuration change control authorities for baselines and the associated change documentation:

(a) All proposed changes to the functional baseline are documented using engineering change proposals (ECPs) together with proposed specification change notices (SCNs) and proposed specification change pages. (Details on these documents are provided in Section 12.2)

TABLE 9-V. AN EXAMPLE OF CONFIGURATION CONTROL OF BASELINES

Baseline	Document	Effectivity	Approval Authority	Change Documentation
Functional	System specification	(1) Initial submission to the customer at the system requirements review. (2) After satisfactory completion of the system design review and after approval of the document by the customer.	Customer	(1) Revisions (2) ECPs, SCNs, change pages
Allocated	All SRSs, IRSs, and unit specifications.	(1) Initial submission to the customer 30 days prior to preliminary design review (PDR). (2) After successful completion of PDR.	Customer reviews and provides comments; PMO approves.	(1) Revisions (2) ECPs, SCNs, change pages
Product	All software product specifications, engineering drawings and associated lists, and interface control drawings.	(1) After submission of preliminary documents to the customer 45 days prior to physical configuration audit (PCA). (2) After submission of final documents 30 days after successful completion of PCA for individual CSCIs and after approval of the documents by the customer.	(1) Customer approves preliminary specifications and associated changes at PCA. (2) Customer approves class I changes. Customer concurs in the classification for class II changes.	(1) Revisions (2) ECPs, SCNs, change pages, old source files, new source files, differences, and ECNs, as appropriate.

Proposed changes to the functional baseline require customer approval because the functional baseline is part of the formal agreement with the customer (specifying the technical characteristics of the items being provided). Because the customer is spending money to obtain items with specific technical characteristics, the developer is not able to change the functional baseline without the customer's approval.

(b) All proposed changes to the allocated baseline are usually documented using engineering change proposals together with proposed specification change notices and proposed specification change pages.

In a manner similar to the functional baseline, changes to the allocated baseline should require the program manager's approval, since the allocated baseline is a formal agreement between the program manager and a design activity manager (hardware or software) on the technical characteristics of the items to be provided.

As indicated above, these changes normally are provided to the program manager as engineering change proposals. In the government world, an engineering change proposal is a specific form; however, when circumstances permit it, for cost-effectiveness most companies will use forms other than the government forms. The choice of using other forms is a judgment item, balancing the ease of use of a company form against the expense of initiating and maintaining another set of forms, and these decisions are based on the individual situation.

(c) Engineering drawings are identified in Table 9-V as a baselined item. In government configuration management, the control of drawings has been noted as an anomaly. Government standards note that drawings become part of a product baseline, but say nothing about their control prior to that point in time.

In usual practice, drawings are part of the detailed design documentation, the "build-to" from which parts are ordered and hardware is fabricated. As such, drawings require control, and any changes to the drawings are approved by the hardware manager. These changes normally are coordinated through a hardware configuration control board (HCCB).

(d) All proposed changes to the software product specifications portion of the product baseline should be documented, using engineering change proposals together with proposed specification change notices and proposed specification change pages; these are provided to the customer for approval.

There are two views about the change approval authority. The first view is that the authority to approve changes rests with the configuration control board. This approach can be used for some programs; however, it is not recommended for all programs. The second view is preferred; that is one vests the authority to approve changes of a certain scope in one person, and this person should also serve as the chair of the appropriate configuration control board.

Table 9-V also shows another layer of granularity associated with the control of baseline configuration documentation. As shown in that table:

(a) Configuration control of the individual baseline components will initially be established on their first delivery to the customer. These documents are all furnished at specified times from the SCML and in accordance with their CDRL requirements.
(b) Changes will initially be furnished in the form of revisions until such time as the documents are formally approved.
(c) After the follow-on delivery to the customer after SDR, proposed changes will be furnished using engineering change proposals (ECPs), specification change notices (SCNs), and proposed change pages.

9.5.2 Developmental Configuration Change Control

Table 9-VI extends the material in the previous section to the developmental configuration. As shown in the table:

(a) Configuration control of the developmental configuration components will initially be established in an incremental manner.
(b) Changes will principally be furnished through the use of revisions.

Note that Table 9-VI also includes test plans and procedures. Strictly speaking, although test plans and procedures are not part of the configuration documentation, per se, they are often carried along with the developmental configuration as a matter of administrative convenience.

TABLE 9-VI. AN EXAMPLE OF CONFIGURATION CONTROL OF THE DEVELOPMENTAL CONFIGURATION

Document	Effectivity	Approval Authority	Change Documentation
1. All software design documents (SDDs)	(1) Top-level SDD 30 days prior to preliminary design review (PDR). (2) Complete SDD at critical design review (CDR).	(1) Provided to the customer for review. (2) Approved by the project management office (PMO).	Revisions
2. All software test plans (STPs)	30 days prior to PDR	Customer approves class I changes. Customer concurs in the classification for class II changes.	
3. All software test descriptions (STDs)	90 days prior to software formal qualification test (FQT)	Customer approves class I changes. Customer concurs in the classification for class II changes.	
4. All source code	(1) Prior to initiation of unit test (2) Prior to initiation of CSC test (3) Prior to initiation of software (Sw) FQT (4) Prior to initiation of hardware/software integration (HSI) Builds (5) Prior to initiation of system factory acceptance test (FAT)	(1) RE (2) Unit Manager (Mgr) (3) Sw Development (Dev) Mgr (4) Test Mgr (5) Customer approves class I changes. Customer concurs in the classification for class II changes.	(1), (2) Revisions (3), (4), (5) ECPs, SCNs, old and new source files and differences.
5. All interface design descriptions (IDDs)	(1) Top-level at PDR (2) Complete at CDR	(1) Provided to the customer for review (2) Approved by the PMO	Revisions
6. All critical item product fabrication specifications (CIPFSs)	Completion of Hw CDR		
7. All hardware (Hw) FAT plans	Completion of Hw PDR	PMO	
8. All Hw FAT procedures	90 days prior to planned start of test		
9. All engineering drawings and associated lists	(1) On release (2) Prior to initiation of Hw FAT	(1) Hw Dev Mgr (2) PMO	ECNs
10. System FAT procedures	90 days prior to planned start of test	Customer approves class I changes. Customer concurs in the classification for class II changes.	Revisions
11. System interface control drawings	(1) On release (2) System design review (SDR)—top-level	(1) PMO (2) Provided to the customer for review and comment; PMO approves.	(1), (2) ECNs (3) ECPs, ECNs

The manner of making changes to an item in the developmental configuration can vary depending on the status of the item. The overall thrust is to delegate the configuration change control authority downward to the lowest possible level and to require only that documentation which is essential to making a decision.

9.6 IMPLEMENT APPROVED CHANGES

This can take several aspects depending on the item being changed:

(a) For software, the approved revised source files, the product files, and others (as appropriate), should be transferred from the temporary directory in the SCML to the appropriate permanent directory in the SCML which holds that approved baseline or developmental configuration. The revised CSCI should then be archived, and/or stored in another location in accordance with local backup policies.

If the end product is to be distributed in digital form through the use of electronic or optical media, then it would be duplicated under controlled conditions on to the media and the media then sent to the appropriate using locations together with a version description document. Special arrangements will be required to provide a reasonable degree of assurance that the end product has not been modified during the transmission process. This assurance can be provided, for example, through the use of error-detection/error-correction coding, or by reading back what was sent.

For some software products, implementation includes installation, either locally or at a remote site through communications lines (for an example, see Figure 7-5 and supporting text).

(b) With a specification or other hard copy document, one copy would be produced and, typically, provided to the data management function for duplication and distribution.

(c) An engineering drawing or associated list would be distributed in accordance with local procedures.

For changes to hardware that is already in the field, see Section 10.2.

At the conclusion of the implementation, a report of the action taken to include the status of the effective items is usually provided to the configuration status accounting subprocess. This usually is done through the use of an installation completion notice.

9.7 AN EXAMPLE DEVELOPMENT PHASE CHANGE PROCESS

The processes used to implement configuration control do not always cleanly separate into the subprocesses previously illustrated. Usually, they are merged in one part or another, depending on the item being processed and the life-cycle phase of the project.

Figure 9-7 shows a typical flow of the configuration change subprocess used in the early stages of software testing and integration. This uses a problem report (PR) to document both the problem and its solution, and includes changes in software, firmware, and documentation. This flow shows the process of controlling Category I software and Category II firmware. (See Section 6.1.1 for details on software categories.) This process flow assumes that documentation is being maintained by the configuration management organization on electronic media.

(a) The originator uses the problem report to describe the problem to be fixed and forwards it to the configuration management organization.

(b) The configuration management organization logs the problem report, assigns it a number, enters it in the database, and forwards it to the software manager. (Throughout this process, the configuration management organization will update the database to reflect the changes in the status of the problem report. To avoid repetition, these updates will not be mentioned further.)

(c) The problem report is then reviewed by the software manager, who does one of the following:

 (1) Sends a copy of the rejected problem report with the reasons for its rejection back to the originator, (concurrently notifying the configuration management organization).

 (2) For all accepted problem reports:

  (a) Assign a priority of action. Priorities are assigned by using due dates. Priority indications such as high, medium, and low are not recommended for use for two reasons: (1) inflation inevitably sets in, and everything becomes a high priority, and, (2) the terms can have a shock value when spoken in front of upper management ("There are 40 high-priority problems that are still open!").

  (b) Designate the software engineer who will be responsible for further resolution.

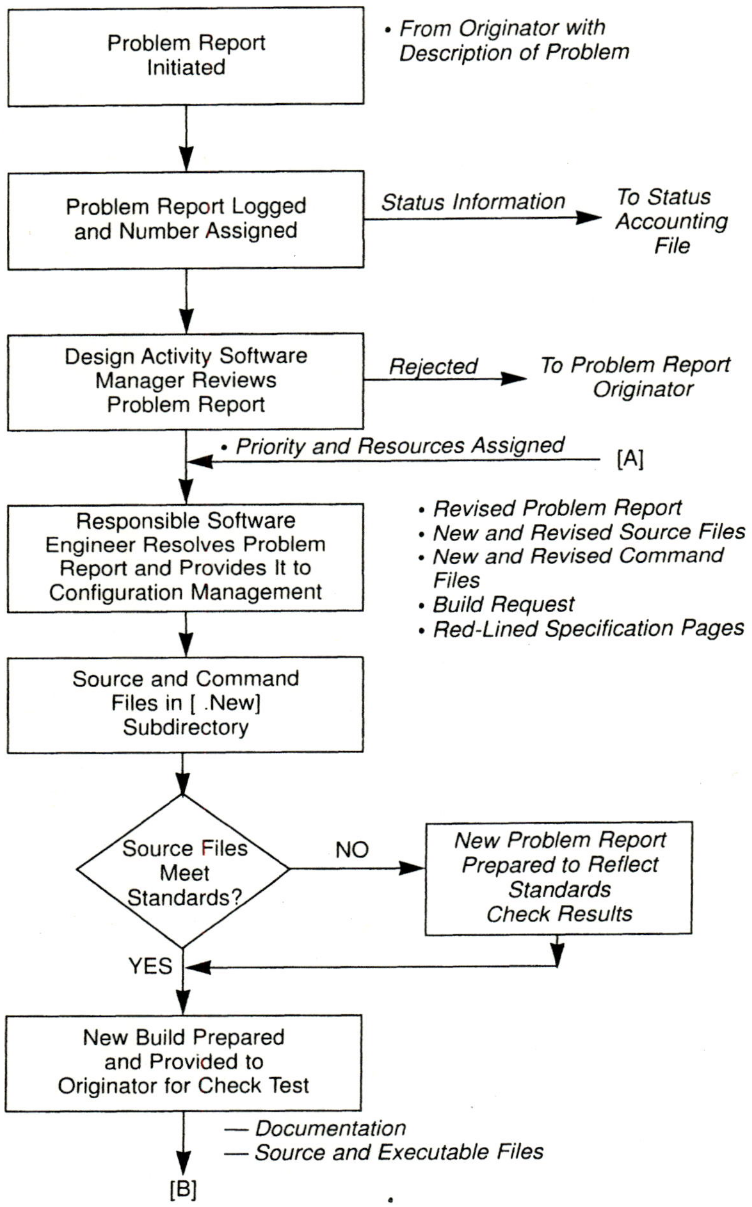

FIGURE 9-7. An Example Software Configuration Control Process for the Development Phase.

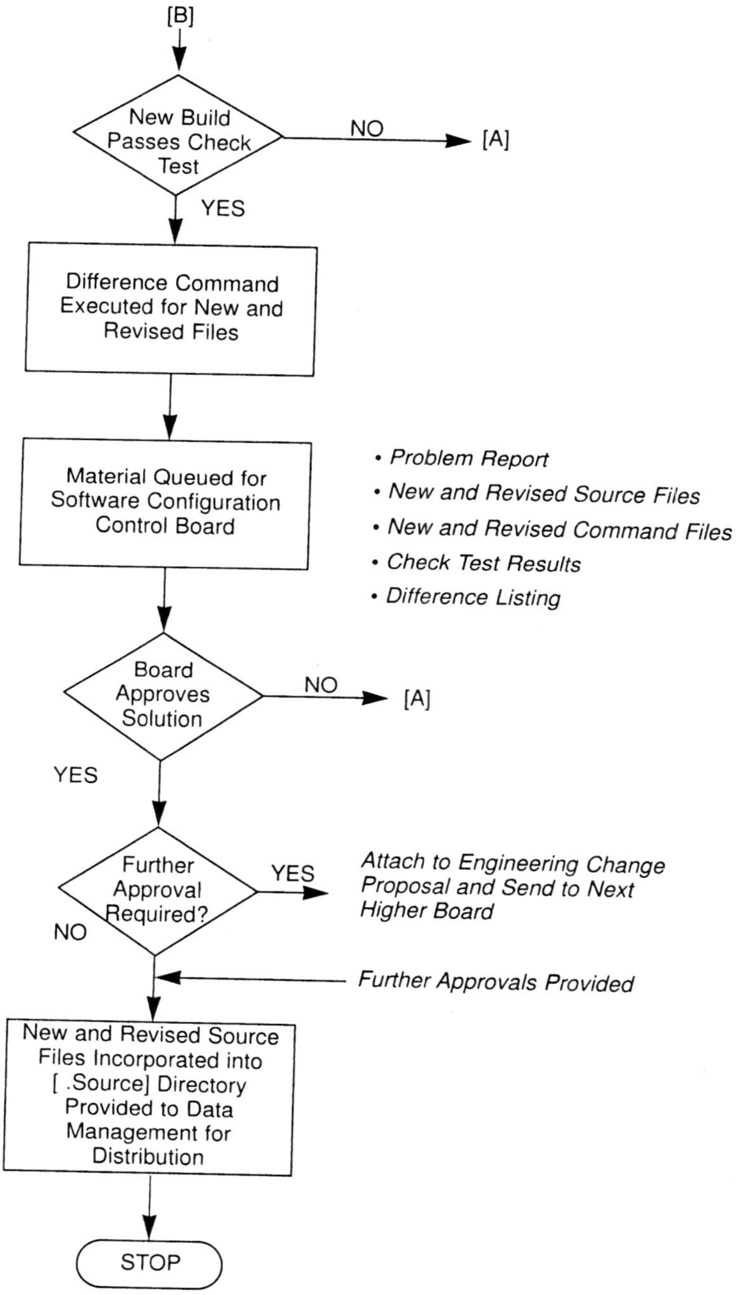

FIGURE 9-7. *(Continued)*

(d) After resolution of the problem, the responsible software engineer provides the updated problem report to the configuration management organization, which, in turn, logs and queues the report to the software configuration control board (SCCB) with the following items attached:

(1) If this resolution involves changes in documentation, the proposed specification change pages are sent. (These proposed specification change pages usually consist of marked changes, or "red-lines," on existing material. The point here is to provide information. If the changes have to go forward for further approvals, the configuration management organization, with the assistance of the responsible software engineer, reformats them after approval by the software configuration control board.)

As an alternative, the responsible software engineer could provide new and/or revised documentation source files, together with a command file that, when executed, will cause a revised print file to be built. The choice is based on convenience.

(2) If this resolution involves changes in code, new and/or revised source files are sent with a command file that, when executed, will cause a revised executable file to be built.

(3) A build request that provides complete identification of all the source files to be used to produce a specified executable file.

(e) On receipt of this material, the configuration management organization:

(1) Places the new and revised source and command files received from the responsible engineer in the [.NEW] subdirectory. (This is a temporary holding location, indicating that the files are controlled but not yet approved by the software configuration control board for full use.)

(2) Updates the information in the first line of the revised source file headers (for example, version number and date).

(3) Checks the source and command files for standards compliance. (This is an automated check, performed by executing a standards-checking program against the desired files. Standards enforcement is not usually a configuration management task. It is done at this time, however, as a matter of enlightened self-interest on the part of configuration management, in order to avoid churning of controlled files.) For those files that do not comply with standards, the configuration management organi-

zation initiates a new problem report to record those discrepancies.

(4) Prepares the new build (for software and firmware) or new proposed specification change pages (for documentation) and provides them to the originator for a check test. (The purpose of the check test is to ensure that the proposed solution will correct the fault and fix the failure.)

(f) If the material does not pass the check test, the originator will cycle it back to the point of providing changes to the configuration management organization.
(g) If the material does pass the check test, the configuration management organization will execute a DIFFERENCE command to provide a machine comparison (the difference listing) between the contents of the old source files and the new (revised) source files.
(h) The configuration management organization then provides all the material (the original problem report, the new and revised source files, the difference listing, the build request, and the check test results) and queues it for action by the software configuration control board.
(i) If the software configuration control board does not approve the material, it is returned to the originator for further action, as shown in Figure 9-7.
(j) If the software configuration control board does approve the material, then:

(1) If further approvals are required, the complete change package is attached to an engineering change proposal if the change involves the functional, allocated, or product baselines.
(2) If further approvals are not needed, the configuration management organization implements the new and revised source and command files into the permanent portion of the software configuration management library. They also provide the approved specification change notice and approved specification change pages (or the approved revision) to data management for duplication and distribution.

The above is one example of a detailed process as it applies to changes in a software product, and is meant to illustrate the level of detail at which such processes should be specified. Different organizations will assign different responsibilities to various elements, and this example should not be misconstrued as indicating that there is only one way to accomplish a given operation.

9.8 CONFIGURATION CONTROL TOPICS

9.8.1 Double Baselining

This is a classic trap in configuration management. Double baselining occurs when there are agreements on the technical content of the product at several levels. In establishing what work is to be done, there are normally three parts of the agreement: (1) the contract, which provides cost and schedule information and identifies the deliverables; (2) the statement of work, which delineates precisely each of the tasks covered by the contract; and (3) the system specification, which states the technical requirements the product is to meet. Since they represent the agreement with the customer on what is to be done for the money provided, all of these items are under change control.

Typically, as shown in Figure 9-8, the requirements in the system specification are broken down and further allocated to subordinate elements of the system; eventually, they are assigned to hardware and software elements. Thus, the requirements for configuration items at the allocated baseline level are directly derived from a system specification, the functional baseline. This breakdown is the result of a system engineering process that includes analysis, prior experience, and a host of other factors. Unfortunately, the customer exists in an environment in which, for example, software is a major concern. This software perceives as a major risk item, the one element most likely to be the cause of cost and schedule overruns, and so forth. To gain a greater degree

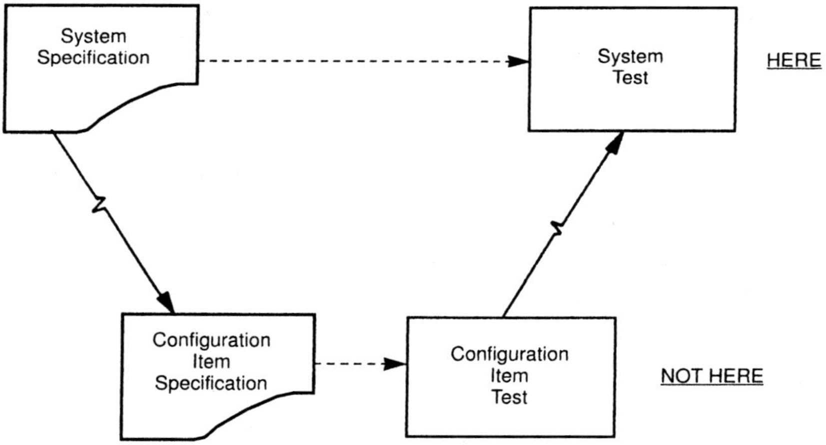

FIGURE 9-8. Double Baselining.

of assurance, some customers will attempt to exert the same degree of control over the allocated baseline (the configuration item specifications) as they already have over the functional baseline (the system specification). This attempted solution can, of itself, be the cause of the problems (for example, cost and schedule overruns and technical inadequacies) it seeks to cure.

If the customer is to have approval rights over the contents of the allocated baseline and their associated changes, then all changes must be submitted to the customer for that approval. As shown in Figure 9-9, this implies the preparation of a formal piece of paper, its signature by a contracting officer, receipt and distribution by the customer, formal evaluation by the customer, preparation and coordination of a formal reply, and much more. From start to finish, this process implies a cycle time of at least 60 days. This time may be extended by questions, requests for clarifications, and misrouted correspondence. In the meantime, the producer has an active workforce committed to the effort. As shown in Table 9-VII, this leaves the producer with a number of choices, all of which can affect the development effort. The producer can (1) continue to apply the workforce to the previously approved work (which is projected to change), (2) let the people go to other projects (in which case they will never be seen again), or, (3) use the people to implement what has been proposed (proceeding at risk). None of these are good choices, and all potentially expand the costs and schedules. Recognizing the frequency with which changes may be required in software requirements specifications and the inevitable desire to reduce the producer's risks, it can be seen that the attempted cure (customer control of the allocated baseline) can be one cause of the disease (the high risk associated with software development).

TABLE 9-VII. PRODUCER'S CHOICES ON IMPLEMENTING PROJECTED CHANGES

	Choice	Impacts
1.	Apply workforce to approved tasks (which are proposed to be changed)	Cost: If changes are approved, this work will be wasted.
2.	Release workforce to work on other projects	Cost and schedule: Workforce will most probably be retained at new projects. New workforce will require training in work-to-date.
3.	Apply workforce to projected changes	Cost and schedule: If changes are not approved, the cost of the work on the unapproved tasks will be disallowed as a contract cost, and the time not spent on approved work is unrecoverable.

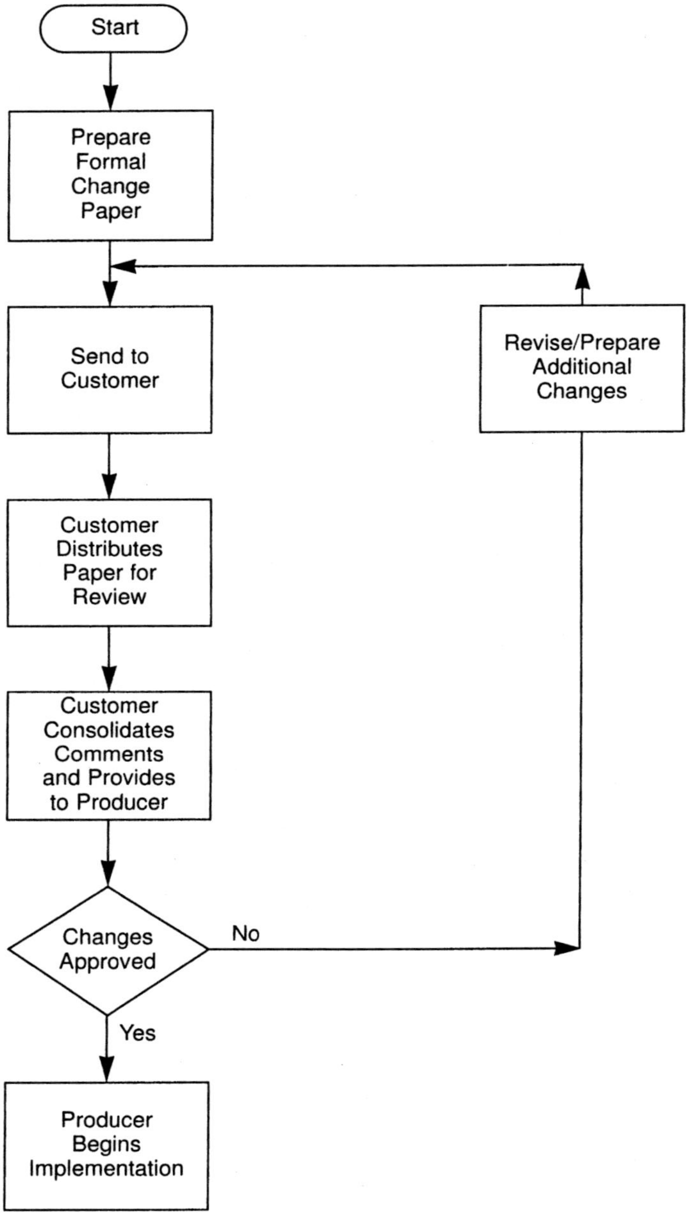

FIGURE 9-9. Customer Approval Process.

The solution to this problem is to recognize that there are legitimate concerns on both sides of the table. The customer needs a reasonable degree of assurance that the work is proceeding properly. This, however, is a matter of visibility rather than of control. One way to resolve the issue from a producer's viewpoint is to have an open shop; this provides the customer with all the internal memos and technical correspondence associated with the effort, allows the customer free access to personnel, and so on. This open shop requires: (1) a method of ensuring that the customer does not impede the work, and, (2) a certain degree of maturity on the part of the customer's personnel. Also, the customer should understand that this is raw data from low-level sources that requires processing in a number of forms before it might become a basis for action.

From an overall view, as shown in Figure 9-8, the agreement with the customer is at the level of the functional baseline (the system specification). The producer should be required to demonstrate, by an objective method, that each and every requirement has been achieved. The area of the customer's direct control is at the level of the system specification and system test (marked "HERE" in Figure 9-8).

Breakdown and further assigning system requirements to subordinate elements is a part of the system engineering and management tasks the customer is paying the producer to perform. Intrusion in a directive manner by the customer in that process should be avoided. The customer should not be involved in control at the level of the configuration item specification and the configuration item test (marked "NOT HERE" in Figure 9-8).

9.8.2 Expedited Actions

There are times when not every configuration management procedure can be followed as written. Configuration management exists to support projects, and projects may have urgent needs for expedited actions. These needs should be expected and plans made to deal with them.

For example, performing a standards check takes time. Suppose 200 source and command files are suddenly dumped into the software configuration management library and executable files are needed the next day; it may be impossible, with the time constraint and the people available, to check the source files for compliance to standards. One solution to this problem is to write a problem report stating that standards have not been checked for the attached list of source files (writing this type of problem report takes about two minutes), and then initiate the compilation process. Then, after the panic is over, the configuration management organization should go back and initiate the check of each of the source files for standards compliance. When that process has been completed (this includes the issuance of any resulting problem reports), the original problem report is formally closed through the software configuration control board.

As a second example, a particular set of changes may be required to be implemented and processed into one or more executable files, and this action cannot wait for approval at the regular meetings of the software configuration control board or the project configuration control board itself. In this case, there are two possibilities: (1) this particular action can fall into a category of actions formally delegated to a particular manager (for example, the hardware/software integration manager) to approve it on an exception basis, or, (2) if not otherwise formally specified, approval can be provided by the program manager or by the chair of the highest configuration control board whose approval would be required. In either case, a problem report (stating what was done and on whose direction) should be initiated at the time the direction was provided and closed at the next regular software configuration control board or configuration control board meeting.

The major point of all this is to continue to maintain the integrity of the products when schedule pressures mount. The methodology is to provide a written audit trail of the actions taken to meet specific needs and have a process to review those actions and resolve any byproducts.

9.8.3 Test Procedures/Descriptions Minor Changes

As a special case of expedited actions, consider changes in test plans and test procedures. Difficulties can arise during the execution of a formal dry run of the test or during the formal test itself. Long before the actual test, some prearranged mechanism should be established to permit minor changes to be made to these documents to account for typographical errors and other minor anomalies. To avoid delaying significant testing activities, *red-lining* of test procedures is usually authorized as follows:

(a) At the last dry-run of a formal test which is to be executed for customer witness (for example, a factory acceptance test), the contractor test director should be authorized to enter minor changes in the previously-approved test procedures. Such changes would be entered in red pencil or red pen. Each change should be marked by both the test director and the appropriate contractor quality assurance representative with their initials and date of entry.

(b) At the briefing before beginning the formal test, the contractor test director should present all these changes to the customer's test director for his review and concurrence.

(c) The customer's test personnel should initial and date all the changes that they agree are minor and do not change the scope of the testing.
(d) Copies of the annotated test procedure/description, with both sets of initials, should be furnished to all concerned and used to conduct the test.
(e) A copy of the annotated test procedure/description together with a retyped copy of the test procedure/description should be distributed with the test report.

Documentation of this type of change procedure should be placed in the CM plan.

9.8.4 Implementation Of An Automated Problem-Reporting System

There are advantages to an automated problem-reporting system. For example, if the problem report is on paper, the routing through the mail system and its associated delays can add substantial time to the total processing. If the problem report is on electronic media, then a preassigned routing table can be followed, and the problem report can be automatically and electronically provided to the next person on the action list after the previous person has electronically signed the report.

The difficulties of implementing such a system as a change in the way in doing business across the face of a large project or company are severe. Part of this is organizational: the software is developed by one group, the hardware and associated firmware is produced by a second group, the drawings are produced and maintained by a third group, the drawings are used by the factory (a fourth group), and so forth. Each of these groups has an existing way of doing business—something that works for them. Introducing an automated problem-reporting system implies all the difficulties associated with introducing any other change. There will be fluency problems and start-up problems (things do not always work as well as they should when transferred to another environment), and there will always be an inborn resistance to change.

One way to start the change process is to initiate an automated problem-reporting system in the software section of one project, then expand it to include all the software engineering activities, then further expand it into the system engineering efforts (specifications and test plans) on one project, and so forth. By doing a step-by-step implementation, the bugs can be worked out one at a time without catastrophic effects.

9.9 SUMMARY

Configuration control assists in maintaining the integrity of the product by maintaining cognizance of all changes to all items under control. This begins with the initial indication of a problem with a controlled item and extends through the evaluation of validity of the reported problem, the approval of an appropriate change to one or more of those controlled items, and the closure at the implementation of approved changes to all affected items.

Detailed step-by-step procedures are required to provide an objective, repeatable process, and an example of one such process is provided. The use of such detailed processes requires an established, documented configuration management procedure by which such processes can, for good and sufficient reason, be ignored.

9.10 EXERCISES

1. Prepare two separate flow charts of the actions involved in the IDENTIFY THE PROBLEM subprocess; one for a large project and one for a small project. Identify the people and associated job functions involved in each subprocess step and the time durations associated with each step. Identify what can be done to expedite the process in the large project for urgent actions, and what additional follow-up would be required after the urgent actions had been processed.

2. Extend Table 9-IV to provide a complete set of criteria used to evaluate proposed change packages.

3. *Situational Problem:* Your manager has just returned from a process improvement seminar and is enthusiastic about the use of problem reports to record the data that can be used to improve the hardware and software development processes. To support this viewpoint you are to determine what the essential elements of information required for: (1) a problem report, and (2) a change request.

   REQUIREMENT: Identify the essential elements of information for a problem report, and separately, for a change request. Highlight those that are required to support a metrics program.

4. *Situational Problem Continued:* In response to the outstanding reception of your ideas on problem reports and change requests, your manager has asked you to put together an implementation approach on the efforts required to automate this proposal.

   REQUIREMENT: Identify the tasks, schedules, milestones, and costs required to automate your proposed problem report/change request system.

10

CONFIGURATION CONTROL OF HARDWARE

Hardware changes can be the result of: (1) an approved design change for material which is not yet in production, (2) the identification of nonconforming material currently being produced, or, (3) the need to retrofit existing material, upgrading it to reflect either a design change or the resolution of a latent defect uncovered after the material had been produced. The change process to an approved design (the engineering drawings) is covered in Chapter 12. This chapter covers the control of material that is either in production or has been produced.

10.1 NONCONFORMING MATERIAL IN PRODUCTION

When hardware is being manufactured, it is subjected to various tests and inspections. Any material that does not conform to the requirements specified in the contract, drawings, specifications, or other approved product descriptions is termed *nonconforming material* and is entered into the corrective action and disposition system. In the discussion that follows, the reader should be aware that various parts of a corrective action and disposition system could be assigned to different organizations (for example, quality assurance or manufacturing). In the larger sense, since all of these actions affect the integrity of the product, they are treated in the coverage of configuration management and, in particular, configuration control.

Figure 10-1 shows a process flow of nonconforming material through a corrective action and nonconforming material disposition system:

(a) The system is triggered by the identification of nonconforming material. The first action taken is a preliminary review of that material. This is done simply as a cost-effective measure, since some nonconformances do not need a full material review board review. As shown, the preliminary review will result in one of the following actions:

(1) The material can be returned to the supplier. In this case, further follow-up will most probably be a quality assurance function to ensure that: (1) the supplier's process is corrected to

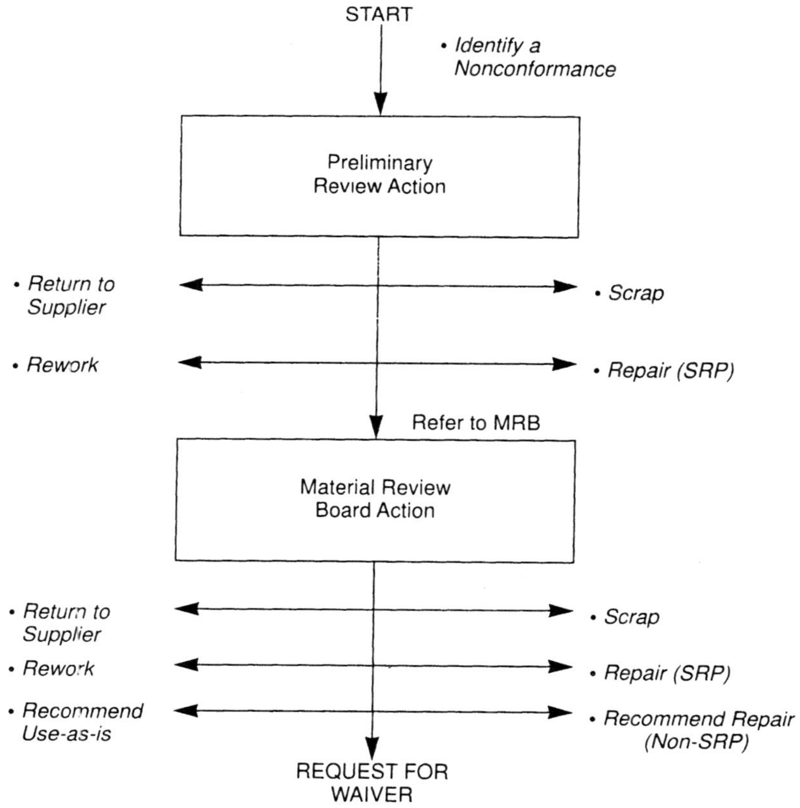

FIGURE 10-1. Corrective Action and Nonconforming Material Disposition System.

preclude subsequent provision of defective material, (2) any existing on-hand material from that supplier is evaluated (for example, subjected to additional testing), and, (3) the need for any retrofit actions involving material from that supplier, which has been incorporated into a product already shipped to a customer, is evaluated.

(2) The material can be scrapped if it is obviously unfit for use and cannot be economically repaired or reworked.

(3) The material can be repaired using a standard repair procedure (SRP) that is acceptable to the customer. Repair, in this context, is a procedure that does not completely eliminate a nonconformance.

(4) The material can be reworked to completely eliminate the nonconformance. For example, a hole that was drilled too small could be enlarged to the proper dimension.

(5) The material can be referred to the material review board for action.

(b) The material review board, in turn, can direct that the material be returned to the supplier, scrapped, repaired using an standard repair procedure, or reworked. The material review board can also:

(1) Recommend to the customer that the material be repaired using a nonstandard repair procedure.

(2) Recommend to the customer that the material be used as is. This is usually done when the material is determined to be usable for its intended purpose, and the nonconformance does not affect health or safety, performance, interchangeability, reliability or maintainability, effective use or operation, and weight or appearance (when a factor). The determination to use the material as is normally includes a determination of the appropriateness of a documentation change. (If the material is useable as is, then it is not clear why additional requirements are being placed on the product, and so those requirements must be reviewed.)

(3) Initiate a request for waiver (see Section 12.2.7).

There is a great deal more to a corrective action and disposition system (for example, there is normally a corrective action board, which watches the processes, a statistical process control with control limits, and so on). From a configuration management view, the remaining issues are a quality function, and a complete discussion of them is beyond the scope of this book. For a complete description, see MIL-STD-1520.

10.2 RETROFITS

When material has been delivered to a customer and then is to be changed, three things are needed from a configuration control viewpoint: identification and approval of the changes to be made, identification of the specific items of material to be changed, and reporting of the items that have been changed.

Identification and approval of the changes to be made to material is handled as a Class I change (see Section 12.2.2.1). This change will be reflected in approved drawings, which will specify the work to be done on each item (for example, modification drawings, which delineate the changes to delivered items, assemblies, installations, or systems). These may very well be accompanied by *kit drawings*, which indicate or depict a packaged unit or group of items and include instructions on how the modifications are to be made.

Identification of the specific items to be changed is best done on a serial number basis. This assumes that the items to be changed are identified not only as a group (such as the CAGE code, drawing number, manufacturing lot number, and so on) but also that each item in the group is uniquely identified by a serial number. The use of a serial number as an identifier allows closure to be made on all the items that need to be changed. If the items have not been identified by a serial number but have been distributed in bulk (for example, automobile brake pads), then positive closure on all outstanding items cannot be made; at best, recalls can be only broadly announced and modifications performed on a "best efforts" basis.

Scheduling of the modifications, allocation of resources, and arrangements for time to make the modifications are not configuration management actions. However, when the work has been completed, the configuration management organization should receive an installation completion notice (see Section 12.2.3), reporting the accomplishment of the changes. This installation completion notice is then used by the configuration status accounting function (see Chapter 13) to update the status of the affected material.

10.3 SUMMARY

Configuration management includes maintaining the integrity of products, both in production and already delivered. When nonconforming material is discovered in the production line, it must be identified, and the actions to bring it back to an acceptable state must be controlled. These actions are not uniquely performed by configuration management, but include those actions performed by quality assurance control and others.

In a similar manner, items that have been delivered may require modification to either correct a latent defect or enhance specific characteristics. These changes require control, and the implementation of such changes requires a positive feedback mechanism, usually provided through the use of installation completion notices.

10.4 EXERCISE

1. Identify three items in the current issue of *Consumer Reports* magazine that have been recalled, and estimate the cost associated with each recall.

11

CONFIGURATION CONTROL OF SOFTWARE

This chapter builds on the material discussed in Chapters 6 and 9, and covers specific topics in the configuration control of software. Since material provided in this chapter applies equally to the software component of firmware, no specific additional chapter on the control of firmware is provided.

Three topics are of major interest:

(a) Tailoring the application of configuration control to the type (category) of software to be controlled
(b) Implementing a configuration management library as a repository for controlled software
(c) Using a standards-checking tool as an initial screen for software to be entered into the configuration management library

11.1 SOFTWARE CONTROL IMPLEMENTATIONS

Section 9.7 provided an example of the processing of changes to product software (and the software component of product firmware). As noted in Section 6.1.1, there are other categories of software, and the control and processing of each need to be specified in a cost-effective manner. The fundamental view is that the control of changes should rest in the hands of those who will be affected by the change. The challenge is to devise reasonable, cost-effective ways to implement that control. The material that follows provides guidance in controlling these different types of software: product, vendor, test, product support, and reusable software.

11.1.1 Product Software

This is software being developed as a product to be delivered to a customer. Control of this software is in stages:

(a) As the software code itself is being developed by the programmer, the programmer controls the changes to the software. In effect, until the programmer has developed software that passes an initial set of tests, no one cares what changes are made to the software.
(b) When the software is submitted for unit testing (the initial tests of the software), the authority to authorize changes to the software is moved to the first level of software management. The reason for this is straightforward: the code that has been tested is now being used by other programmers. If the original programmer retains the right to make changes to the software without reference to the other programmers who are using that software, the other programmers may be surprised when their code (which was working), no longer works because of unilateral changes made by the original programmer. Anarchy can result when more than one programmer is making changes to more than one source file. To avoid this, change control passes to the first level of management after software passes its unit tests.
(c) As the software passes succeeding levels of testing, the configuration change control authority becomes more and more tightly held. Ultimately, when the software begins its formal acceptance tests, the authority to authorize changes is vested in the customer, the person who will be accepting the software as a deliverable item.

11.1.2 The Software Component Of Product Firmware

The software component of product firmware is controlled in a manner similar to that of product software. The important thing is to make sure that the configuration control of this category is explicitly stated.

11.1.3 Vendor-Provided Software

Vendor-provided software is one of the most frequently overlooked items for control. In theory, each new release of vendor software is completely compatible with the previous release. As a result, it is usually assumed that application software which was compiled, executed, and tested using one or more vendor products will again be compiled and executed in an identical manner with the new releases of those vendor products. Although this is a highly desirable goal, for a number of reasons, it is not always realized.

Vendor software organizations are composed of human beings, some of whom are maintaining and enhancing some very complex programs. The vendors themselves have problems with personnel turnover, concerns with the adequacy of tests, and organizational difficulties. (In one particularly famous case, a compiler maintenance group from a large computer manufacturer received their bonuses based on their enhancement completion schedule, with interesting results for those customers who received the next version. The compiler maintenance group had no incentive to test their revisions against old application code and, as a result, did not. As a further result, when the revised compilers were installed at the customers' locations, very serious problems resulted—the programs at the customers' facilities, which had been compiled and operated using the previous version of the compiler, would not compile using the new compiler.)

The case becomes worse when products from two or more vendors are being used on one project (for example, an operating system from the computer manufacturer, a cross-compiler from a second vendor, and a relational database system from a third). All vendors do not make changes at the same time. As a result, one vendor's relational database system (which worked with the previous version of a second vendor's old version of an operating system), will not operate with the new version of the operating system. Things deteriorate even further when a number of platforms are being used (such as Alpha and Sun workstations), and a CASE tool vendor does not upgrade the versions of the CASE tool that operates on both of those products simultaneously.

One method of providing stability in this environment is to process changes as follows:

(a) As part of their normal enhancement process (for example, VMS version 10.7) vendors propose changes as revisions.
(b) The facility manager evaluates the proposed changes in order to include the interoperability effects with other products in use at the facility. This may include running benchmark programs to ensure that there are no unexpected effects either on the current product

software in testing or with other vendors' products. The facility manager then advises the software manager and program manager of any potential adverse effects.

(c) The decision to upgrade to the newest revision is made by the project configuration control board which provides implementing instructions, including the date of implementation.

The situation can become even more complicated when one facility is supporting more than one project. In this case, the use of a facility configuration control board should be considered, with meetings scheduled once a month which would consider changes projected for 30 to 60 days in the future. This would permit sufficient time for each project to make an assessment of a change and respond to the proposal for the change.

11.1.4 Test Software

Software that is developed to support the formal acceptance testing of product software and firmware (for example, test drivers and analysis programs) requires the same level of change control authority as the software/firmware under testing. The difference may be in the manner in which test software changes are documented for approval.

Normally, test software is one-time software. It is used for one test and then discarded. Under these conditions, the test software can be controlled as a one-time item and then archived.

One-time control implies the deletion of the requirement for detailed documentation of specific changes and the associated detailed justifications for changes in the test software. Either it works that one time, or it does not. If the test software works that one time, then it is archived. If the test software does not work, it is usually handed back to the developer to be modified until it does work. In either case, there is no need to track the changes (why it did not work) or to justify the changes made to make it work.

If the test software is to be used repeatedly for product acceptance testing, then changes must be tracked, and a more comprehensive control scheme is required.

11.1.5 Product Support Software

This software actually consists of two cases:

(a) The more recognized case is the software that supports the formal process of producing product software (to include the software component of firmware), but is not formally identified as a product. The standards-checking tool discussed in Section 11.3 would fall into this category.

(b) The case that is usually not officially recognized is the software used to support hardware production; for example, the software used to run numerically controlled machinery or backplane wiring tools. Mistakes in that software will directly affect the integrity of the product.

Both of these should be controlled at the same or at a higher level than the products they are supporting. It is not appropriate for this software to rattle around in an individual's desk on an ad hoc basis.

11.1.6 Electronically-Formatted Engineering Design Data

As the individual engineer begins work, the engineering design data is controlled by that person. As the data begins to spread throughout the engineering organization, the data should be controlled by the person whose resources would be affected if the data were changed. Changes in this data can quickly affect other digital groups, analog design groups, mechanical engineering, manufacturing, and the customer.

One model to use in implementing such a control in an organization is to draw analogies to the controls already in place for engineering drawings and associated lists. The reason for drawing such analogies is that one product of such data can be engineering drawings, and control of drawings is usually already well established and accepted in industry.

11.1.7 Manufacturing-Support Software

Manufacturing-support software is under the control of the developer while it is being developed. Control is normally transferred to the manufacturing organization when hardware begins fabrication. Depending on the environment (for example, if the hardware is being built for a specific customer), changes to manufacturing-support software used on a production line may require customer concurrence after the first article production tests have begun.

11.1.8 Documentation Software

Documentation software (which is used, for example, to produce specifications, engineering drawings, and test plans), is controlled on the same level as the end-item documentation it produces.

11.1.9 Reusable Software

Reusable software is contained in a company library and used in more than one project. There are two variants on this. In the first variant, the software in the library itself can be rigidly controlled, particularly as it increases in value (for example, after it has been fully tested and fully documented). In such cases, changes are formally proposed to a company configuration control board and, when approved, all users of that software are so notified.

In the second variant, software from a company library is provided on an "as-is" basis to any project requesting it. This is similar to software provided by a user group. Further modification and/or control of such software for use in a particular project is then delegated to the specific project using the software. If the modifications may be of use to another project, the revised software may also be placed in the company library.

11.2 IMPLEMENTING A CONFIGURATION MANAGEMENT LIBRARY

There are a number of approaches to implementing a configuration management library in electronic media. The choice of which approach to use is a function of the size of the project, the tools available, the knowledge of the implementers, and the resources available for the implementation.

11.2.1 An Initial Approach

The most straightforward approach is the establishment of a configuration management library which only the librarian can operate. In that implementation, the configuration management library is established as a directory separate from the other project directories. As shown in Table 11-I, the configuration management library can be divided into two parts, each with special read/write permissions:

(a) The TRANSFER subdirectory of the library—This is established such that anyone can place a file in that subdirectory (write into that subdirectory), but only the librarian can read a file from the TRANSFER subdirectory (transfer a file from that subdirectory into another part of the library).
(b) The remainder of the library—This is established so that anyone can read any files in the remainder of the library (and copy them for use outside the library), but only the librarian can write files into the remainder of the library.

In effect, the TRANSFER subdirectory of the configuration management library is a one-way gate, or a holding pen, for files to be transferred to other subdirectories of the configuration management library from outside the configuration management library. Programmers can place their code in the TRANSFER subdirectory (but cannot take it out), the librarian then moves the material in the TRANSFER subdirectory elsewhere in the configuration management library.

Figure 11-1 shows a typical operation which involves making changes on software that is already under configuration control:

(a) A programmer wanting to make a change in a source file already under control in the library would copy the file from the library into a work area (not to another part of the library). As shown in this example, the programmer would copy source file VF701.FOR;15. The original copy of VF701.FOR;15 would remain in the library.
(b) The programmer would then make changes in the file, which would then become VF701.FOR;16.
(c) The programmer would then deliver VF701.FOR;16 to the TRANSFER subdirectory of the library. Note that no one other than the librarian can move VF701.FOR;16 from the TRANSFER subdirectory of the library, not even the programmer who originally placed VF701.FOR;16 in that subdirectory.

TABLE 11-I: TYPICAL CONFIGURATION MANAGEMENT LIBRARY PRIVILEGES

Privilege	Authorization
1. Write software into the transfer subdirectory	Everyone
2. Read software from the transfer subdirectory	Librarian
3. Write software into the rest of the library	Librarian
4. Read software from the rest of the library	Everyone

(d) The change approval process can now proceed on the changed, controlled file, and the librarian can now process the file in accordance with standard library procedures. At the end of this process, both the old file (VF701.FOR;15) and the new file (VF701.FOR;16) are in controlled storage in the library.

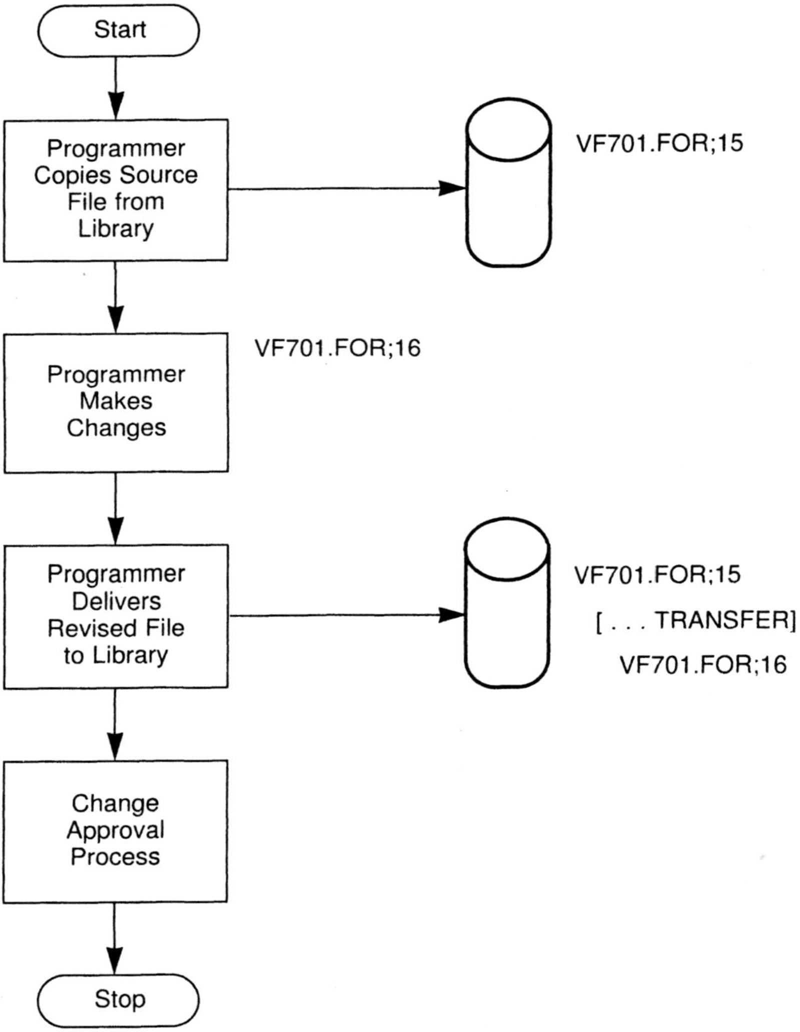

FIGURE 11-1. An Initial Approach to Controlling Changes to Source Code.

This approach is simple to operate, can be established rapidly with a minimum amount of user involvement, and does not require sophisticated operators. Furthermore, it does not require extensive specialized tools, since it can be established using only the commands that already exist in the operating system command structure (for example, DEC DCL).

11.2.2 Use of a Check-Out/Check-In Facility

The first approach identified in the previous section is usually supplemented with what is known as a check-out/check-in facility. The concept is simple, and the problem that it solves is well known. For instance, consider the situation in Figure 11-2, which details this common problem:

(a) To resolve a problem during hardware/software integration, programmer AAA copies VF701.FOR;15 into a work directory and makes changes in the file.

(b) In a similar manner, to resolve another problem during hardware/software integration, programmer BBB copies VF701.FOR;15 into a work directory and makes changes in the file. Programmer BBB has copied file VF701.FOR;15 into a work directory before programmer AAA had provided the revised source file containing the AAA changes back to the library.

(c) When programmer AAA provides the revised source file to the library that contains the AAA changes, the revised source file is named VF701.FOR;16.

(d) When programmer BBB provides the BBB changes to the library (after programmer AAA has provided the AAA changes to the library), the BBB revised source file is automatically renamed by the operating system to VF701.FOR;17 (two files cannot have the same name in the same directory).

The end result is that the latest file, VF701.FOR;17, does not contain the changes that resolved the problem on which programmer AAA was working.

To resolve this problem, configuration management tools typically include a check-out/check-in facility. Personnel who wish to copy a file for the purpose of making changes must use this facility; this allows only one person at a time to check out for change any one specific file. Thus, using this facility avoids simultaneous changes being made in the same file by two different programmers.

11.2.3 A More Sophisticated Approach

For a small to medium project (up to 50,000 lines of source code), the first approach may very well be the optimal option. As the project becomes larger and more sophisticated programming languages come into major use (such as Ada), this approach begins to encounter difficulties. One of these difficulties is interlocking references.

Individual source files do not live alone. They call and refer to other source files, and in turn are called and referred to by other source files. To refer to another source file, the complete directory address of that source file must be added to the file identifier; for example, a complete reference to a particular file (see Figure 11-3 for one example) is embedded in the directory structure as shown in Figure 11-4. In this example, ANXYDZ2 is the directory, and CCS, EDPAUG, and BUILD1 are part of a chain of nested subdirectories, each of which is separated from the next by a period (".").

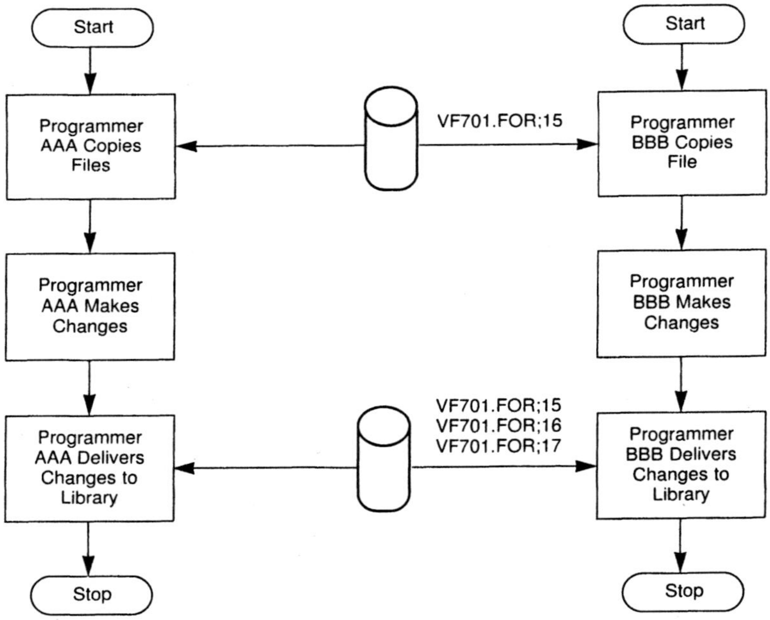

FIGURE 11-2. Simultaneous Changes.

[ANXYZ2.CCS.EDPAUG.BUILD1]file_name,file_type;version_number

FIGURE 11-3. An Example of a Directory Address Appended to a File Identifier.

For one file to refer to another file, detailed knowledge of all the directory structures and where various files are located is required. Moreover, when the source files are transferred from a programmer's directory into a configuration management library (where at least some of the directory names are different), all the references inside the source files require changing. As might be suspected, some references are always missed and are only discovered near the end of an 18-hour compile. At that point, an improper reference causes the compile to fail; and after correction of the improper reference, the 18-hour compile is restarted.

A more sophisticated approach takes the view that:

(1) The configuration management library should be established on a project basis.
(2) The directories and subdirectories to support the entire project should be established in the configuration management library at the beginning of the project.
(3) These directories should be used by the development personnel from the very beginning of the project.
(4) The library will control access to these files on a file-by-file basis; this depends on the individual files' stage in the process.

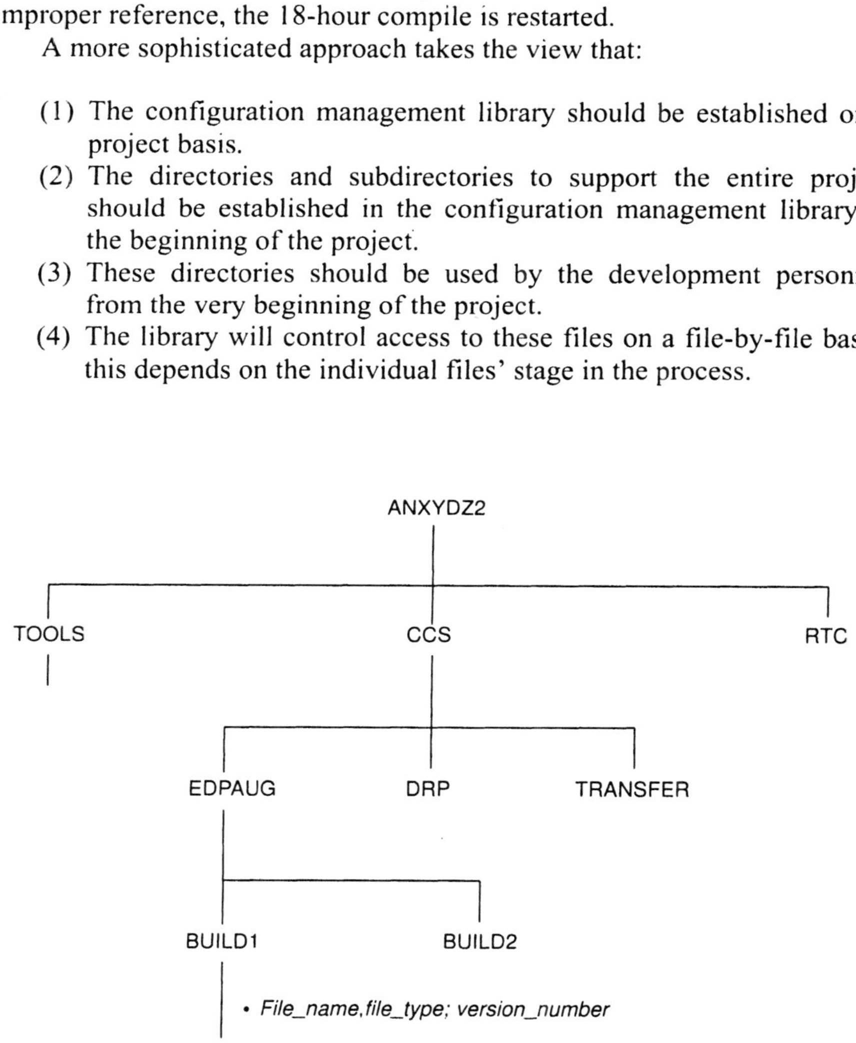

FIGURE 11-4. A Directory Structure Example

The remainder of the problem, then, is to install a means of restricting change authorization access to source files that have been used for certain categories of testing. (As files move beyond unit testing, the ability to unilaterally change those files has to be sharply limited.) Individual file protections can be manually set; but as files are used, the need to change those files will arise. Furthermore, there is a need to keep different versions of files active for different purposes. This can be visualized as a hierarchy of accesses (for use), some being used for acceptance testing, others being changed for resolving bugs, and so forth.

There are a number of benefits associated with this approach. First, it avoids the improper reference problem previously discussed. Second, as a byproduct, it initiates the entire process of software integration at the time of the first entry of a source file into the configuration management library. Even better, it uses the original programmers (those who know the programs best) to correct their own code for integration errors that will otherwise require action at a later date.

This approach does require considerable thought and planning at the beginning of the project, and it can be very disruptive if it is implemented in the middle of a project.

11.2.4 Software Tools Considerations

A configuration management tools industry has arisen, one which allows these types of restrictions and usages to be automated, thus making control of large software systems significantly easier.

The better tools include other facilities that make the configuration management efforts easier to implement (for example, check-out/check-in, which prohibits two programmers from attempting to modify the same source file concurrently). The vendors sense a market for these tools, and both the number of vendors offering such tools and the facilities provided by those tools are rapidly growing.

To provide recommendations on any specific tools would be a disservice to the reader, as they would be hopelessly out of date almost as soon as such a list was composed.[1] Prior to investing in a particular tool, certain cautions should be considered:

---

[1] A list of some 81 SCM tools is available in *Software Configuration Management Technology Report*, September 1994. For a copy, contact STSC Customer Service, OO-ALC/TISE, 7278 Fourth Street, Hill AFB, UT 84056-5205, Voice: 801-777-7703, FAX: 801-777-8069, e-mail: mcdonalb@stsc.hill.af.mil.

(a) Recognize that buying the tool is the easy part. The much more difficult part is getting the tool cut over to operational use, and getting it to do the tasks for which it was purchased. This implies planning for the acquisition of the tool and planning for its implementation.
(b) Recognize that one tool will not do the complete job and that a complete CM tool suite will probably be required. For example, one tool will probably be required to prepare differences between different versions of documents, a second tool will be required to prepare paper forms (ECPs, SCNs, and so on), a third tool will be required to control the software versions, and a fourth tool will be required to handle engineering drawings.
(c) Prepare a statement of requirements to define what these tools are to do (change control, problem reporting, status accounting, and so on). This will normally include determining what the complete CM system is to do and with what it is to interface. For example, the tools used to support the engineering drawing system should interface with the tools used by those who buy parts.
(d) Prepare a test plan that states how the tool is to be tested to ensure that it meets each requirement. Provide this to the vendor and encourage the vendor to examine it, interact with it, and, in the best of all possible worlds, execute the tests against the tools.
(e) Look for a happy user of the tools. This is aimed at avoiding the "vaporware" problem where the tools exist, for the most part, only on the view graphs of the vendor's marketing department.
(f) Determine what training the vendors provide and plan to augment that training at your facility. As a part of this, ensure that vendor support is available and assign a member of your staff to be a tools "guru"; that is, someone who has detailed knowledge of the tool and who is available at your location on a full-time basis to help users through the tools-familiarization phase.
(g) Run a pilot project using the tool suite before investing in tools to convert the entire company.[2]

A caution on tools: a number of CM tools were originally developed on mainframe machines. Their migration to a new environment—from an IBM mainframe to a Sun client-server environment, for example—may have been done in such a manner that the CM tool resides and executes only in

[2]For much more detail, see S. Dart, "Adopting An Automated Configuration Management Solution," Software Technology Center Conference, April 1994, Hill Air Force Base, Utah.

the server. As a result, the client machines can only act as terminals, and the computing power of the individual client machines is not available.[3]

The effect of this architectural decision is not apparent on a small network (5 to 10 clients). However, as the network grows larger (30 to 50 machines), significant reductions in response times can be encountered. In one case, the response time required to bring up a problem-reporting form was 30 minutes, so use of that tool was discontinued. To avoid being surprised, the prospective buyer should first look for a happy user of the specific tool and, above all, benchmark the tool against the projected application of it under full load conditions.

11.2.5 Ada Complications

There are some additional complications if the programming language being used for the project is Ada. An Ada compiler embodies functions that, for other compilers, are provided by the operating system; as a result, CM of Ada files provides a unique challenge:

(a) Section 10.4 of ANSI/MIL-STD-1815A, *Ada Programming Language*, requires that the Ada compiler maintain a program library.
(b) The facilities required of a SCML may not be provided in a particular Ada compiler's program library (for example, a check-out/check-in facility). As a result (as shown in Figure 11-5), two libraries will be required: a SCML, and a separate Ada program library. The effect of this situation is the requirement to move (copy):

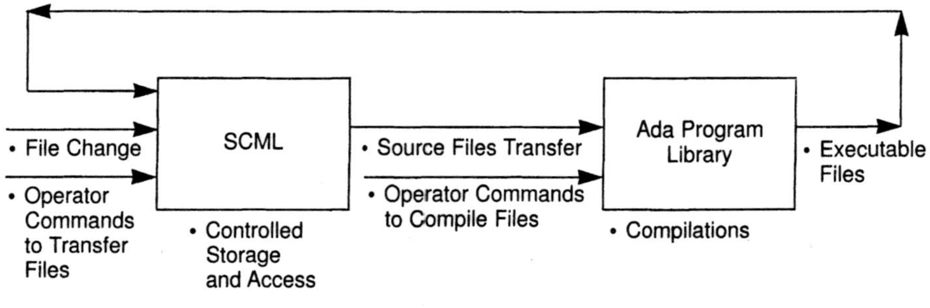

FIGURE 11-5. An Example of Separate Libraries Required by Unintegrated Tools

[3]My thanks to R. Gillus who first brought this to my attention.

(1) Source files from the CM library to the Ada compiler program library to make executable files. (This, for one file, is trivial. For large computer programs this can become more interesting.)
(2) Executable files from the Ada compiler program library to the SCML so that the executable files can be made available to the users. (In theory, this last move could be avoided by providing global permissions for read-only access to the Ada program library.)

(c) The movement of files into the Ada compiler program library and the subsequent compilations are required to be done under repeatable objective conditions. (For example, it would not be recommended that integration builds be prepared by people other than the CM personnel using a well-defined procedure.)
(d) As the amount of compilations increase (for concurrent unit tests, integration tests, check tests, and builds), the opportunity for errors in this process increase.
(e) The amount of continuously-applied highly-skilled effort required to operate (manually integrate) these two tools is not usually recognized until the organization is well into the project.

The effect on the user could be a continuing requirement to transfer (or copy) all the files from the configuration management library to an Ada library in order to compile an executable file. This is time-consuming and subject to error.

There is no intrinsic reason why an Ada compiler could not incorporate the CM functions; that is, have one integrated library, as shown in Figure 11-6. Most Ada compilers do not have an integrated library probably because the compiler developers did not recognize the need for it. This will undoubtedly change; to date, however, the problem remains unless the CM tool developers have specifically addressed the topic.

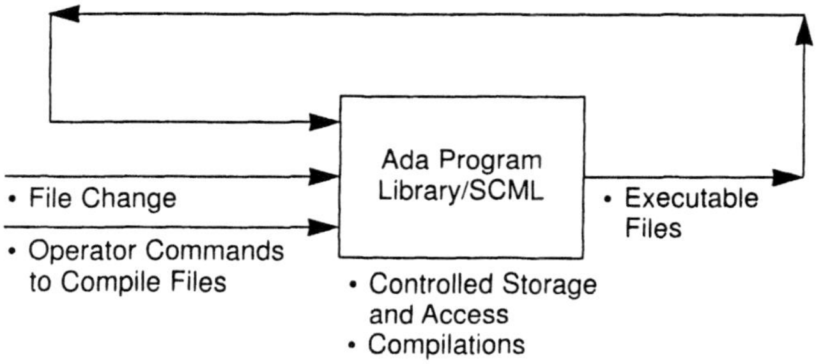

FIGURE 11-6. An Integrated Library Facility

Tools are being developed and enhanced very rapidly, and it is difficult to predict precisely which configuration management capabilities will exist at any given time in any Ada compiler. As a result, it is recommended that the following questions be included in making inquiries about specific Ada products:

(a) What facility stores the Ada source files used by the compiler? (The normal answer should be that this is provided by the Ada compiler itself.)
(b) What facility provides *versioning* (the ability to state what the previous versions of a particular source file were)? (This is normally provided by a configuration management tool.)
(c) What facility provides the ability for controlling check-out and check-in of source files for changes? (This is normally provided by a configuration management tool.)
(d) What facility provides controlled access to source files? (This is normally provided by either the operating system or a configuration management tool.)
(e) Is the library from and to which the programmers check-out and check-in source files a part of the library maintained by the Ada compiler? (If the compiler is tuned to a particular configuration management tool, the answer should be yes; otherwise, manual transfers between the Ada library and the configuration management library will be required.)

Prior to accepting a CM tool for use with an Ada compiler:

(a) The vendors should be required to demonstrate the interoperability of the two tools under realistic load conditions.
(b) The detailed procedures to be used between the SCML and the Ada program library should be established and debugged.

11.3 IMPLEMENTING A STANDARDS-CHECKING PROGRAM

One of the strong recommendations herein is that all source files of code be checked for compliance to standards as part of the process of being entered into the configuration management library. Although this is not, strictly speaking, a configuration management task, it is a matter of enlightened self-interest.

If files are not checked when originally entered into the configuration management library, the files will not normally comply with the standards criteria. As time goes by, these files acquire value; they will have been tested at higher integration levels, modified to meet unexpected events, and so forth. Then finally, at the end of the project, just as the software is about to be delivered, the program manager is faced with the situation in which the software works and performs all the required functions, but does not meet standards.

If, at the time of delivery, the customer is asked to approve a request for waiver for these items, the customer could very well require compensation. If delivery time is near, and the contractor is required to go back and modify the code to meet standards, this could cause a significant period of retesting. Consider, for example, if significant numbers of large source files have to be modified to meet a standard that no source file will contain more than 100 executable statements.

The solution to this concern is to check the files as they are entered into the configuration management library by using a *standards checker*, a software program that will automatically check each new and revised source file against the required standards as it is entered into the configuration management library. If the source file does not meet standards, the standards checker generates a problem report delineating the particulars.

A few items about standards checkers should be noted:

(a) The generation of the standards checker should be a planned systematic effort.
(b) The standards themselves should have been previously established as project standards—the configuration management organization should not be a standards-generating organization.
(c) The achievement of each standard must be capable of being objectively determined by a prescribed method, with no judgment required.
(d) Finally, the tool used to check other source files for standards compliance should meet those standards itself and be under configuration control.

From an implementation viewpoint on UNIX-based systems, using two programs provided by the computer user group (YACC and LEX), can considerably reduce the effort of producing a standards checker. Those programs are usually in every user community, and an effort should be made to find them prior to starting a new development effort from scratch.

It should be noted that programmers can pass any test if they know about it early enough. The normal ploy, then, is to release the standards checker to the programming community. They will use it prior to entry of their source files in the configuration management library to ensure they are not embarrassed.

11.4 SUMMARY

Applying configuration control to software requires consideration of the usage of the software. Product, vendor, test, product support, and reusable software each has a different purpose and context of usage, and each requires different control mechanisms; one process does not serve all needs.

Implementing configuration control of software requires the use of a repository (the configuration management library), to which access is controlled and in which specific software transfer procedures are required. Such a library can be implemented at several different levels of sophistication and should be automated through the use of appropriate software tools, large numbers of which are currently being advertised. Finally, to reduce the number of changes to the library, all source code should be checked for project standards compliance by an automated tool prior to entry in the configuration management library.

11.5 EXERCISES

1. Provide a flow chart covering the use of reusable software when the software is controlled in a company library. Cover acquisition of the software, initial test, modification by a user, subsequent test, and the actions required to place the modified software into the software reuse library.

2. Provide a detailed flow chart of the actions required to produce an Ada executable file from a group of Ada source/object files residing in an SCML that is separate and distinct from the Ada Compiler library. Use the directory structure for the SCML shown in Figure 11-4.

3. *Situational Problem:* Your CM group supports a variety of different-size projects, ranging from one to two people up through 60+ people. Your manager is becoming interested in aspects of trade-offs, cost-effectiveness, and risk reduction and has come to you for information. The basic question he wants answered is: what are the cross-over points for the use of software CM tools, and at what point, in terms of project size, is it worthwhile to move to more sophisticated tools?

   REQUIREMENT: Provide a chart of project size versus tool capabilities. Project size should be specified in terms of people; tool capabilities should range from version control libraries, through check-out/check-in, automated problem reporting and standards checking. Include in your considerations the cost of tools (make any reasonable assumptions), training and maintenance.

12

CONFIGURATION CONTROL DOCUMENTATION

Configuration control documents are used to propose and record engineering changes to baselined items; this includes hardware, software, firmware, and other documents. Recognizing that the preparation and processing of paperwork can be a major expense, the reason for every single piece of paper should be understood and justified (and the paper discarded or modified, if appropriate), and every reasonable attempt should be made to replace the paper with electronic media and automate the processing.

Table 4-I identified typical components of various baselines, and Chapters 9 through 11 discussed the control of changes to hardware, software, and firmware. This chapter provides details associated with the change packages that propose and record these changes.

12.1 CHANGES TO BASELINED ITEMS

As previously noted in Sections 2.1.2 and 2.2.2, the characteristics of both hardware and software are first identified in specifications, and their design is then expressed in design documentation and drawings. To maintain the integrity of the products that will evolve from these documents and drawings, the specifications, design documents, and drawings are placed under configuration control. Changes to these controlled items then need to be documented and processed in an organized manner. There are five types of change papers used to process these changes, depending on what is to be changed: hardware, software, firmware, documents, and drawings. Each of these is discussed below.

12.1.1 Changes to Hardware

As discussed in Chapter 10, changes in hardware can occur either during production or after delivery to some remote site.

(a) Changes to hardware during initial production (prior to the establishment of a product baseline) are proposed and approved as changes to drawings (for example, through the use of an engineering change notice). Such engineering change notices are usually processed with the awareness of the developing organization, and no further approvals are required. This may require the use of an internal configuration control board.

(b) Changes to hardware being produced after the establishment of a product baseline are also processed through the use of engineering change notices, but in this case, the approving authority is the customer. (The hardware has passed its acceptance tests, and it has been verified that the drawings are sufficient to enable identical copies of the tested hardware to be fabricated.) In this case, the engineering change notices may be attached to an engineering change proposal and sent to the customer for approval.

(c) Changes to hardware that has been delivered and accepted are also made through the use of engineering change proposals and engineering change notices. However, additional items may be required (for example, an installation kit and changes to an associated maintenance manual) to enable the retrofit to be made at the remote site. In addition, after the change has been made, those making the change should provide a report that the change has been accomplished by using an installation completion notice.

12.1.2 Changes to Software

Changes to software can be made in a variety of increasingly formal methods (that is, more rigorous procedures). This section describes the most formal methods, those that are used when software is part of the product baseline. The methods used for less formal control (for example, when the developmental configuration is first initiated) should be less rigorous, and the amount of paperwork should decrease accordingly.

The most complete change documentation set is shown in Figure 12-1. As shown therein, the change package consists of the following:

(a) An engineering change proposal. As indicated in Section 12.2.2, this is prepared with one specification change notice per software configuration item.
(b) The proposed specification change notice. This identifies all the source files that are being changed. The source file identification should include the source file name, the file type, and the new version number. Note that computer programs are changed at the file level rather than at the page level (as documents are). Attached to the proposed specification change notice should be a copy of:

    (1) Each of the new (revised) source files
    (2) Each of the old source files (the ones being changed)
    (3) The difference listings (the results of running a computer program that identifies all the differences between the old source file and the new proposed source file)

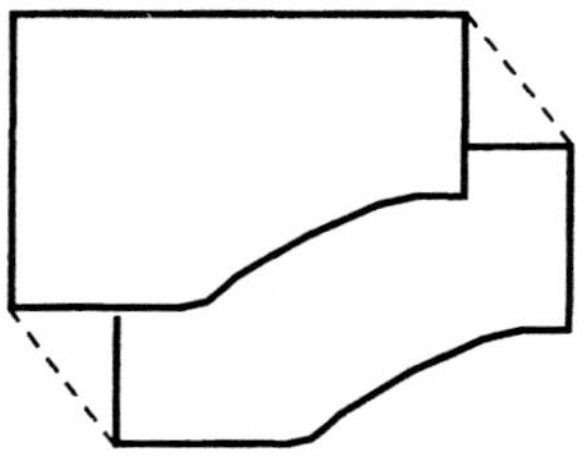

- *Change Proposal*
- *Proposed Specification Change Notice*
- *New Source File Listings*
- *Old Source File Listings*
- *Difference Listings*
- *Version Description Document*
- *Problem Report(s)*
- *Test Results*

FIGURE 12-1. A Typical Software Change Package.

(c) A copy of the version description document that documents the electronic media on which the revised source files are archived. The new source files will usually be archived with the rest of the source files that are part of a specific computer program configuration item (so that each tape or disc contains a complete computer program configuration item). As such, the version description document will apply to the complete computer program configuration item (rather than to just the revised source files themselves).

(d) A copy of the problem report(s) that document(s), in depth, the problems whose resolution required these source files to be changed.

(e) A copy of the test results that verify that the revised source files did indeed resolve the problem that required the changes.

12.1.3 Changes to Firmware

Changes to firmware include both of the methods identified above. Changes to the software component of firmware are processed like any other software changes. Associated with the total change package will be an engineering change notice to change the altered-item drawing that documents the placement of the image file on the media.

12.1.4 Changes to Documents

Figure 12-2 shows a typical change package for documents. This change package typically is used for changes to the functional baseline, the allocated baseline, and those documents that are part of the product baseline. Change packages for documents that are part of other baselines should be tailored downward to reflect individual project needs.

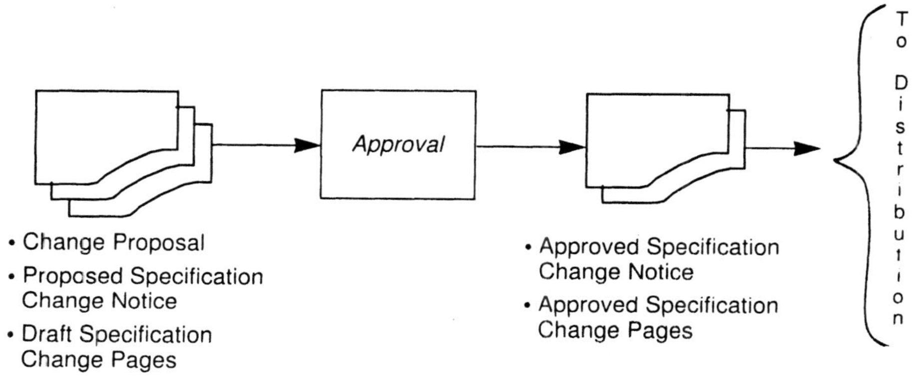

FIGURE 12-2. A Typical Document Change Process.

The engineering change proposal is the cover document and includes one or more proposed specification change notices (one for each document to be changed) which are attached to proposed specification change pages. At the end of the approval process, the approved specification change notices and the associated approved specification change pages are distributed as updates to the documents to be changed.

12.1.5 Changes to Drawings

Drawings are the detailed instructions by which hardware is fabricated. Because of this, drawings themselves are controlled. Usually, using an engineering change notice is the only way in which to obtain the authorization necessary to add to, delete from, or in any way revise a released drawing.

The processing requirements of engineering change notices are directly related to the status of the drawings that are proposed for change. If the drawing has been released, then the following actions can occur:

(a) If it is for limited use within the originating design activity, the notice is processed through the engineering change notice board and approved by the design activity.
(b) If it is for unlimited use within the organization, the notice is processed through the engineering change notice board and project configuration control board.
(c) If it is a part of the technical data package component of the product baseline, the notice is processed through the engineering change notice board and further processed through the project configuration control board for approval. Additional processing through the customer may be required, depending on the contract and the classification of the change.

12.2 CONFIGURATION CONTROL DOCUMENTS

This section provides details of the documentation associated with the control process. The documents identified in this section are the documents used in government configuration management. To avoid reinventing the wheel, the purpose of each of these documents and the essential elements of information associated with each of them should be understood. After that, they can be successfully modified to meet individual environments.

12.2.1 Engineering Change Notice

An *engineering change notice* is a request to make a change in a controlled drawing. As such, the following elements of information are usually required:

(a) The number of the engineering change notice.
(b) The title of the drawing being changed.
(c) The drawing number of the drawing being changed. Only one drawing number is indicated. If a second drawing is to be changed, a second engineering change notice may have to be initiated.
(d) The new revision letter of the drawing to be changed (revised).
(e) The date the engineering change notice is initiated.
(f) The next higher assembly (drawing number and title) in which the drawing to be changed is incorporated.
(g) All related changes by drawing number. As a part of this, all related engineering change notices should be processed as one change package.
(h) The reason for the change. Recognizing that identifying the reasons for requiring that a change be made provides a first step for process improvement, some thought should be given as to how these reasons should be grouped. See Table 12-I for an example of a list of reasons for changes.
(i) Complete identification of the changes to be made.
(j) The cut-in point at which these changes are to be made. This may be done, for example, by indicating the serial number of the assembly in which the change is to be first implemented.
(k) Contract number and other program identification.

12.2.2 Engineering Change Proposal

An *engineering change proposal* is a document used to propose and approve changes in controlled items. In government usage, engineering change proposals normally use DD Form 1692 from MIL-STD-973 with various supplementary forms, depending on the baseline to be changed.

The user should be aware that using the DD Form 1692 implies a degree of formality that is not always required. Very few of the blocks apply to software, and very few (even on the first page) apply to hardware in the early stages of a project prior to the establishment of a product baseline. For this reason, many projects use local forms, tailored to specific needs, for proposing and processing changes in the early stages of projects.

12.2.2.1 Classes and Types

As shown in Figure 12-3, engineering change proposals are divided into classes and types:

(a) A Class I change is a significant change; for example, a change that would affect the cost, schedule, or technical performance of the end product. Except as noted, Class I changes require customer approval prior to implementation. The two exceptions are: Class I engineering change proposals typed as "Record Only" do not require formal approval of the customer; and Class I engineering change proposals typed as "Compatibility" can have allowances in the contract to

TABLE 12-I. AN INITIAL SET OF REASONS FOR DRAWING CHANGES

1.	Adaption of an existing design for a new use
2.	Procurement Data Change—This may include: a. changing the procurement data as the vendor design is defined; b. adding vendor identification for use in procurements; c. changing vendor to improve cost or schedule.
3.	Design Improvement—This can result from: a. an evaluation of a breadboard and the consequent finalization of the design—fabrication of printed circuit boards (Prototypes) require released drawings; engineering change notices are required to finalize the drawings; b. planned Improvements to meet reliability growth program requirements.
4.	Vendor Changes—This may be a result of: a. vendor-supplied item not in accordance with the organization's drawing (a change in the drawing is required to accept the item); b. the addition of detail to assure vendor quality meets specified requirements.
5.	Obsolete Parts—An obsolete part must be replaced by a new part.
6.	Alternate Methods—This can include: a. parts substitution to provide cost or schedule improvement not associated with a design deficiency; b. a manufacturing change to improve cost or schedule.
7.	Engineering Deficiency—Changes to resolve either design errors or improperly specified test requirements.
8.	Drafting error correction
9.	Contract change
10.	Value analysis

permit work to continue without waiting for customer approval. Both types are valuable aids in maintaining progress while concurrently maintaining the integrity of the product and the customer's interests.

(b) A Class II change is a minor change; for example, a correction of documentation errors or the addition of a clarifying note. Class II changes normally only require the customer's concurrence in the classification; usually, silence after a specified amount of time (for example, five days) implies consent.

12.2.2.2 Content

The *engineering change proposal* is a cover document, one which carries its enclosures through the approval process. To do this successfully, the following items of information should be included:

(a) The unique identifier assigned to this change proposal and the date of initiation.
(b) Identification of the item(s) proposed to be changed.

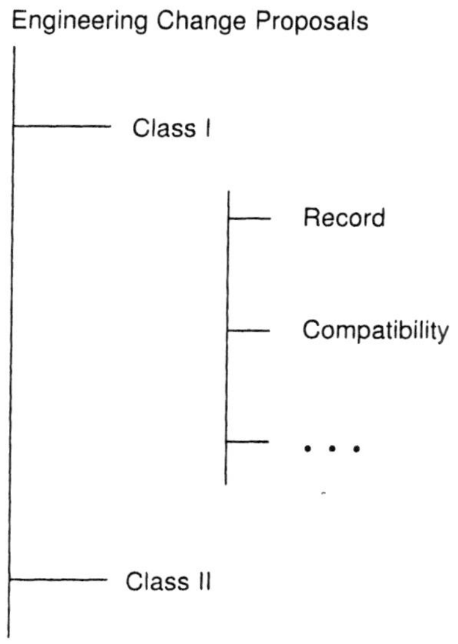

FIGURE 12-3. Classes and Types of Engineering Change Proposals.

(c) Identification of the proposed specification change notice(s) that provide the details of the change(s) to be made.
(d) Identification of other change proposals (if any) that are related to this change proposal.
(e) The reason(s) for the change; this may include, as an attachment, the problem report that documents the reason in depth.
(f) The priority of the change.
(g) The proposed date of implementation.
(h) Identification of this change, and if it is proposed to be made as part of a particular group of changes.
(i) The cost of the change, including both the time required to make the change and the dollar cost.

12.2.3 Installation Completion Notice

An *installation completion notice* is a report of the accomplishment of one or more change(s) to a system, computer software, equipment, and/or spares. This is normally used when an item in production has been sent to customers, and an approved change is to be implemented in those already delivered items. The receipt of this report provides closure on the implementation of the change and enables the exact configuration of all the items to be accurately maintained.

12.2.4 Notice of Revision

A *notice of revision* (NOR) is a document used to propose revisions to drawings, associated lists, or other referenced documents not under the control of the originator. This would usually be written by an originating contractor for material that was under the design control of another contractor, and replaces the use of specification change notices.

The reason for this form is that the originating contractor does not have the complete current details of what changes have been either proposed or approved for the item to be changed. Changes that are still in the proposal stage may not have reached the originating contractor at the time of the initiation of this notice, or a notice of revision may be initiated while an approved change is in the distribution cycle.

12.2.5 Problem Report

The purpose of a problem report is to document problems of any type (hardware, software, or firmware). To do this, the following information should be provided:

(a) The name, telephone number, and organization of the person initiating the report.
(b) The problem report number.
(c) A brief phrase describing the problem and similar problems, if applicable.
(d) The date the report is first submitted.
(e) A description of:

    (1) The problem, with sufficient information to permit duplication and analysis.
    (2) The conditions, inputs, and equipment configuration under which the problem arises.
    (3) The activities leading up to the problem occurrence.
    (4) Any relationships to other reported problems and modifications.

(f) The specific document paragraph(s) to which the report applies, including appropriate configuration identification and version number, if applicable, and all established baselines affected.
(g) The date by which the problem needs to be fixed in order to maintain established schedules.
(h) The name, telephone number, and organization of the person assigned to analyze the problem.
(i) The date the analyst was assigned.
(j) The date the analysis was completed.
(k) The time required to analyze the problem report (this should be in hours). The best way to keep this data is through the use of a special shop order on an automated accounting system, one shop order per problem report. Attempting to keep this data manually and reconcile it at a later date with the data from another accounting system is very difficult.
(l) The recommended solution and alternative solutions, if available; a short descriptive phrase on the nature of the recommended solution; and, when applicable, supporting rationale and test results. In a normal case, this would include a suggested implementation.

(m) The cost, schedule, and interface impacts if the solution is approved; also, the performance impacts if the solution is not approved.
(n) The impacts on other elements, components, integrated logistics support, system resources, training, and so forth.
(o) Signature of the approving authority.
(p) The date the solution was approved.
(q) Any further action (for example, approvals) required.
(r) The name, telephone number, and organization of the person correcting the problem.
(s) The date the problem was corrected.
(t) The version in which the problem will be corrected. This can be the version number of the source file, the revision number of a document, or the revision number of the image file.
(u) The time (in hours) required to correct the problem (see comments under item k above).

To improve the overall development process, the cause of the problem should be identified; and, to be of most value, these categories should be defined. Tables 12-II and 12-III provide suggested categories into which hardware and software problems could be placed, and it is recommended that these, or similar categories, be incorporated into a standard problem report form. (Note that each problem/change report is placed in one, and only one, category prior to being closed.)

12.2.6 Request for Deviation

A *deviation* is a specific written authorization granted prior to the manufacture of an item, to depart from a particular performance or design requirement of a specification, drawing, or other document for a specific number of units or a specific period of time. A deviation differs from an engineering

TABLE 12-II. AN INITIAL SET OF CATEGORIES FOR HARDWARE PROBLEMS

1.	Equipment documentation
2.	Material problem
3.	Part substitution
4.	Productivity
5.	Acceptance test failure

change proposal in that an approved engineering change proposal requires corresponding revision of the documentation defining the affected item: a deviation does not need revision of the applicable specification or drawing.

These are processed in the same manner as Class I engineering change proposals.

12.2.7 Request for Waiver

A *waiver* is a written authorization to accept an item that, during manufacture or after having been submitted for inspection, is found to depart from specified requirements but, nevertheless, is considered suitable for use "as is" or after repair by an approved method.

These are processed in the same manner as Class I engineering change proposals.

TABLE 12-III. AN INITIAL SET OF CATEGORIES FOR SOFTWARE PROBLEMS

1.	Hardware Interface—This is specified when there is an interface problem between a computer program and hardware.
2.	Software Interface—This is specified when there is an interface problem between two different computer programs.
3.	Requirements—This is specified when the resolution of the problem requires a change in a software requirements specification or in a higher-level document.
4.	Design—This is specified when the resolution of the problem requires a change in the design documentation and does not require a change in a software requirements specification.
5.	Code—This is specified when the resolution of the problem requires a change in a source file and does not require a change in the design documentation or the software requirements specification. This is further subdivided Into: a. Standards Violation—This is specified when the problem is limited to a failure on the part of the source file of code to comply with the project standards as determined by the configuration management library standards-checking tool. b. Other.
6.	Invalid—This is specified when the problem/change report is declared invalid by the software manager.
7.	Other—This is specified when the resolution of the problem is not placed in one of the above categories.

12.2.8 Specification Change Notice

A *specification change notice* is a document used to propose, transmit, and record changes to a specification.

12.2.8.1 Types

Specification change notices are of two types:

(a) *Proposed specification change notices* are submitted with engineering change proposals, one specification change notice for each specification to be changed. If there is more than one document to be changed, then a separate proposed specification change notice is provided for each document to be changed.
(b) *Approved specification change notices* are used to issue approved changes to specifications.

12.2.8.2 Content of Proposed Specification Change Notices

A proposed specification change notice identifies the document to be changed and the associated page numbers on which changes are to be made. This requires the following minimum information:

(a) A prominent marking of the word "PROPOSED" on the face of the document (this avoids confusion of a proposed specification change notice with an approved specification change notice).
(b) The unique identifier assigned to the proposed specification change notice.
(c) The date of initiation of the proposed specification change notice.
(d) Complete identification of the document to be changed.
(e) The page numbers of the pages to be changed. (The proposed specification change pages themselves are attached. These contain the actual changes to the previous text.)
(f) A history of the previous changes to the document. This should include a list of other specification change notices (both those that have been approved and those whose approval is still pending) and the specific page numbers affected by each notice. This information is important in order to avoid an unknowing approval of changes to pages on which other changes have already been made, or on pages which other proposed changes may be processed independently.

(g) The status of each of the other specification change notices (approved or proposed) in existence at the time of the initiation of this proposed specification change notice.

12.2.8.3 Content of Approved Specification Change Notices

Approved specification change notices are identical to the proposed specification change notices with three exceptions: the word "PROPOSED" is no longer on the notice; the date is changed to the date when the specification change notice was approved; and a signature is placed in an approval block, indicating that the notice and its included change pages have been approved.

12.2.9 Specification Change Pages

Specification change pages are of two types:

(a) *Proposed specification change pages* are submitted with proposed specification change notices for approval.
(b) *Approved specification change pages* are issued as an integral part of approved specification change notices.

12.2.9.1 Content of Proposed Specification Change Pages

There are two types of proposed specification change pages. The first type consists of pen-and-ink changes on the faces of the currently approved pages. This approach has a number of good qualities.

First, it is easy to prepare; even better, it is easy to determine quickly the precise change. Second, it is also easy to determine the identification of the currently approved page, since the page number and date of approval of that page are at the top of each page. Third, there is no opportunity to confuse this type of proposed specification change page with an approved specification change page.

However, there is a price to be paid for this ease in preparation, and this is in the potential difference between what is on the draft in pen-and-ink and what is on the final, printed, approved specification change page. Despite detailed proofing, much hard work, and the best endeavors of all concerned, there is a possibility for error in the translation between the draft and the final specification change page. The chances of errors increase as schedules are shortened and pressures are applied to "get the changes out, now!" Once an error is made and an erroneous page has been distributed for inclusion in a document, the corrective action required becomes a matter of great urgency and some embarrassment.

The second type is through the use of a complete replacement page. This is preferred by many organizations in order to avoid the problems associated with differences that may arise between what was seen by the approver of the proposed changes and the actual distributed approved changes. In this approach, the proposed specification change pages are prepared to look exactly like approved pages, with the exception of the following five items:

(a) Each page is stamped prominently on the top and bottom with the word "PROPOSED."
(b) The number and date of the specification change notice to which these pages are attached are placed in the upper-right-hand corner of each page.
(c) Bars are placed on the side margin of the page to indicate where new changes are being proposed.
(d) Any bars marking previous changes are removed.
(e) Proposed specification change pages are printed on a different color of paper.

The trade-off here is the amount of additional work required to prepare the proposed specification change pages and the percentage of that work which will need to be redone if a further change is made as the paperwork is being processed through the approval cycle.

If a proposed specification change page is prepared to look like an approved specification page, then the old (previously approved) specification page should also be provided as part of the package. This will permit those who review the proposed specification change page to identify precisely the new material, and to identify, without question, the complete text of the currently approved page.

12.2.9.2 Content of Approved Specification Change Pages

Approved specification change pages should be prepared as complete reprints of pages, ones which are suitable for incorporation by removing the old pages and inserting the new pages.

The differences between the old and new pages should be that: (1) each specification change page should carry the number and date of the approved specification change notice in the upper right-hand corner, and, (2) bars should be placed in the left-hand margin of each page to indicate where changes have been made from the previously approved page.

12.2.10 Specification Revisions

A *revision* consists of a complete reissue of the entire specification, and is distinguished from the initial issue by the revision letters placed on every page of the revision. Bars are usually placed on the left-hand side of each page to indicate where changes have been made from the previous revision.

Revisions are normally issued when the number of changes has grown too unwieldy to handle through the use of approved specification change notices. Either the number of specification change notices has become excessive (for example, six), or the number of changed pages has gone over a fixed percentage (for example, 30). Revisions are normally issued after the proposed specification change notice that covers the last set of changes has been approved.

12.3 PROCESS IMPROVEMENTS

A number of improvements can be made in a configuration management operation. Some of these are listed below.

12.3.1 Automating the Production of Documents

As previously noted, configuration control, particularly of documents, involves the use of highly stylized forms. Specification change notices, engineering change proposals, requests for waivers, and requests for deviations all use very specific forms. Entering the correct information into those forms, and making sure that every single entry is correct, is a time-consuming (and resource-consuming) effort. When a mistake occurs, the entire package comes back for retyping. This can seriously impact the effort when an engineering change proposal is bounced back from a customer because of an insignificant error on a particular page.

The administrative rejection process becomes worse when the customers themselves are audited by customer audit agencies to ensure that the paperwork that they process is complete and correct. The empire moves on paper and the paper is required to be correct, down to the very last entry. The value added by this process is not seen as significant, but this environment exists and requires solutions.

One approach to resolving this problem is to establish a highly trained group of people to prepare those forms and audit them using detailed checklists. The checklists then accompany the paperwork, so that everyone can see that good things have been done.

A better way is to automate the process so that the information on the forms and the forms themselves are produced as a unit. As one implementation, the program Forms Management System (FMS) on the Alpha will put the form on the terminal screen, insist that each entry is made, insist that each entry is made correctly (to the extent that this can be specified), and, if requested, provide help on completing the form. The completed form, with all the information on it (including the "from" and "to" regions of the forms and the associated graphics), can then be printed on a laser printer. Productivity is enhanced, the skill level required is reduced, and a better product is provided. This is currently done for income tax forms on personal computers, and should be extended to all parts of the configuration management world.

12.3.2 Automating the Engineering Drawing System

After automating the configuration management of software and documents, and implementing an on-line problem-reporting and corrective-action system, the next logical step is to automate the drawing systems. A significant amount of this may have already been done; if so, this step should build on what is presently in the system.

12.3.2.1 The Digital Engineering Process

Today, the digital engineering process is very heavily automated. The characteristics of chips (integrated circuits) are very accurately represented in simulation libraries, and the tools to interconnect these chips are available in software. Complete boards can be built and represented on the face of color monitor screens, backplane wiring can be accurately represented, and entire cabinets can be simulated without ever touching a soldering iron or wire-wrap tool. Furthermore, these products, as represented in software, can be stimulated with signals coming in over the simulated backplane and the resultant outputs captured and recorded (or fed into another simulated cabinet).

In support of other engineering processes, the mechanics of preparing drawings on large Mylar sheets have been giving way to preparing drawings electronically, but the transition has not been completed. One of the difficulties with changing a drawing system from paper to electronic media in large organizations is the sheer size of the stack of existing drawings. The impact on the corporation if the new systems do not work is such that the game is sometimes called "Bet the Company."

However, the impact of not converting the drawing systems is the gradual loss of business—the old methods simply become noncompetitive on a cost-effective basis. Changing paper (mylar) drawings, and processing the paper to authorize such changes by hand is a very expensive business. As covered in Section 5.3, the impact of not being able to rapidly implement "where-used" and "as-built" configuration information implies a loss of control of the product.

The overview of this process, then, is that the integrated design activity links electronically to the factory, while the factory, in turn, is moving to automated production lines of many types.

12.3.2.2 An Implementation Approach

There is nothing conceptually difficult about automating an engineering drawing system. The drawings are treated as source files, and changes are handled like changes to any other source files. The important thing to remember is that the interfaces (the paper drawings) already exist, and can be used to support an incremental approach such as the following:

(a) The initial step is to take a small group of drawings for one project and, using a scanner, convert them into bit-mapped files. The interface to other portions of the project continues to be paper drawings. Difficulties will occur at this stage: the amount of storage will be inadequate; the response time for accessing those files will be too long; the scanning process will yield, at times, unusable drawings; and maintenance problems will beset the printers that produce the drawings from the source files.

All of these and other difficulties are common to start-up projects; as a normal approach, a duplicate capability should be maintained until the first subprocess is fully operational and reliably produces the desired products.

After the small group of drawings is in the system and the start-up problems are resolved, the conversion of the rest of the drawings can be initiated.

(b) The second step can be to extend the input into drawing files to accept the electronic outputs of the digital engineering process. Again, this should be done on a pilot-project basis. There will be interface problems, and automated file conversion routines will have to be developed, tested, and implemented.

(c) The third step could be to extend the automated interface, to the factory, again on a pilot-project basis, and this can become rather complicated. There are a number of factory systems (for example, purchasing, inventory control, and control of substitute parts) that already exist and have a manual interface into the drawing system. Again, each manual interface should remain operational until the automated interface has been in place and working for a sufficient length of time to prove its reliability.

The above approach can be varied; it could, for example, be started at the factory level and work back. The important thing is to plan what is to be done; implement it on a phased basis; maintain, as a duplicate fail-safe capability, the old subprocess capability while the new capability is proven to be reliable; and then move to the next step.

12.4 SUMMARY

Configuration control documents are used to propose changes to hardware, software, firmware, documents, and drawings. Different documents are used, depending on the item to be changed and its location in the development/production process. Substantial cost-effective improvements are available through the automation of the engineering drawing system and integration of the automated production of change control documents.

12.5 EXERCISES

1. Compose a local form to act as a Class II engineering change proposal.

2. Prepare a combined form to use as both a problem report and a change request for items that are part of a developmental configuration. Provide a list of of the advantages and disadvantages of using a combined form for both purposes.

3. *Situational Problem:* Your manager has called you in to discuss and determine the best way to handle proposed change pages. As part of this, you have been requested to describe the different processes using flow charts; which include using the following: (1) complete proposed change pages, (2) "red-lines," handwritten changes on the face of the page to be changed, and, (3) "from-to" changes showing the changes on a change by change basis.

   REQUIREMENT: Provide process flow charts and indicate the advantages and disadvantages of each approach.

13

CONFIGURATION STATUS ACCOUNTING

As shown in Figure 1-2, *configuration status accounting* (CSA) is the fourth major process of configuration management. As a process, configuration status accounting is the recording and reporting of the information needed to manage the functional and physical characteristics of the items, and includes: (1) a listing of the approved documents that identify and define the item's functional and physical characteristics, (2) the status of proposed changes, deviations, and waivers to those characteristics, (3) the implementation status of approved changes, and, (4) the functional and physical characteristics of all units of the items in the operational inventory.

A restricted view of the configuration status accounting process is that the operation of the repository for the items to be controlled is not part of the process. This means that there must be some other place in which the documents (specifications, design documents, and manuals), technical data packages, and other documentation (and the software configuration items themselves) must reside. Furthermore, in the restricted view, the information to be provided to the configuration status accounting database is an input to the process; the problem reports, the engineering change proposals, and so forth are actually prepared and processed through some other unspecified mechanism. The result could be a patchwork system, cobbled together, unintegrated, slow, and prone to error.

Another view of the configuration status accounting process is shown in Figure 13-1. This view is one in which, to the maximum extent possible, the specifications and all the information about the configuration items and their changes are incorporated into one logical database. (The data itself may be physically distributed to various locations, but would be available through on-line inquiries.) This is a preferred view and incorporates the first view as a subset. This view, then, contains four subprocesses, three of which are discussed below. Due to its generic nature, the fourth process, Establish The CM Facility, is discussed in Chapter 14.

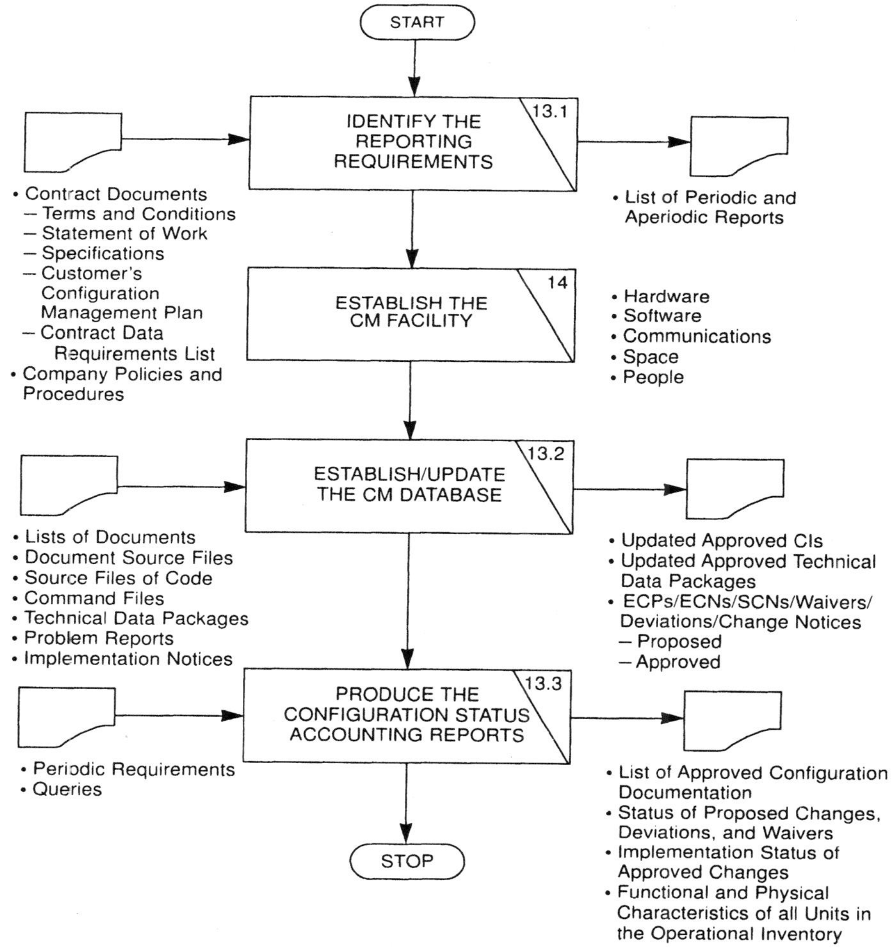

FIGURE 13-1. The Configuration Status Accounting Process.

13.1 IDENTIFY THE REPORTING REQUIREMENTS

The first thing to do is to identify the information to be recorded and reports to be made. This information comes from the contract and from company policies.

13.1.1 Contract

The contract identifies the items to be delivered and reports to be made. It also establishes the forms required for reporting changes, and the format and reporting frequency of the contractually required configuration status accounting reports. Contract requirements are usually a subset of the overall company configuration status reports, but special requirements may exist.

13.1.2 Company Policies

Company policies state how the company is to be organized and operated. These normally identify the business practices that must be in place in order to operate effectively. These require detailed information interchange between the configuration management element and other organizational elements (for example, the factory).

Consider, for example, that knowledge of the precise composition of every manufactured item produced by the organization is usually required. This is because the failure characteristics of an embedded item (part or purchased subassembly) included as part of an assembly might not surface until the assembly itself has been manufactured and widely distributed.

When a system fails, the line replaceable unit (LRU) that contains the fault is replaced. Should the failure rates be considered excessive, each failed unit will receive a failure analysis to determine the precise cause of the failures. Usually the cause of repeated failure in one type of line replaceable unit can be traced to the failure of one part that, for some reason (perhaps a failure in the part manufacturing process), is not meeting its reliability specification. When a faulty unit has been distributed worldwide, repair, replacement, or issuance of a modification kit for that deficiency requires identification of all the units of that type containing that part.

To carry the example further, the part (from a specific lot from one manufacturer) that is not meeting its reliability specification in one assembly may have been used in other assemblies or systems. The actual in-use failure rate may indicate that the offending part should be replaced before it fails in those other systems as well, particularly when the accelerated failure of that part may affect safety.

As a further example of information flow with other elements, consider the following configuration information developed as part of the factory operations:

(a) The design activity will reflect the design of an item in "build-to" drawings. Part of the drawing package will include parts lists, which will contain items identified by part numbers.
(b) As part of the factory operation, the purchasing department will screen the parts lists to ascertain which parts have been superseded (those that are obsolete and no longer being produced). The purchasing department will check the inventory, ascertain how many of the superseded parts are in stock, and then order the superseding part. At this point, then, the items to be manufactured begin to diverge in composition; some will be built with the specified part (from the existing inventory), and some will be built with the superseding part. Things can become more complicated when there is more than one superseded part (and there usually is).
(c) The purchasing department will then place orders for the parts, and the vendors' packages will begin to arrive at the receiving dock. Two additional items of configuration information have now been added: (1) the generic part numbers used for the procurement orders have been augmented by additional vendor identification markings (manufacturer's code, lot number, date of manufacture), and, (2) the vendor may have shipped "better-than" parts to fill the original order (for example, parts that may have higher reliability than those originally specified). All of this information must now be recorded to fully identify these parts as components of manufactured items.
(d) As the manufacturing process begins, each repairable item being produced by the factory will be serial-numbered, and the exact composition of each serial-numbered item will be part of the "as-built" configuration identification.

What has happened is the gradual change from a "build-to" drawing package to an "as-built" configuration; this change usually requires accurate rendition and easy access to that information.

13.1.3 Reports

Two types of reports are usually provided, periodic reports and those produced on demand.

13.1.3.1 Periodic Reports

Table 13-I provides a list of typical periodic CSARs and a more complete listing of some 27 CSARs can be found in Appendix H of MIL-STD-973. Gathering the data and providing the reports can consume a significant amount of resources, so the goal is to identify only that data that is needed. Considerations that should be made include:

(a) For small projects, the data can be gathered manually, but for medium-sized projects and larger, data collection and processing requires automation.
(b) It is easier to identify the needs for data and obtain agreement on its collection early in the project, rather than afterwards when budgets have been already been established.
(c) Data collection and processing cost money, so ensure that there is a genuine need for the data before initiating the efforts to collect it and incorporate it into a report. The concept is that there should be a prime user of the report, a champion of the collected data, who will establish the need for the report.
(d) Reports are best provided electronically. Printing and distribution can be significant costs.

13.1.3.2 "On-Demand" CSARs

The second type of report is those produced on demand, for example, a "where-used" report (see Section 5.3). This data does not need to be produced month after month when only one piece of the data may be required (and a different piece every month). Even better is the case when the data is on a relational data base and is made accessible on a read-only basis to all those on the project. For best results, *Structured Query Language* (SQL) should be used since this avoids requiring the users to learn still another specialized programming language.

13.1.3.3 CSAR Data Elements

Implicit in the development of a CSAR is the identification of what data elements will be contained in the report and what the data elements will be renamed. Appendix I of MIL-STD-973 identifies over 400 named data elements associated with CSARs and this appendix should be consulted when establishing requirements for the content of a specific CSAR.

13.2 ESTABLISH/UPDATE THE CONFIGURATION MANAGEMENT DATABASE

While this is a straightforward action, it implies a requirement for data verification. If the item itself is being entered, then data about that item can be abstracted directly from its substance. However, difficulties can occur when only data about an item is being entered (for example, the implementation of an updating kit). Depending on the risk and the impact, feasibility checks can be used as a safeguard. Furthermore, the source document from which the data was abstracted should also be an entry. For example, when a baseline is established, a complete reference should be provided (as a part of the entry) to the letter that approved those documents. This provides a 100% audit trail in case an entry is questioned.

TABLE 13-I. TYPICAL CONFIGURATION STATUS ACCOUNTING REPORTS

Item No.	Report Coverage	Notes
1.	Specification revision	Current version in use and history of changes, both proposed and approved.
2.	Drawing revision	
3.	Software version	
4.	CI components	List of all components of all CIs (for hardware by serial number, for software by file version number).
5.	Contracts listing	Tracks all changes to existing contracts, both prime contract and subcontracts.
6.	Change tracking	Tracks all changes from the time proposed until closed.
7.	Problem reports	Tracks all problem reports from the time initiated until closed.
8.	Change implementation status	Status of implementation of approved changes.
9.	As-built record	Configuration of items in the field.
10.	Maintenance history	Maintenance actions performed on each unit in the field.
11.	Audit actions	Status of each action item from initiation until closure.

13.3 PRODUCE THE CONFIGURATION STATUS ACCOUNTING REPORTS

This is a straightforward operation, one that should be initiated as early as possible and prior to being required. Since the configuration management organization needs to be perceived as contributing to the solution of the problems, the configuration status accounting reports are one of the earliest, best advertisements that the configuration management organization will have. As it turns out, the initial information on the configuration status accounting report is also badly needed (the complete current identification of the functional baseline); thus, it is immediately useful. Also, placing that type of information in the configuration status accounting report early and providing updates every month trains the project personnel to use the configuration status accounting report. When they start using it, they will feed back useful information on any mistakes. This then becomes a "win-win" situation for all concerned.

13.4 SUMMARY

Establishing a configuration status accounting capability includes identifying the overall reporting requirements, initialializing and updating the database, and producing the reports. The most difficult thing to do is to determine what reports are to be provided to avoid producing useless papers. Flexibility should be built into the system, as the reports themselves will change as the users' needs evolve.

13.5 EXERCISE

1. Prepare an example configuration status accounting report covering the status of a project at the time of a critical design review. Include the status of the functional and allocated baselines, and the developmental configuration through to the source code that is beginning acceptance test. In each category, provide the status of various changes to include the ECPs and problem reports.

14

THE CONFIGURATION MANAGEMENT FACILITY

The configuration status accounting database is part of the overall configuration management facility and operates most effectively when there is no need for an intervening entity. Data about the status of the configuration items should be directly obtainable from the specifications, change documents, drawings, and, in the case of the software, the configuration items themselves, rather than provided by manual keyboard entry from other locations. This facility then serves two purposes: it provides the ability to furnish the configuration status accounting reports, and it also serves as the software configuration management library.

As shown in Figure 14-1, the process of establishing the configuration management facility requires three efforts: establishing the requirements, acquiring the resources, and implementing the system.

14.1 ESTABLISH THE REQUIREMENTS

The most difficult thing to do is to establish the requirements for a configuration management facility. This requires specification of: (1) the functions to be performed, (2) the attributes the system is to have, (3) the performance requirements the system is to meet, (4) the external interfaces with which the configuration management system will have to operate, and, (5) the design constraints within which the system is to be built.

Even more difficult, these specifications must be expressed in such a manner that if the product provided conforms to the specifications, it will perform the desired task. What this means, in part, is that every requirement be expressed in such a manner that its achievement can be verified by a prescribed objective method.

14.1.1 Functional Requirements

Initially, the configuration management system must accept the items identified as inputs to the third and fourth blocks in Figure 13-1, and produce the products shown as outputs of those blocks. The configuration management system, viewed in this light, is a database facility providing a central storage facility which responds to queries. In this view, the system should provide the ability to handle four different categories of data: documents,

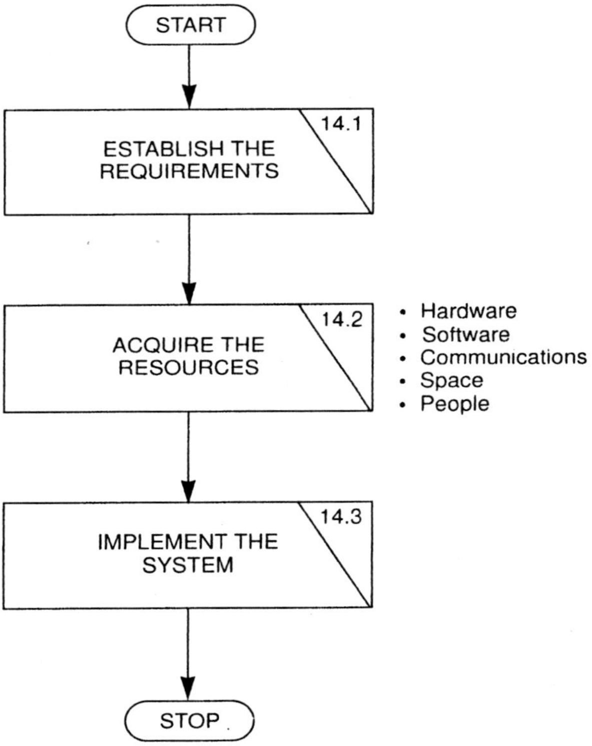

FIGURE 14-1. Establishing the Configuration Management Facility.

drawings and technical data packages, change documentation (including problem reports), and the configuration items themselves (in the case in which the configuration items can be placed on electronic media). These are discussed in the material that follows.

Secondly, the configuration management system must be capable of maintaining multiple copies (versions) of controlled items, allowing various degrees of access to controlled items based on different sets of criteria, and restricting the ability of users to make simultaneous changes (a check-out/check-in facility). These were discussed in Section 11.2.

14.1.1.1 Documents

Documents can be handled as text files, and the normal practice is to prepare them on a word processor or personal computer. There are two difficulties with this approach which need to be explicitly covered. First, the documents should include the graphics with the text as one integrated package. Otherwise, the graphics may be produced by other means, and the capability of controlling the changes to them can be lost. With the variety of packages on the market today that provide integrated graphics and text processing capabilities, the graphics and text should be recorded and stored together.

The second problem associated with this effort is that sometimes the floppy disks used by those who prepared the documents are stored in the left-hand desk drawer of those who did the preparation. While this may provide a degree of security to those who prepared the documents, it eventually results in chaos as private databases proliferate, personnel leave or shift jobs, databases are lost, and so forth. These need to be gathered and entered into the CM data base. The difficulty then is ensure that the habit of making changes outside of the CM data base does not persist.

The information of interest is how many documents are to be kept, their sizes, the requirements for update, the necessity for on-line storage and retrieval of superseded copies, and archiving requirements.

14.1.1.2 Drawings And Technical Data Packages

Almost all configuration management efforts are initiated with a drawing control system. The drawings themselves are on paper (Mylar) and perhaps also on microfiche for ease of retrieval, but the information about the drawings is usually in an automated database. The automated drawing control system database handles text files and, as such, may keep parts lists, superseded parts list, histories of change notices, and other items that support or deal with drawings, but not the drawings themselves.

Part of the effort of establishing the configuration management facility will then be to place the drawings in the database in such fashion that they can be maintained in digital format. This is directly equivalent to keeping other documents (which contain integrated text and graphics) in digital format. All of this evolves to a requirement to keep a certain number of drawings in on-line storage available for immediate retrieval. Further requirements include the capability to archive old drawings (further implying a storage facility) and to input new drawings from paper (requiring a scanner capability) from a workstation, and in bulk, electronically, from other sources (for example, a subcontractor).

There are two different ways in which the drawings can be entered and these ways are associated cost-effectiveness considerations. First, the drawings can be recorded in analog mode, one in which the entire drawing can be either printed or deleted, but can not be readily changed. Because this provides an immediate capability it is the simplest and cheapest way to store drawings; however, it has no growth capability.

Second, the drawing can be entered digitally in a manner in which both the text and the graphics can be changed via the keyboard (and mouse). This permits software to operate against the drawing, abstracting text based on content, and so forth. This is more costly in terms of both time to establish the initial capability and initial cost. It does provide a much larger capability to do many more things (for example, to screen parts lists to determine where specific parts are being used).

14.1.1.3 Change Documentation

The goal is to reduce the manual processing of change documentation, including that required to initiate and process problem reports, engineering change proposals, engineering change notices, specification change notices, specification change pages, and the other means by which problems are reported and changes processed. As noted in Section 12.2, these require forms; for ease of completion, the forms themselves can be menus on the screen, with the data already in the system placed automatically on the screen. This is normally accompanied with help screens to assist the user in knowing what data is entered, categorization of fields as mandatory and optional (mandatory fields must be filled in or the process will stop), and error checks on input data. Then, as the forms are completed and processed, they are automatically forwarded electronically to the next person to act on them.

Some amount of paper interface will always be required (for example, in providing material to a customer). In such cases, the required forms with the information in them should be automatically printed and posted to the required addressees.

14.1.1.4 Software Configuration Items

The configuration management facility should also provide the ability to store and manage the software configuration items, those items that can be stored on electronic media (including the software component of firmware). These are usually established in a project computer in the design activity (with specialized software support tools), but they should be integrated with the rest of the configuration management facility for ease in processing common data.

14.1.1.5 Other Considerations

The same comments associated with software also apply to the digital design process. For that process to be repeatable, the device libraries, associated tools, and inputs must be under control. The outputs of the process should interface directly, electronically, with that portion of the configuration management facility that supports drawing packages.

14.1.2 System Attributes

This consists of the "ilities" and, in essence, provides a checklist of things that should be reviewed. For example, consider expandability. Most configuration management systems will expand as their usefulness becomes known. If the configuration management facility is locked into a particular manufacturer's product (hardware or software) which cannot be expanded without major effort, much unhappiness may result. In terms of hardware, the need to increase the processing power by upgrading to the next higher processor in the series or adding additional computational resources to the local area network should be transparent to the facility. In one particular case, an installation started out using 4 Mbytes and quickly grew to 16 Mbytes. This was a plug-in operation done in an evening. Thus, an important part of the specification is to require that the system be capable of expanding its resources (primary memory, secondary memory, processing speed, and communication channels) in no more than four hours. (Four hours is an arbitrary figure, chosen to distinguish between a quick plug-in operation and one requiring 40 days.)

Reliability is another system attribute that requires specification. If it is important that the system always maintain its capability despite hardware failures, then that must be expressed. There are computer systems that maintain a nonstop transaction processing capability, and other systems that claim extreme reliability. Those items, plus the need for an uninterruptible power supply, require evaluation.

When the system starts to fail it may be important that the system have an immediate restart capability. This can save eight (or more) hours of checkpoint restarts, depending on the size and complexity of the system. Losing data is not the worst thing that can happen in a large database; even worse is not knowing what has been lost. To solve this problem, some machines have the capability to sense the loss of power and store the state of the machine. This becomes both a hardware and a software problem, and is sometimes easier to resolve it by the use of an uninterruptible power supply.

Finally, as resources become unavailable or the load peaks beyond all previous recognition, the system should have a graceful degradation capability, an ability to recognize an overload condition and shed nonessential processes while notifying users that these functions will no longer be performed.

These capabilities are not unique to a configuration management facility, but if desired, they do have to be recognized, specified, and tested. (It is much better to have a complete backup made, go to the main power breaker yourself, throw the switch, and immediateley discover that the recovery procedures are faulty, rather than finding it out on Monday morning at 8:00 a.m. as a surprise.)

14.1.3 Performance Requirements

Performance requirements are associated with the numbers on the system: for example, the number of users who will require service on an average and peak-load basis, what the peak processing and input/output loads will be, and what maximum response times are allowed for each type of processing identified.

The ability of hardware/software to handle a specified task or collection of tasks is best judged by using a series of benchmark programs. Such benchmark programs should be prepared by the user and represent the user's workload for a significant amount of time (for example, a four-hour slice). The benchmarks should be issued in source code, and the vendor should be encouraged to execute these benchmarks on the machines they are proposing. This could include the ability to read in an example set of drawings, store and retrieve them under software control, compile and execute a series of Ada programs, and so forth. The concept is to gain a reasonable degree of assurance that the system will carry the specified loads.

14.1.4 External Interface Requirements

The major external interfaces to the configuration management system will include people (the operators who will interact with the system), the factory (which will receive the drawings, and so forth, electronically or in paper form), and perhaps a customer.

The human interfaces are the most difficult to specify, and yet should be completed prior to any acquisition action. If the requirements are not specified prior to an acquisition, the danger is that the hardware or software that was initially purchased (usually obtained in a burst of enthusiasm based on generalized promises) will be unable to provide the displays required for efficient operation.

Those who will use the drawings should have electronic interfaces, which implies a set of interface standards. These are best confirmed by an actual demonstration of the interface prior to completing the acquisition.

Customers need information, and perhaps the poorest way to provide information is on paper. Most customers want to acquire a reasonable degree of assurance that work is proceeding towards a stated goal, and one way to provide that assurance is to allow limited on-line, read-only access to the configuration management database. This requires a certain degree of maturity on the part of the customer, but normally provides very good working relationships.

14.1.5 Design Constraints

It may be that the configuration management system is to be an expansion and integration of existing systems, or it might be a subset of a larger integrated system operating in the context of a company-wide system. This situation can require that the family of hardware machines be fixed and the software specified, or that particular interface standards or a particular software programming language be used.

Perhaps, as things have evolved inside an organization, more than one database is in existence. There may be one for software and a second that takes care of the drawing system; if so, they are probably on incompatible machines. There may even be a third database, consisting of networked workstations, which supports the digital design process. This opens up the whole field of distributed database design, with the associated concerns of keeping the various physically separated portions in synchronization. At the very least, communication links and file translation software will require consideration.

All of these are compatibility design constraints on a configuration management facility. They must be identified so that the configuration management facility will be compatible with the other appropriate elements of the company.

All of these requirements are important; they must be specified in detail and their achievement verified prior to making firm commitments for new items.

14.2 ACQUIRE THE RESOURCES

Resources come in a number of different types: hardware, software, communications, space, and people. The acquisition of each is not an easy task, and on any project, the earlier the procurement process is started, the better the prospect of success.

14.2.1 Multiple-Source Solicitations

The best type of procurement is a multiple-source solicitation. It is also the most difficult because it requires that the entire procurement process be planned and then executed. Typical documents that support such an action include a *request for proposal* (RFP), a specification, a *statement of work* (SOW), a *contract data requirements list* (CDRL), and an evaluation plan. These are briefly discussed in the following material.

14.2.2 Request For Proposal

The *request for proposal* does two things: it provides instructions to bidders on what should be done prior to the award of the contract, and it states the terms and conditions proposed to be a part of the ensuing contract. The first part, the instructions to bidders, identifies the proposed sequence of actions to be used for the solicitation and provides particulars about the process and the products. For example, the instructions for bidders should state the date when proposal submission is required, to whom the proposal should be sent, any required proposal format instructions (including the maximum length acceptable), and details on how benchmark program results are to be handled.

The request for proposal should also contain details concerning the pre-proposal bidders' conference, the manner in which questions are to be handled during that conference, material associated with pre-award surveys of bidders' facilities, and the debriefings offered to those bidders whose proposals are not accepted.

The proposed contract terms and conditions establish what is to be provided in terms of end-item products, the schedule for when they are to be provided, the identification of any contract services to be performed, details on payment, place of performance of contract efforts, and so forth.

14.2.3 Statement Of Work

The *statement of work* states what tasks are to be performed. For example, if the vendor is to provide contract maintenance support for the products delivered by the vendor for a period of two years after delivery and acceptance of the vendor's product, then the statement of work should contain a separate major section that provides the details on that task (how many people, on-or off-site, on-call, working hours, equipment to be furnished by the vendor to support the maintenance efforts, and so forth). The statement of work should also make reference to any data items that the task will produce, but details on data items should be reserved for the contract data requirements list.

14.2.4 Contract Data Requirements List

The *contract data requirements list* identifies all the data items to be provided. It includes such details as what data is to be provided, when it is to be provided, the number of copies to be provided to each addressee, the format to be followed, and approval requirements, if any. It should also contain a reference to the section number of the statement of work that requires that data item.

As an example, identification of a monthly maintenance report would be made in the contract data requirements list as well as any vendor problem reports that were generated as part of the on-site maintenance effort.

The harsh rule of thumb is that if a data item is not listed in the contract data requirements list, it is very unlikely that it will be supplied. Part of this is due to the ways that companies are organized; almost all of them have a data management organization, which ensures that all data items, periodic and one-time, are composed and delivered as required. The data management people manage the data items using the contract data requirements list; if data items are not on the contract data requirements list, they will probably not be delivered.

14.2.5 Evaluation Plan

This is the plan that states how each proposal will be evaluated; it contains the evaluation criteria and their associated weights. It will also contain the time-phased sequence of events to be used in evaluating each proposal, the groups that will evaluate different sections of each proposal, and so forth.

The goal is to provide as objective an evaluation as possible and rule out any factors that would favor one proposal over another. As a part of this, it is recommended that the same group of people evaluate the same section of every proposal.

14.2.5.1 Hardware

There are two aspects of buying hardware that should be remembered. First, do not buy any hardware that has not already been produced and is not in the hands of a happy user. Then, visit that user and make sure that the user is indeed happy. The hazards of buying vaporware (software that has been announced but not yet produced) are well known; the same applies to hardware.

Second, when buying hardware, remember to coordinate with the company facilities people. The hardware will need space, power, and air-conditioning, all of which may require work that takes a considerable amount of lead time.

14.2.5.2 Software

If the configuration management facilities are to use already existing company-procured hardware, additional software will probably be required to support that particular configuration management effort. In today's technology, there is no one package that will fill the complete set of requirements; this implies make-or-buy decisions. One approach is to buy two or more packages that will perform the majority of the tasks, and then provide in-house augmentations and the interfaces between the packages. This will require a software engineering effort, which requires both people and time.

14.2.5.3 Communications

One form of communication connects the users directly to the machines. If, however, the users are to be remotely linked to the machine, then not only is there a requirement for communication links operating at the bit speeds required (how long does it take to transfer a drawing package at various speeds?), but there are also security considerations.

Security considerations will always exist for material that is classified according to government security regulations. Security considerations will also exist when unclassified material that has value to the company is vulnerable to access through communication links. Various operating systems have vulnerabilities that can be exploited in order to cause either loss of the material or its unauthorized alteration. A detailed assessment should be made of these vulnerabilities and of the associated risk reduction actions.

14.2.5.4 Space

Space for the configuration management function is required, and the people who allocate space may belong to separate entities. The basic need is to have sufficient contiguous space so that all of the configuration management people can be located in one place. This is preferred, since they will be interacting together at least at the start of the project and should be cross-trained in each other's specialties. At a later time, as the work proceeds and depending on the nature of the project, it may be necessary to relocate some configuration management personnel to provide specific support at individual locations. That should be dealt with on a project-by-project basis.

4.2.5.5 People

Acquiring the right people is perhaps the most difficult task of all. Various types of people will be needed, including support specialists and software engineers. Not all of them will be needed initially, so there will be concerns associated with their time-phased acquisition. They will require training (perhaps best done initially off-site, at the vendor's location and on the vendor's configuration management tools) and motivation. Finally, it is considered penny-wise and pound-foolish to delay configuration management personnel acquisition for cost reduction reasons. The tasks are required, and their omission will have a significant downstream impact.

14.3 IMPLEMENT THE SYSTEM

There are a number of different strategies associated with implementing a configuration management facility: the big buy, incremental builds, and the oil spot. The *big buy* is the procurement of everything required for the entire effort. All the resources are procured at the same time, they all arrive together, and then everything is to be operational at the same point in time. Alas, for all good intentions, Murphy's law still applies—things that can go wrong will—and the result is that chaos descends on the scene.

A second approach is that of *incremental builds.* In this approach, a series of capabilities are identified, each building on the capability of the previous build; the achievement of each capability can be objectively determined by a person who is neither a configuration management specialist nor a software engineer. For example, the initial capability could be the production of a monthly configuration status accounting report (CSAR) that covers only the baselined documents. The second could be the on-line implementation of a problem-reporting system. The third could be the inclusion of the status of the problem reports in the configuration status accounting report. Meanwhile, in the background, capabilities such as the production of formatted change documentation would also be proceeding.

The *oil spot* approach is the logical extension of incremental builds to more than one thread of activities. For example, while the configuration status accounting report is being expanded, the ability of the configuration management facility to use a scanner to accept drawings should be demonstrated, and then the further ability to provide the drawing to the factory in electronic format should also be demonstrated. A third line of action, independent of the others, could be the implementation of the configuration management facility to accept the outputs of the digital engineering process and transform them to finished drawings.

The thought behind all of this is to provide an overall approach to achieving the total capability through demonstrable incremental steps, all of which have definite value as individual items.

14.4 SUMMARY

The configuration management facility serves two needs: it provides the machine resources to track the exact status of configurations, including problems and proposed changes, and it also provides the facilities to be used for the software configuration management library (or digital data configuration management library). Acquiring such resources is a long-term effort requiring a significant investment to ensure that the facility will fill the needs.

14.5 EXERCISES

1. Provide a procurement package for a configuration management facility. As part of this, provide an example:

    a) Request For Proposal
    b) Requirements Document
    c) Statement of Work
    d) Contract Data Requirements List
    e) Evaluation Plan.

2. *Situational Problem:* Your manager has called you concerning the XYZ Proposal which is about to submitted to the Do Right Corporation. He has noticed that this will require a completely new facility and wants to discuss with you today your plans for facility acquisition.

    REQUIREMENT: Prepare an abbreviated plan for the acquisition and activation of the new CM facility. Include the tasks to be accomplished, the milestones, the schedules and a cost estimate for each of the tasks.

15

CONFIGURATION AUDITS

As shown in Figure 1-2, the fifth step in managing a collection of items is to audit the products and the overall process itself. An audit is an independent evaluation of a product to ascertain compliance to specifications, standards, contractual agreements, or other criteria. In the configuration management world there are three types of audits, and they can be examined in two different ways: the types of audits to be performed, and the actions that are common to the types of audits. To be complete, both examinations must be made.

15.1 TYPES OF CONFIGURATION AUDITS

Three types of audits are done in the name of configuration management: *functional configuration audits* (FCAs), *physical configuration audits* (PCAs), and *in-process audits*. Each has a different purpose and must be examined in detail.

15.1.1 Functional Configuration Audits

The purpose of a *functional configuration audit* is to verify that the development of a configuration item has been completed satisfactorily and that the configuration item has achieved the performance and functional characteristics specified in the functional or allocated configuration. Functional configuration audits are held at the end of a development cycle, following the completion of all the testing on the items that have been developed. For hardware this can be quite complex, as there are a great variety of requirements that necessitate specialized tests. For example, as shown in Figure 15-1, the tests to determine if a hardware CI meets its performance requirements usually include separate tests for: (1) physical requirements, (2) reliability, (3) maintainability, (4) environmental conditions (temperature, humidity, wind, ice loading, salt spray, altitude, shock, vibration, noise, inclination, rain and fungus), (5) transportability, (6) electromagnetic radiation, (7) electromagnetic interference, (8) Tempest, (9) safety, (10) human engineering, and others. Each of these tests and subtests (for example, fungus) has a separate test plan, a separate test procedure, a separate test report, anomaly reports and action items—and all of these are in addition to the testing of the functional requirements themselves.

As a result, by the end of the testing period a horde of hardware/system test reports have been accumulated, each probably noting at least one anomaly together with a series of actions to resolve the anomalies, responses to the actions, and more. To come to an understanding that all the hardware tests have been successfully completed, that all anomalies have been resolved, and that all the action items have been closed usually re-

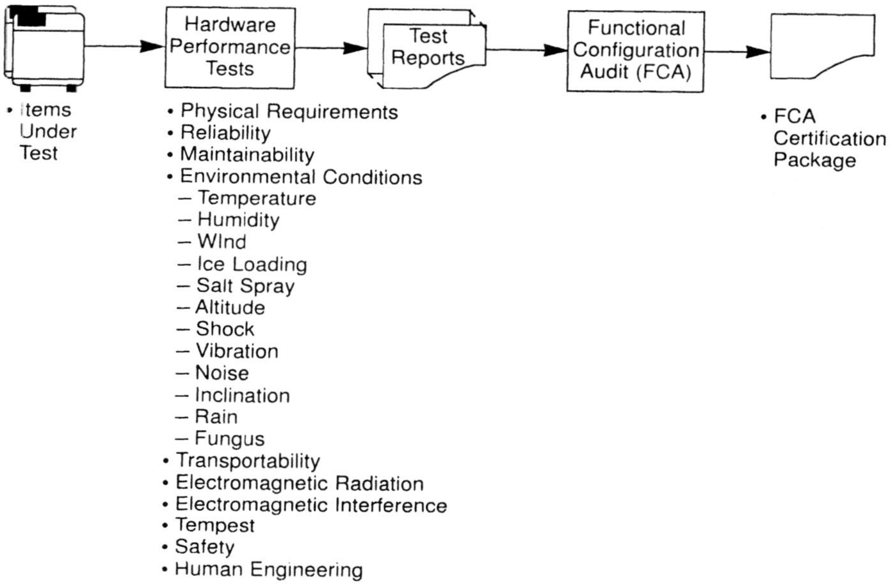

FIGURE 15-1. An Overview of the Events Surrounding a Hardware Functional Configuration Audit.

quires a meeting of all the interested parties (customer and user). At this meeting, all the test reports and associated anomaly reports are reviewed. This meeting has been formalized into the FCA and, for hardware, is usually required.

There are a number of cautions that should be observed at this point. First, the functional configuration audit is not the time to review the test program itself for adequacy. The judgment that the test program (and the associated test plans and test procedures) were adequate for the intended purposes, and were both necessary and sufficient, has already been made, long before the test program was actually initiated. Going back to review that aspect would be unsettling. This would open up the entire test program for a review on completeness, a matter on which there already has been a written agreement.

Second, there is sometimes a viewpoint expressed that if anything changed (for example, if there were any parts substitution in the item as it went through the test program), the entire test program should be reinitiated. There are judgments to be made, and extreme calls on either end of the spectrum (retest everything; do not retest anything at all) should be avoided. Regression or check tests should be used in doubtful cases, and those judgments should be reviewed at the functional configuration audit if they have not already been confirmed by mutual agreement of the concerned parties.

Third, there are cases in which there has been only one test made, with one test report and a series of actions (this case is very common in software). In such circumstances, convening a functional configuration audit to review that one test may not be warranted. For detailed considerations of this case, see Section 15.3.

15.1.2 Physical Configuration Audits

The *physical configuration audit* is a technical examination of a designated configuration item to verify that the configuration item "as built" conforms to the technical documentation that defines it. Thus, on the hardware side, a physical configuration audit is an audit of the actual product itself against its technical data package. The criterion used for the audit is: if the instructions in the technical data package were followed, would an item identical to the one that had passed the physical configuration audit, be produced?

An overview of the events surrounding a hardware physical configuration audit (PCA) is depicted in Figure 15-2. This shows the PCA in the context of the design, test and production activities including the FCA. As shown therein:

(a) The "build-to" engineering drawings are derived from the specifications and are then used to build the engineering model(s) of the product.
(b) The engineering models of the product are then tested to ensure that they meet the requirements of the specifications and these test results are reviewed (as previously discussed in Section 15.1.1) at the hardware FCA.

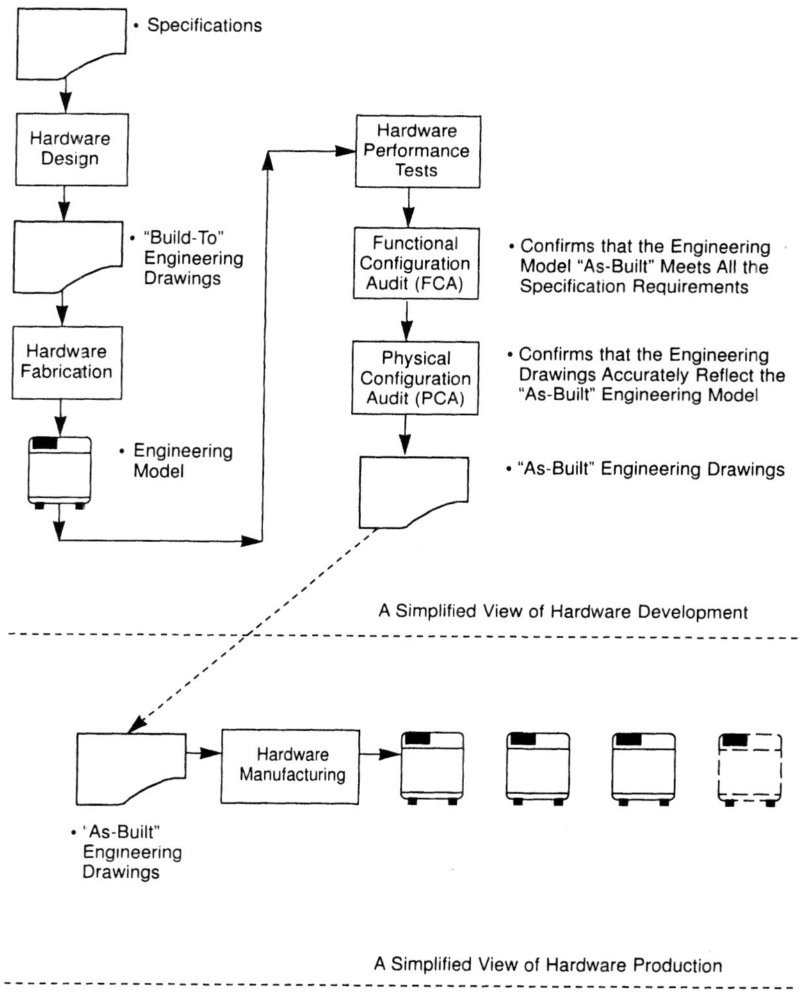

FIGURE 15-2. An Overview of the Events Surrounding a Hardware Physical Configuration Audit.

(c) After the FCA has been successfully completed, a physical configuration audit (PCA) is then executed to ensure that the engineering drawings, associated parts lists and the other components of the technical data package:

(1) Accurately reflect the engineering models that have successfully completed their performance tests.
(2) Contain the necessary information to enable accurate copies of the hardware items (that passed the performance tests) to be manufactured as part of a production process.

The reason for this physical configuration audit is straightforward in the hardware environment. It has been previously verified at the functional configuration audit that the item constructed as part of the development cycle met all the requirements in the specifications. Now, if the technical data package provides accurate instructions on how to build identical items, then many, many more of the items that meet those specifications can be produced without the exhaustive testing required for the initial item. Confirmatory and first-item testing will take place as the production line rolls on, but these can be done on a sampling basis rather than on 100% of the production items.

Unfortunately, the act of performing a physical configuration audit has been copied from the hardware world to the software world without examining the underlying rationale. As noted above, in the hardware world, a physical configuration audit is performed so that additional items can be manufactured. In the software world things are different, and this gives rise to a major concern which is discussed in detail in Section 15.4.

15.1.3 In-Process Audits

In-process audits are performed to determine whether the configuration management process established in an organization is being followed and to ascertain what needs to be improved. This can be done in-house (an organization does well only those things the boss checks) and also on a subcontractor's configuration management system.

In this context, the task of in-process audits is sometimes done by the quality assurance (QA) function, which has both advantages and disadvantages. The major advantage is that the quality assurance function itself is further removed from the configuration management organization, so there is a greater degree of independence. The disadvantage is that, for the most part, the quality assurance organization lacks the degree of specialized knowledge required to thoroughly audit a configuration management process. One way to overcome this disadvantage is for the quality assurance function to borrow configuration management expertise from another organization (for example, consultants).

In any event, even if the quality assurance function is to perform in-process audits, there will always be a need for the configuration management organization to audit itself.

15.2 COMMON AUDIT ACTIONS

The actions associated with audits are usually divided into three parts: pre-audit, audit, and post-audit. Each of these is covered separately in the material that follows.

In these audit actions, the role assigned to the configuration management organization can vary, and may include management of the audit, co-chairing one or more of the audits themselves, and acting as recording secretary or clerk. The view taken here is that the configuration management organization is responsible for all the actions associated with the audit, including both pre- and post-audit actions. The reasons for this view are that: (1) often, in busy organizations, complete documented authority and responsibility for such audits are not established; (2) busy people, who are otherwise engaged in doing other things for which they have responsibility, will not usually divert efforts from their primary tasks to perform other jobs; and, (3) successful completion of these audits is of direct interest to the configuration management organization.

None of this should be taken to imply a lack of coordination. What it does imply is that the configuration manager will take the lead in initiating and successfully completing these audits.

15.2.1 Pre-Audit Actions

The success of any audit is directly dependent on the preparations that have been made to conduct the audit. If there is insufficient time to prepare for the audit by either the group to be audited or the group performing the audit, then it would be best for all concerned to reschedule the audit until such time is available. The following actions are considered to be a minimum set of things to be done prior to the actual audit itself.

First, announce (in consultation with the manager whose group is to be audited) that the audit is to take place, including the time, location, and purpose. This should be done as far in advance as possible so that all concerned can arrange their schedules to support the audit. Preferably, this should be done at least at the conclusion of the previous audit. If not, it should be announced as soon thereafter as possible. The reason for this is quite simple: all of us can meet on any particular date if the date is specified sufficiently far in advance. To ensure participation, then, get on everyone's calendar as early as possible.

Second, specify the criteria to be used for the audit. This should be a matter of joint agreement between both parties. It does no good and solves no problems to conduct an audit using criteria that have not been accepted by the group being audited. They will pay no attention to the results, and all that has been done is a waste of everyone's time.

Third, prepare a detailed draft agenda and provide it to all concerned well in advance of the audit date itself. This agenda should include such items as:

(a) The purpose of the meeting—This will be well known to all those who are going to participate; however, it will not be well known to others who may be concerned about it, so it is best put in writing to avoid confusion.
(b) A review of the report of the last audit.
(c) The status of the closure of the actions from the last audit.
(d) The detailed steps to be taken to conduct the audit itself.
(e) A review of the draft minutes that result from this audit.
(f) A review of the actions that result from this audit.

By placing all this detail (and more) on the draft agenda, surprises are avoided, people can remain focused on specific items, and business can be conducted efficiently.

Fourth, identify by name all personnel who are to participate in the audit, together with their specific duties. Of particular interest are the chair (the person who will run the meeting) and the secretary (the person who will prepare the minutes). Preparation of the minutes in a timely and accurate manner reduces lost efforts. The minutes should contain a record of every significant decision, together with a sufficient level of supporting information so that a person who did not attend the meeting would be capable of understanding what decisions were made and the basis on which each decision was reached.

Fifth, specify the actions to be taken to record any anomalies resulting from the audit, and prepare and coordinate the associated forms. The coordination will yield additional insight into what should be done, and those items are best ironed out before beginning the audit.

Sixth, review all the previous audits, their associated actions, and the current status of each of those actions. Besides determining what actions are still open, this provides information from which patterns of nonconforming actions can be inferred, which in turn may point to particular items that should be checked as part of the forthcoming audit.

Seventh, prepare and coordinate a detailed checklist, covering every single mandatory item. For example, if a project instruction is a requirement, then every single mandatory item in that instruction should be listed as a separate question. That type of preparation takes a significant amount of effort, and so is often not done. If it is not done, there are two consequences: (1) the audit can only be conducted by very skilled people who have a detailed knowledge of all the contents of all the standards, and/or, (2) coverage of the audit may be spotty and based on who is conducting the audit.

Eighth, establish a random-choice methodology for both the criteria and the items to be checked. There will be always more detailed individual criteria to be covered and more items to be examined than time or people to perform the checks. One way to conduct an audit in which that situation exists (for example, attempting to audit all the drawings in a particular system for compliance to DOD-STD-100C) is to use a random-choice methodology. Number the criteria from 1 to 10,000 (if there are that many). At the time the audit is actually initiated, throw a ten-sided die (available from the local Dungeons and Dragons game store) to determine which criteria are to be used for that audit. Then, using a similar random methodology, choose the items to be audited.

The reason for all of this is quite simple: the major benefit from any audit is the work that is done, before the audit takes place, by the group being audited. The group being audited should be encouraged to meet all the criteria for all the items. Through random choice of both criteria and items being examined, the group being audited is encouraged to provide a consistent level of effort across all items for all criteria (if only because they do not know what subsets will be checked).

15.2.2 Audit Actions

Assuming that the auditing group is from an outside organization, the first thing to be done on arriving at the plant is to make a courtesy call to the manager of the organization being audited. This is a brief call, stating the purpose of the visit and leaving with the manager a copy of the letter that announced the audit and the draft agenda. The manager may be surprised by your visit and may not have been informed that such an audit was planned. Leaving a copy of the letter and the draft agenda reduces the confusion factor and ensures that there will be no complications due to diversion of resources for other purposes during the time of your visit.

When beginning the audit itself, the first thing to do is to review the draft agenda to provide a firm focus on each event. At that time, it is a good idea for the chair to announce that after the draft agenda has been approved, any other items will be placed at the bottom of the agenda, and that this is being done for two purposes: it is necessary to ensure that the items on the agenda for which people have prepared are covered, and placing any new items at the bottom of the agenda will allow those interested in participating in the topic to prepare for those agenda items in a reasonable manner.

The initial part of the audit should include two briefings of limited length. The first should be an introductory briefing by the personnel conducting the audit, explaining the purpose of the audit, the proposed conduct of the audit, and the projected post-audit actions. This is aimed at providing a clear understanding to all who are present and who may not be completely familiar with all the details of what is going to take place. It is best to provide this once, at the beginning of the audit, with everyone present; otherwise, the audit may be interrupted by questions from those who do not have that understanding.

The second briefing should be an introductory briefing by the personnel being audited, providing an overview of their organization, the system being audited, the results of previous audits, and the status of actions from the previous audits. The first two items orient the members of the auditing team, and the last two require the audited organization to go back to the last series of audits and provide their understanding of that status.

The audit itself should then follow the agenda, including on-site completion of the previously prepared checklists and preparation of the draft audit minutes, including the associated audit anomaly reports and audit actions.

The last item that involves the entire group is the review with the audited organization of the draft minutes, draft audit anomaly reports, and draft audit actions. The purpose of this review is to ensure that the facts as recorded in the minutes and associated documents are not in dispute and that the actions are understood. Any items in dispute should be corrected or the position of both parties noted. As a portion of this review, dates should be established for responses to the actions.

Prior to leaving the plant, the auditing team should seek an exit meeting with the manager responsible for the audited organization and provide the manager with a copy of the revised draft report and attachments. This permits the manager a second view of what took place and allows any items that might be in error to be corrected early in the review stage.

15.2.3 Post-Audit Actions

The results of the audit, including the minutes, anomaly reports, and actions, should be approved, published, and distributed within one week of the audit's completion. If the minutes and attachments are not quickly published, the value of the audit rapidly deteriorates. Minutes and actions published a month after the audit's completion have lost at least half of their value.

When distributing the minutes and attachments, it is always a good policy to provide a set of these items to the quality assurance group of the audited organization. With some encouragement, the quality assurance group will institute follow-up to ensure that the actions have been completed.

15.3 MAJOR CONCERN: SOFTWARE FUNCTIONAL CONFIGURATION AUDITS

The purpose of a *functional configuration audit* is to verify that the development of a configuration item has been completed satisfactorily and that the configuration item has achieved the performance and functional characteristics specified in the functional or allocated configuration. FCAs came into being because of the large number of tests performed on hardware configuration items and the view that the corresponding effort should be made on software configuration items. However, for software, a different situation exists. As shown in Figure 15-3, software is normally tested once, in a software formal qualification test. The anomaly reports and the associated action items are all contained in one document, the software test report. It is not normally considered cost-effective to convene a formal meeting to review the status of one document (the test report). As a result, contracts that involve software normally do not contain a requirement for a FCA of software nor is FCA for software considered a best practice.

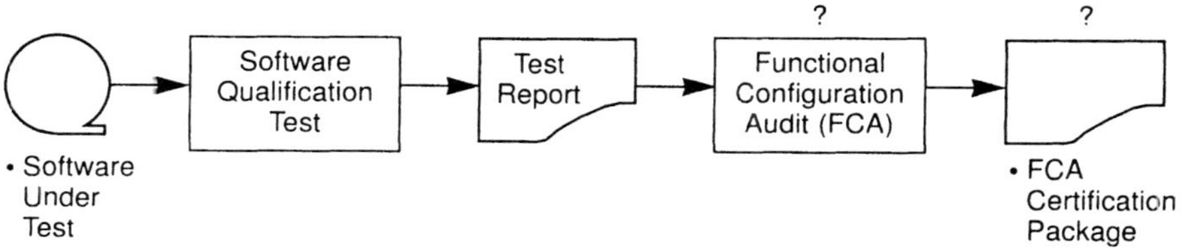

FIGURE 15-3. An Overview of the Events Surrounding a Software Functional Configuration Audit.

There are other items associated with an FCA of software and these are identified in Table 15-I. As noted in that table, these are duplicative efforts. In addition, some of them are open to interpretation and may represent major risks. Recommendations on software FCAs are provided in Table 15-II.

TABLE 15-I. A REVIEW OF THE MIL-STD-973 REQUIREMENTS FOR SOFTWARE FCAS

MIL-STD-973		Recommended To Be Done At Software FCAs?	Comments
Section Number	Requirement		
5.6.2.3.a	Review test procedures and results for compliance with specification requirements.	No	Test procedures and test results are deliverable items and are reviewed and accepted by the customer separately.
5.6.2.3.b	N/A		Does not apply
5.6.2.3.c	Audit test plans, specifications and test procedures against test data.		(1) The test plans, specifications, procedures, and input test data are audited at the time they are approved. (2) Output test data is approved as part of the test report.
5.6.2.3.d	(1) For those requirements that can not be completely verified by testing, determine whether adequate analyses or simulations have been accomplished and whether the results of the analyses or simulations are sufficient to ensure that the CI meets the requirements in the specification. (2) All ECPs that have been approved shall be reviewed to ensure that they have been technically incorporated and verified.	(1) No (2) Yes, but only for those ECPs approved after the end of the formal acceptance tests.	(1) This is done as part of the software test plan and reports. (2) ECPs that were incorporated in the software prior to the initiation of the software acceptance test are technically verified as part of that test. (3) ECPs that are approved after the software acceptance test carry with them the associated requirements for additional technical verification.
5.6.2.3.e	Audit the test report.	No	This is done as a part of the acceptance of the deliverable item.
5.6.2.3.f	N/A (hardware only)		Does not apply
5.6.2.3.g	N/A (hardware only)		
5.6.2.3.h	N/A (hardware only)		These are workmanship requirements; e.g., finish. All requirements for software are included in the acceptance test plan. If a software item does not pass the acceptance test, it is retested prior to FCA.
5.6.2.3.i	Acknowledge accomplishment of partial completion of the FCA for those CIs whose verification is contingent upon completion of integrated systems testing.	Yes	

TABLE 15-I. (Continued)

MIL-STD-973		Recommended To Be Done At Software FCAs?	Comments
Section Number	Requirement		
5.6.2.3.j (1)	Review database characteristics, storage allocation data and timing, and sequencing characteristics for compliance with specified requirements.	No	This is done as part of the software acceptance test.
5.6.2.3.j (2)	Review all documents which comprise or describe the contents or the use of the software product for format and completeness (e.g., SPS, User's Manual, VDD).	No	These are deliverable items and are reviewed and approved at the time of document delivery.
5.6.2.3.j (3)	Review the records that reflect the changes made to the developmental configuration for the CSCIs.	Yes	This is a review of the configuration status accounting reports which have been previously submitted in accordance with contract requirements.
5.6.2.3.j (4)	Review the listing of all versions of the developmental and non-developmental software for the CSCIs that are in the software library.	No	The purpose of this review is not clear. There are no criteria stated. The criteria stated in the SRSs are checked at the time of acceptance test.
5.6.2.3.j (5)	Review the findings of all internal CM and software QA audits of the CSCI.	Yes	
5.6.2.3.k	PDR and CDR minutes shall be examined to ensure that all findings have been incorporated and completed.		

TABLE 15-II. SOFTWARE FCA RECOMMENDATIONS

FCA Required By Contract	Recommendations
No	Do not perform.
Yes	(1) Review PCA contract requirements in detail. (2) Recognize that some of the requirements are open to various interpretations and some may be duplicative of other contract efforts. (3) Clarify these requirements as part of proposal effort. (4) Review software FCA contract requirements and identify those that are major risk items.

15.4 MAJOR CONCERN: SOFTWARE PHYSICAL CONFIGURATION AUDITS

Software physical configuration audits are a major productivity concern. As a result, prior to initiating such an effort, the rationale for performing a software physical configuration audit should be examined in detail, together with a detailed assessment of the usefulness of its product.

15.4.1 Background

As previously noted, the reason for a hardware physical configuration audit is to ensure that items built from the instructions in the technical data package will be identical to the ones that passed all the development tests. In software, things are different. If additional copies of the software are needed, they are made directly; there is no need to refer to a technical data package in order to make additional copies.

Instead of examining the technical data package to ensure that additional copies can be manufactured, software physical configuration audits are held to ensure that the design documentation accurately reflects the software code. (The opposite view—that the code should agree with the design documentation—fails to take into account that, at this stage of the development, it is the code that has passed the final acceptance tests, not the design documentation.) The reason given for this approach is that the maintenance personnel need to be able to rapidly obtain an overall understanding of the software architecture and an ability to go deeper into any software component. Furthermore, this need cannot be satisfied by the examination of the source code itself, as the details in the source code listings prohibit the abstraction of the higher-order framework. The need is then expressed as a requirement to have some document that would enable a person not familiar with the program to quickly grasp an understanding of the program as written. By default, this higher-level view has been projected to be provided by the software design documentation prepared during the software development; hence, the need for accuracy, which thus implies the need for a software physical configuration audit.

As shown in Figure 15-4, the theory of the software physical configuration audit is straightforward: (1) prior to the physical configuration audit, the "build-to" software design documentation is modified to reflect the "as-built" code, (2) the revised documentation is then sent to the customer 30 days before the physical configuration audit, (3) the customer chairs the physical configuration audit meeting at the developer's location for three days or so, and leaves a list of discrepancy reports with the developer, (4) the developer corrects the discrepancies, and, (5) the customer accepts the documentation.

There are three difficulties with this approach: (1) changing the "build-to" software documentation to reflect the "as-built" code is an expensive process, (2) the physical configuration audit itself takes considerably more time and effort than envisioned by either party, and, (3) the output—the design documentation—is not actually used by the maintenance programmers.

To examine this systematically, the view must include an appreciation of the input (the design documentation itself), the actual physical configuration audit process, and the value of the output.

15.4.2 Physical Configuration Audit Input: The Design Documentation

Design documentation is initially prepared to act as the "build-to" plans for the construction of the software. As such, it usually contains things (for example, the program design language [PDL]) to assist the programmers in writing the source code. Once the software has been constructed (in the form of code), unless there are overriding reasons for not doing so, the design documentation is, in effect, usually abandoned. The reasons for this are quite straightforward:

(a) The purpose of creating the design documentation was to enable the code to be built. The code has now been built; therefore, there is no value added to the product by updating the design documentation.
(b) The developer is to be paid when the system has completed its acceptance test, and the system tests cannot be started until the soft-

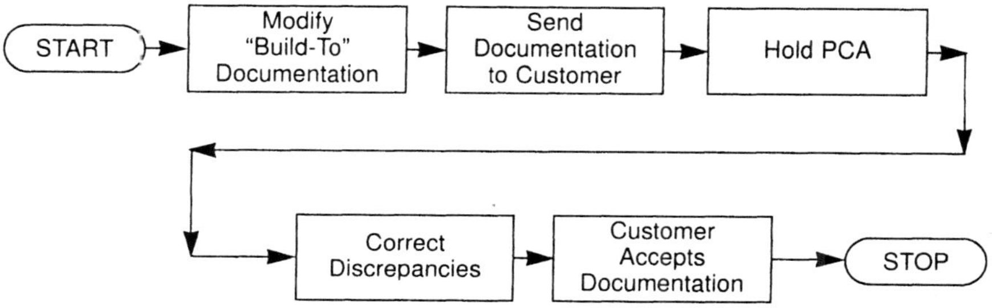

FIGURE 15-4. The Theory of the Software Physical Configuration Audit.

ware tests are completed. Therefore, every single person who can help with testing the software is pressed into service. Those who know the software are all supporting the test activities, and no one is left to keep the design documentation up to date.

For those who doubt this scenario, consider the reaction of a project manager on being told that competent, knowledgeable people are available but not being applied to complete the software test activities. This will appear to be completely unreasonable to the project manager who will shortly bring the matter to the group general manager. The final result will be direction that all available resources be placed on the test effort. (In addition, the customers themselves have an urgent need for the system, which is why they are buying it in the first place, and this adds increased pressure to complete the testing and delivery.)

The current response to all this is to state that the updated design documentation is needed and to require, as a part of the contract, a software physical configuration audit. In theory, at that time a complete review is made of all the software design documentation. The design documentation that does not reflect the "as-built" code is to be revised and provided as part of the physical documentation audit input.

15.4.3 The Physical Configuration Audit Process

At first glance, the time required to hold a physical configuration audit could be estimated as shown in Table 15-III. As shown therein, this is about two months, which can be further estimated (very roughly) at about $45,000 per computer program.

In looking at the practice, consider the documentation for one computer program of approximately 30,000 lines of executable source code, approximately 400 source files. The associated documentation will be about

TABLE 15-III. AN INITIAL PCA SCHEDULE ESTIMATE

Activity	Duration
1. Bring documentation up to date	30 Days
2. Send documentation to customer	7 Days
3. Hold PCA	3 Days
4. Correct discrepancies	14 Days
5. Send revised documentation to customer	7 Days
TOTAL:	61 Days

1,000 pages of text, tables, and figures, and about 1,000 pages of listings. Going through that much material in some reasonable time period (say 30 days) is a heroic task. Things become worse when: (1) the standards to which this documentation is to be written are, at best, ambiguous, (2) the customer's people performing the review may not be skilled in the application or the programming language, (3) the reviewers have other duties (for example, analysis of system test results), and, (4) there are at least three other computer programs of similar magnitude also being delivered for review at the same time. The task is practically impossible.

From an initial review, it does not appear that 30 days is sufficient time to conduct a detailed technical review of the consistency between the design documentation and the listing. Even worse, the lore of the field is that it takes a competent maintenance programmer three to six months to achieve a proficient understanding of from 7,000 to 15,000 lines of source code. So the expectation of 30,000 lines being reviewed for consistency with design documentation in 20 working days may well founder on consideration of human factors.

Even worse, the customer does not usually have the in-house resources to assign one technically competent person to each computer program on a full-time basis. (Good people are scarce; there are many more jobs to be done on an immediate basis than there are good, technically competent people to assign to them.) The natural result is that either the review does not get done, or the customer hires consultants to perform the review. This introduces a third party to the transaction, with a different set of motives. The developer wants to complete the project and be paid. The customer wants a working product that fills the need and complies with the contract. The consultant wants to do a good professional job and continue to be employed.

Consultants, being hired to find problems with code and documentation, will find them. As noted above, 30 days is inadequate for a thorough job of providing specific "Change to Reads," so the critique will consist of general statements of dissatisfaction and one or more examples to illustrate the points, together with a recommendation that the material be completely redone in accordance with the dissatisfied statements and resubmitted to the customer upon completion.

This leaves the customer in a difficult position. The customer has engaged professionals to review the material, and the professionals have found it unsatisfactory. If the customer declares the material satisfactory, various unpleasant statements can be made; for example, why were the consultants hired in the first place if their recommendations are to be discarded, and what is the technical expertise in the customer's shop that could be so superior to the consultants' expertise? The only safe thing for the customer to do is to pass the recommendations on to the developer with directions to implement.

This places the developer in a difficult situation. Implementing general directions to make corrections is a never-ending task. If the developer agrees with the general comments, the developer will normally fix the examples, perhaps any others that are apparent, and then send the revised document back to the customer. The customer's consultants will then find another set of items that need correction, and the paper passes back and forth.

If the developer does not agree with the general comments, an energetic discussion ensues in which both parties try to reach a mutual understanding of what various words mean.

In looking at this process and attempting to make it more efficient, it becomes obvious that physical configuration audits could be run more efficiently if the customer provided written comments before the actual physical configuration audit meeting. This would permit the developer to review the customer comments prior to the physical configuration audit meeting, and the discussions at the physical configuration audit could then focus on any items of difference. Taking this one step further, the entire process can become more efficient still if the developer provides written responses to the customer comments prior to the physical configuration audit. This would then allow the customer to understand the developer's concerns and make the physical configuration audit even more effective. Furthermore, the revised document, which incorporates the customer comments with which the developer agreed, could also be provided to the customer prior to the physical configuration audit. This would enable the implementation to be checked and preclude further problems.

In reality, when responses and revised documentation are provided, additional sets of customer comments are then generated. This implies, as shown in Figure 15-5, cycling back through another round of responses, revised documentation, comments, etc. In looking down this path, it becomes apparent that this process can quickly go out of control. The average number of cycles is four to five (one customer's estimate), with an elapsed time that grows (for one computer program) from two months to over a year, with an overall cost growth in the vicinity of over $2,000,000. At that time good fellowship ceases, particularly on fixed-price contracts.

15.4.4 The Usefulness of the Physical Configuration Audit Product

Setting all that aside, assume that the design documentation is complete, correct, and current when delivered. Now those engaged in maintenance are placed in exactly the same turmoil previously experienced by the developers: not enough time, money, or incentive to keep the maintenance documentation up to date. Even worse, the design documentation is, in part, redundant with the source code. For example, the program description language mentioned above now appears in both the design documentation and the source file headers. The maintenance programmers must now enter the same information in two different locations, with the usual results. (It will be updated in one place and not in the other, and the next time the correct information is needed, the obsolete information will be used.)

The result of all of this is that, after a year or two, it will be found by those engaged in fixing bugs and making minor changes that the documentation is not current. The response is to abandon the documentation, and revert back to the source code listing. The bottom line is that the need for a

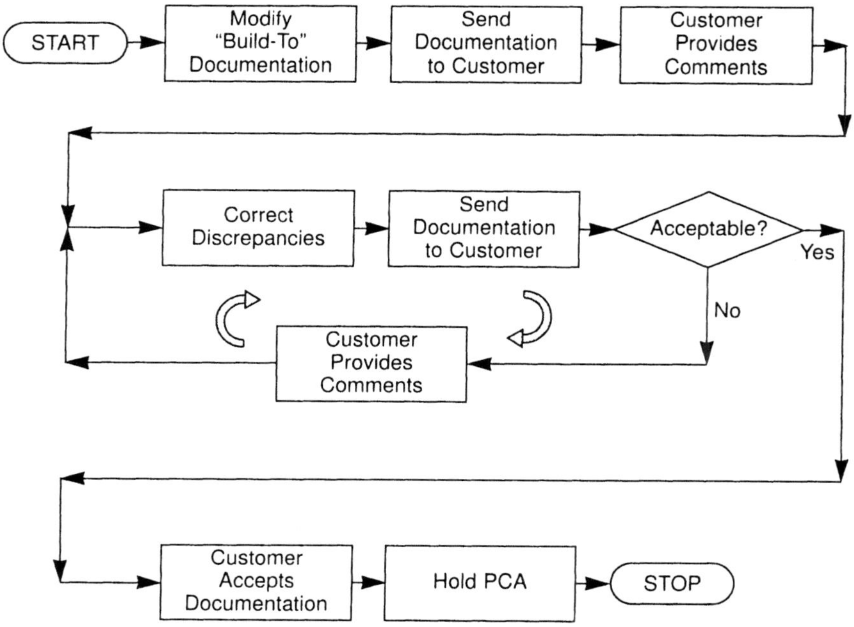

FIGURE 15-5. An Alternate Software Physical Configuration Audit Process Flow.

higher-level understanding of what the code does still exists. However, the approach of having a separate, manually maintained document that provides that information is not viable.

When this problem is posed, one response can be that failure of the maintenance personnel to keep the documentation up to date is merely a failure of the will. What is needed is more management direction and all will be well. This is an application of the "more" theory (that is, what has been done has not worked, so more will be done). The difficulty of the "more" approach is that it does not address the causes of the problems, and thus fails to be a workable solution. What actually happens is that those requiring that the design documentation be kept up to date become unwilling to pay the price incurred to do so. Then the updates fall behind, and the situation reverts to the previous case.

15.4.5 Recommendation

Table 15-IV summarizes the recommendations associated with software PCAs.

(a) If a software PCA is not required, then prior to initiating a request for a software physical configuration audit, stop in at the real user's place of work and inquire of the maintenance programmers what use they make of the "as-built" design documentation. Then ask to see the design documentation for any programs that have been in use for over a year or two. Then decide if a software physical configuration audit is desired or not. The majority of the time the decision will be not to perform the PCA.

TABLE 15-IV. SOFTWARE PCA RECOMMENDATIONS

PCA Required By Contract	Recommendations
No	Do not perform.
Yes	(1) Review PCA contract requirements in detail. (2) Recognize that some of the requirements are open to various interpretations and some may be duplicative of other contract efforts. (3) Clarify these requirements as part of proposal effort. (4) Identify the software PCA contract requirements that are major risk items.

(b) If a software PCA is required (for example, by contract), then review the PCA requirements in detail as early as possible in the proposal or contract stages and prepare a table similar to that of Table 15-V to propose what should be done in PCA and what should not be done. (The earlier these items are discussed, the better the chances are for a favorable resolution. The worst time to discuss it is just before the PCA is scheduled to begin.)

TABLE 15-V. A REVIEW OF THE MIL-STD-973 REQUIREMENTS FOR SOFTWARE PCAS

MIL-STD-973		Recommended To Be Done At Software PCAs?	Comments
Section Number	Requirement		
5.6.3.3.a	N/A (hardware only)	No	Does not apply
5.6.3.3.b	N/A (hardware only)		
5.6.3.3.c	N/A (hardware only)		
5.6.3.3.d	N/A (hardware only)		
5.6.3.3.e	(1) Review of all records of baseline configuration for the CI by direct comparison with the contractor's engineering release system and change control procedures to verify that the configuration being produced accurately reflects released engineering data. (2) This includes interim releases of spares/repair parts provisioned prior to PCA to ensure delivery of currently configured spares/repair parts.	(1) No (2) No	(1) CSCIs are CDRLs and are not processed through the release of engineering drawings. The letter of transmittal is accompanied by a VDD which states the content of the media being transmitted. (2) N/A (hardware only).
5.6.3.3.f	(1) Audit the software library, or similar internal support activity, to assure that it accurately identifies, controls, and tracks changes to the software and documentation. (2) Audit the contractor's engineering release and change control system against the requirements in Appendix B to ascertain that the system is accurate to properly control the processing and formal release of engineering changes. The contractor's system shall meet the information and capabilities requirements of Appendix B as a minimum. The contractor's formats, systems and procedures will be used.	(1) Yes (2) See the response to each item of Appendix B.	— (2) Appendix B requirements are covered at the end of this table.

TABLE 15-V. (Continued)

MIL-STD-973		Recommended To Be Done At Software PCAs?	Comments
Section Number	Requirement		
5.6.3.3.g	For CI acceptance, test data and procedures shall comply with product specifications. The PCA team shall determine any acceptance tests to be reaccomplished and reserves the right to have representatives of the Government witness all or any portion of the required audits, inspections, or tests.	No	a. For software, the input test data and test procedures have been approved when they were delivered to the Government as deliverable items. b. The output test data is approved as part of the approval of the test report. c. There does not appear to be any basis to require software to be retested as allowed in this paragraph. In effect, this would allow the testing program to be open-ended in scope with consequent cost impacts.
5.6.3.3.h	CIs which fail to pass acceptance testing shall be repaired if necessary and shall be retested by the contractor either in the manner specified by the PCA team leader or in accordance with procedures in the product specification.	No	This appears to relate directly to hardware. For software, CIs (CSCIs) that fail to pass their acceptance testing are repaired and retested before this point in time (PCA).
5.6.3.3.i	N/A (hardware only)		Does not apply
5.6.3.3.j	N/A (hardware only)		
5.6.3.3.k	N/A (hardware only)		This is a hardware requirement. CSCIs are not built iaw drawings. The only specification used is the SRS (process specifications as in engineering drawings are not used). The detailed design descriptions (from which the CSCIs are constructed) are checked against the software under 5.6.3.3.1 (3)
5.6.3.3.1 (1)	Review all documents which will comprise the product specification for format and completeness.	Yes	This is a valid task.
5.6.3.3.1 (2)	Review FCA minutes for recorded discrepancies and actions taken.	Yes	
5.6.3.3.1 (3)	Review the design descriptions for proper entries, symbols, labels, tags, references, and data descriptions.	Yes	This is a valid task.
5.6.3.3.1 (4)	Compare detailed design descriptions with software listings for accuracy and completeness		
5.6.3.3.1 (5)	Examine actual CSCI delivery media (disks, tapes, etc.) to ensure conformance with Section 5 of the software requirements specifications.	Yes	
5.6.3.3.1 (6)	Review the annotated listings for compliance with approved coding standards.	Yes	This is a valid task.

TABLE 15-V. (Continued)

MIL-STD-973		Recommended To Be Done At Software PCAs?	Comments
Section Number	Requirement		
5.6.3.3.1 (7)	Review all required operation and support documents for completeness, correctness, incorporation of comments made at Test Readiness Review (TRR), and adequacy to operate and support the CSCI(s). (Formal verification or acceptance of these manuals should be withheld until system testing to ensure that the procedural contents are correct.)	No	The review of the operation and support documents for incorporation of comments made at the TRR is done as part of the closure of the TRR action items. The operation and support manuals are CDRL items and are reviewed and accepted as part of the stated requirements in those CDRLs.
5.6.3.3.1 (8)	(1) Examine the related documentation to ensure that the relationship of the CSCI to the parts, components, or assembles that store the executable forms of the CSCI is properly described. (2) For firmware, ensure that the information completely describes the requirements for installation of the CSCI into the programmable parts or assemblies and that this information describes the requirement for verification that the installation has been properly implemented. (3) Where follow-on acquisition of the firmware items is intended, ensure that the documentation has been accomplished to the level of detail necessary for the intended reprocurement.	No	(1) This applies to the software component of firmware and is covered in the hardware PCA as part of the examination of the altered-item drawing. (2), (3) This information, as well as the information in (1), is contained in the altered-item drawings that would be part of the hardware PCA.
5.6.3.3.1 (9)	Demonstrate, using deliverable or Government owned support software, that each CSCI can be regenerated. The regenerated CSCI shall be compared to the actual CSCI delivery media to insure they are identical.	Yes	

TABLE 15-V. (Continued)

Appendix B Of MIL-STD-973		Recommended To Be Done At Software PCAs?	Comments
Section Number	Requirement		
B.5.1.2	The contractor's engineering release records shall reference the CSCI VDD which contains all the required data elements.	Yes	Note: This should be reviewed against specific project requirements for engineering release records.
B.5.2 d	... The composition of any CSCI in terms of components and units and subordinate CSCI numbers.	Yes, but in terms of files only.	This is normally placed in the VDD, but: (1) "Components" and "Units" are terms defined in DOD-STD-2167A in terms of design hierarchy levels, (2) "Units" are defined in MIL-STD-973 by a cross-reference to MIL-STD-280 (which, in turn, defines a unit as "An assembly or combination of parts, subassemblies and assemblies mounted together, normally capable of independent operation in a variety of situations (Examples: Hydraulic jack, ...) This term replaces the term 'component.' ..." (3) The composition of a CSCI in a VDD is stated in terms of files.
B.5.2 i	... The CSCI version numbers which constitute effectivity of each class I engineering change.	No	This information is normally provided in the associated VDD.
B. ...	Other requirements in this Appendix.	No	These do not apply to software.

15.5 SUMMARY

There are three types of configuration audits: (1) functional configuration audits verify that a development has been satisfactorily completed, (2) physical configuration audits examine the "as-built" documentation to determine its consistency with the physical item itself, and, (3) in-process audits determine if the configuration management process itself is being followed. These audits are valuable and serve specific purposes; however, audits cost money, and the need for specific audits (and the value of performing them) should be evaluated prior to initiating such an effort.

An audit is an activity that involves many players from many different organizations. To be run efficiently and effectively, an audit should be planned, organized, and executed as a complex activity that requires detailed coordination.

15.6 EXERCISES

1. Prepare a checklist for an in-process audit of: (1) configuration identification of code, (2) configuration control of the functional baseline, and, (3) functional configuration audit of one hardware configuration item.

2. Prepare a detailed flow chart of all the actions required for a physical configuration audit of one software configuration item. Include pre- and post-audit actions.

APPENDIX A

DEFINITIONS

A.1 INTRODUCTION

The definitions listed below establish meaning in the context of this document.

(a) The reference in parentheses ( ) after each item identifies the source of the item.

(1) The first number provides the number of the section from which the abbreviation has been abstracted.

(2) The second number is the abbreviation of the document from which the definition was abstracted. This second number itself is an acronym, and its complete name is available in Appendix B. Complete identification of the referenced document is provided in Appendix C.

For example, (40.1, 483A) after the term "Addendum" indicates that the definition was abstracted from section 40.1 of MIL-STD-483A.

(3) If only one number is provided, it is the document number.

For example, (109B) indicates that the definition of the term "Acceptable Quality Level" was abstracted from MIL-STD-109B.

(4) Where no number is provided, the definition is provided by the author.

(b) Many of the definitions are quite extensive. To preclude excessive length, definitions have been truncated as appropriate. Where a complete definition is considered to be required, the referenced document should be consulted.

(c) Words used in a definition that are defined elsewhere in this document have been underlined. All acronyms used in the definition of a term are defined in Appendix B, but are not underlined.

Standards change from time to time; as a result, definitions of commonly used terms also change. To preclude communications difficulties, where such transitions have recently occurred, both definitions are given.

A.2 TERMS

ACCEPTABLE QUALITY LEVEL (AQL). The maximum percent defective (or the maximum number of <u>defects</u> per hundred <u>units</u>) that, for the purpose of sampling inspection, can be considered satisfactory for a process average. (109B)

ADDENDUM. An addendum to an existing <u>configuration item specification</u> is used to describe requirements for a new <u>configuration item</u> which is similar to the existing <u>configuration item</u>. (40.1, 483A)

ADVANCE CHANGE STUDY NOTICE (ACSN). A document which may be used, instead of a preliminary Engineering Change Proposal, to identify an idea or problem in order to obtain authorization to submit a formal routine Engineering Change Proposal. (3.2, 973)

ALLOCATED BASELINE (ABL). The initially approved documentation describing an item's functional, interoperability, and interface characteristics that are allocated from those of a system or a higher level configuration item, interface requirements with interfacing configuration items, additional design constraints, and the verification required to demonstrate the achievement of those specified characteristics. (3.3, 973)

ALLOCATED CONFIGURATION DOCUMENTATION (ACD). The approved <u>allocated baseline</u> plus approved changes. (3.4, 973)

ALTERED ITEM. An existing <u>item</u>, under the control of another design activity or defined by a nationally recognized standardization document, that is subjected to physical alteration to meet the design requirements. (3.4, 100E)

ALTERED ITEM DRAWING. See paragraph 6.1 of ASME Y14.24M.

ALTERNATE ITEM. A type of substitute item which appears on the same parts list as the primary item for which it may be substituted, and typically has a quantity of "ALT" together with a mechanism of associating it with the primary item.

ANOMALY. In software engineering, anything observed in the documentation or operation of software that deviates from expectations based on previously verified software products or reference document. (610)

APPLICATION-SPECIFIC INTEGRATED CIRCUIT (ASIC). An integrated circuit that is customized for a particular application. The term usually refers to non-programmable devices (devices configured by the semiconductor vendor).

APPROVED ITEM NAME. A name approved by the Director of Cataloging, Defense Logistical Services Center and published in the Cataloging Handbook H6, Federal Item Name Directory for Supply Cataloging. (3.5, 100E)

ASSEMBLER. A computer program which translates assembly language mnemonic source statements into binary strings representing machine code operations. It also assigns either relative or absolute memory addresses to resulting instructions and data items. (3.1.33, 1309C)

ASSEMBLY. A number of parts, or subassemblies or any combination thereof, joined together to perform a specific function, and subject to disassembly without degradation of any of the parts. (Examples: power shovel-front, fan assembly, audio-frequency amplifier.) (3.7, 100E)

ASSEMBLY DRAWING. See paragraph 4 of ASME Y14.24M.

ASSEMBLY LEVEL LANGUAGE. A computer language in which machine operations and locations are represented by mnemonic symbols. (3.1.34, 1309C)

ASSOCIATED LIST. A tabulation of engineering information pertaining to an item depicted on an engineering drawing or on a set of engineering drawings. (6.5.1, 31000)

AUDIT. An independent examination of a work product or set of work products to assess compliance with specifications, standards, contractual agreements or other criteria. (610) See also review, functional configuration audit, and physical configuration audit.

AUTHENTICATION. Determination by the Government that specification content is acceptable. (3.2, 2167A)

AUTHORIZED SUBSTITUTION LIST. An associated document, referenced in an engineering drawing or a parts list of authorized substitute parts. (4.3.7, 480B)

AUTHORIZED SUPERSESSION LIST. An associated document, referenced in an engineering drawing or parts list, of superseding parts that have been identified as authorized in a military specification or standard. (4.3.7, 480B)

AVAILABILITY. A measure of the degree to which an item is in an operable and committable state at the start of a mission, when the mission is called for at an unknown (random) point in time. (3.1.46, 1309C)

BASELINE. See configuration baseline.

BATCH. See lot.

BENCH REPLACEABLE ASSEMBLY (BRA). A less desirable form of shop replaceable assembly which is not easily removable; for example, item bolted to chassis or heat sink or soldered in place. (3.1.1.2, 2084AS)

BENCHMARK. A standard against which measurements or comparisons can be made. (610)

BUG. See fault.

BUILD. An operational version of a system or component that incorporates a specified subset of the capabilities that the final product will provide. (610)

BURN-IN. The operation of items prior to their end application to stabilize their characteristics and identify early failures. (3.1.76, 1309C)

CALIBRATION. The comparison of a measurement system or device of unverified accuracy to a measurement system or device of known and greater accuracy, to detect and correct any variation from required performance specifications of the measurement system or device. (3.1.80, 1309C)

CALIBRATION PROCEDURE. The specific steps and operations to be followed by activity personnel in the performance of an instrument calibration. (3.1.83, 1309C)

CATEGORY 1 PROGRAMMABLE PARTS. Solid-state microcircuit devices which:

(a) Are programmed at the time of manufacture, and,
(b) Can not be reprogrammed.

CATEGORY 2 PROGRAMMABLE PARTS. Solid-state microcircuit devices which:

(a) Are programmed after the time of manufacture, and,
(b) Can not be reprogrammed.

CATEGORY 3 PROGRAMMABLE PARTS. Solid-state microcircuit devices which:

(a) Are programmed after the time of manufacture, and,

(b) Can be reprogrammed only after removing the individual devices from the next higher assembly.

CATEGORY 4 PROGRAMMABLE PARTS. Solid-state microcircuit devices which:

(a) Are programmed after the time of manufacture, and,
(b) Are programmed and reprogrammed only while mounted on the next higher assembly.

CATEGORY 5 PROGRAMMABLE PARTS. Solid-state microcircuit devices which:

(a) Are programmed after the time of manufacture,
(b) Are initially programmed as individual parts, and,
(c) Are reprogrammed only while mounted on the next higher assembly.

CERTIFICATION.

(a) A process, which may be incremental, by which a contractor provides objective evidence to the contracting agency, that an item satisfies its specified requirements. (3.1, 2168)
(b) The procedure and action by a duly authorized body of determining, verifying, and attesting in writing to the qualifications of personnel, processes, procedures, or items in accordance with applicable requirements. (A3-1987)

CHANGE CONTROL. See configuration control.

CHANGE NOTICE (CN). A document approved by the design activity that describes and authorizes the implementation of an engineering change to the product and its approved configuration documentation.

CHARACTERISTIC. A physical, chemical, visual, functional, or any other identifiable property of a product of material. (109B) See physical characteristics and functional characteristics.

CHECKSUM. The sum of every byte contained in an input/output (I/O) record used for assuring integrity of the programmed entry. (3.1.100, 1309C)

CLASSIFICATION OF DEFECTS (CD). The enumeration of possible defects of the unit of product, classified according to their seriousness. (109B)

COMMERCIAL AND GOVERNMENT ENTITY (CAGE) CODE. [(Formerly Federal Supply Codes for Manufacturer (FSCM)]. A five character code assigned to commercial activities that manufacture or supply items used by the Federal Government and to Government activities that control design or are responsible for the development of certain specifications, standards, or drawings which control the design of Government items. CAGE Code assignments are listed in the H4/H8 CAGE Publications. (6.5.2, 31000)

COMMERCIAL DRAWINGS. Drawings prepared by a commercial design activity, in accordance with that activity's documentation standards and practices, to support the development and manufacture of a product not developed at Government expense. (6.5.3, 31000)

COMMERCIAL ITEM. A product, material, component, subsystem, or system sold or traded to the general public in the course of normal business operations at prices based on established catalog or market prices. (6.5.4, 31000)

COMMERCIAL SOFTWARE. Software in regular production sold in substantial quantities to the general public or industry at established market or catalog prices. Also known as commercial-off-the-shelf (COTS) software.

COMPANY STANDARD. A company document which establishes engineering and technical limitations and applications for items, materials, processes, methods, designs and engineering practices unique to that company. (6.5.5, 31000)

COMPETENT MANUFACTURER. A manufacturer capable of producing similar products at the same state of the art in the same or similar lines of technology. (6.5.6, 31000)

COMPUTER PROGRAM. A series of instructions or statements in a form acceptable to a computer, designed to cause the computer to execute an operation. (3.1.6, 480B) See software and computer software.

COMPUTER SOFTWARE. A combination of associated computer instructions and computer data definitions required to enable the computer hardware to perform computational or control functions. (3.1.7, 480B; 5.1.d, 483A)

COMPUTER SOFTWARE COMPONENT (CSC). A distinct part of a computer software configuration item (CSCI). CSCs may be further decomposed into other CSCs and computer software units (CSUs). (3.8, 2167A)

COMPUTER SOFTWARE CONFIGURATION ITEM (CSCI). A configuration item for computer software. (3.9, 2167A)

COMPUTER SOFTWARE UNIT (CSU). An element specified in the design of a computer software component that is separately testable. (3.11, 2167A)

CONCEPTUAL DESIGN DRAWINGS. Drawings that describe the engineering concepts on which a proposed technology or design approach is based. (6.5.7, 31000)

CONFIGURATION. The function and/or physical characteristics of hardware, firmware, software or a combination thereof as set forth in technical documentation and achieved in a product (3.14, 973)

CONFIGURATION AUDIT. The verification of a configuration item's conformance to specifications, drawings, and other contract requirements. (3.1.11,

480B) See audit, functional configuration audit, and physical configuration audit.

CONFIGURATION BASELINE. Configuration documentation formally designated by the Government at a specific time during a CI's life cycle. Configuration baselines, plus approved changes from those baselines, constitute the current approved configuration documentation. There are three formally designated configuration baselines in the life cycle of a configuration item, namely the functional, allocated, and product baselines. (3.18, 973)

CONFIGURATION CONTROL. The systematic proposal, justification, evaluation, coordination, approval or disapproval of proposed changes and the implementation of all approved changes in the configuration of a CI after formal establishment of its baseline. (3.19, 973)

CONFIGURATION CONTROL BOARD (CCB). A board composed of technical and administrative representatives who recommend approval or disapproval of proposed engineering changes to a CI's current approved configuration documentation. The board also recommends approval or disapproval of proposed waivers and deviations from a CI's current approved configuration documentation. (3.20, 973)

CONFIGURATION DOCUMENTATION. The technical documentation that identifies and defines the item's functional and physical characteristics. The configuration documentation is developed, approved, and maintained through three distinct evolutionary increasing levels of detail. The three levels of configuration documentation are the functional configuration documentation, the allocated configuration documentation, and the product configuration documentation. (3.21, 973)

CONFIGURATION IDENTIFICATION. Configuration identification includes the selection of CIs; the determination of the types of configuration documentation required for each CI; the issuance of numbers and other identifiers affixed to the CIs and to the technical documentation that defines the CI's configuration, including internal and external interfaces; the release of CIs and their associated configuration documentation; and the establishment of configuration baselines for CIs. (3.22, 973)

CONFIGURATION ITEM (CI). An aggregation of hardware, firmware, software or any of its discrete portions, which satisfies an end use function and is designated by the Government for configuration management. (3.23, 973)

CONFIGURATION ITEM DEVELOPMENT RECORD. A document that provides status information on the development progress of a configuration item as reflected by configuration audits and design reviews. (5.1.g, 483A)

CONFIGURATION ITEM IDENTIFICATION (CII) NUMBER. A permanent number assigned by the design activity to identify a configuration item. The number is a common identification for all units in a configuration item type, model, series, and serves as a permanent address for all actions and documentation applicable to the type, model and series. The CII is seven-digits with alpha-numeric characters. (5.1.i, 483A)

CONFIGURATION MANAGEMENT (CM). A discipline applying technical and administrative direction and surveillance over the life cycle of items to: (3.24, 973)

(a) Identify and document the functional and physical characteristics of configuration items (CIs);
(b) Audit the CIs to verify conformance to specifications, interface control documents and other contract requirements;
(c) Control changes to CIs and their related documentation;
(d) Record and report information needed to manage CIs effectively, including the status of proposed changes and the implementation status of approved changes.

CONFIGURATION MANAGEMENT PLAN (CMP). The document defining how configuration management will be implemented (including policies and procedures) for a particular acquisition or program. (3.25, 973)

CONFIGURATION STATUS ACCOUNTING (CSA). The recording and reporting of information needed to manage configuration items effectively, including: (3.26, 973)

(a) A record of the approved configuration documentation and identification numbers.
(b) The status of proposed changes, deviations, and waivers to the configuration.
(c) The implementation status of approved changes.
(d) The configuration of all units of the configuration item in the operational inventory.

CONNECTION OR WIRING DIAGRAM. See paragraph 10.4 of ASME Y14.24M.

CONSTRUCTION DRAWING. A drawing that delineates the design of buildings, structures, or related construction, ashore or afloat, individually or in groups and are normally associated with the architectural—construction—civil engineering operations. (aka constructed drawing.) (201.8, 100C)

CONTRACT CHANGE PROPOSAL (CCP). A formal priced document used to propose changes to the scope of work of the contract. It is differentiated from an ECP by the fact that it does not affect specification or drawing requirements. It may be used to propose changes to contractual plans, the Statement of Work (SOW), CDRL, etc. [aka Task Change Proposal (TCP)]. (5.1.w, 483A) See also task change proposal DID DA-A-3020.

CONTRACT DATA REQUIREMENTS LIST (CDRL). A Contract Data Requirements List lists and orders the data required by the contract. (4.3.1, 245A)

CONTROL DRAWING. See paragraph 8 of ASME Y14.24M.

CORRECTIVE ACTION. Changes to processes, work instructions, workmanship practices, training, inspections, tests, procedures, specifications, drawings, tools, equipment, facilities, resources, or material that result in preventing, minimizing, or eliminating nonconformances. (3.3, 1520C)

CORRECTIVE ACTION BOARD (CAB). A contractor board consisting of management representatives of appropriate contractor organizations with the level of responsibility and authority necessary to ensure the prevention of nonconformances, to manage quality improvement efforts as appropriate, to assess and manage nonconformance cost elimination, to ensure that causes of nonconformances are identified, and that corrective actions are effected throughout the contractor's organization. (3.4, 1520C)

CORRELATION DRAWING. A drawing that depicts physical and functional engineering requirements between or among components of a subsystem. (201.9.14, 100C)

CRITICAL APPLICATION ITEM. Any item essential to preserving human life, or which, if it fails, endangers human life or adversely affects the completion of a military operation directly or through the impact of its failure on an end item or system. (6.5.8, 31000)

CRITICAL DEFECT. A defect that judgment and experience indicate is likely to result in hazardous or unsafe conditions for individuals using, maintaining, or depending on the product; or a defect that judgment and experience indicate is likely to prevent performance of the tactical function of an major end item such as an aircraft, communication system, land vehicle, missile, ship, surveillance system or major part thereof. (109B)

CRITICAL DESIGN REVIEW (CDR). A review conducted to (3.5, 1521B):

(a) Determine that the detail design of the configuration item (CI) under review satisfies the engineering and speciality requirements of the development specifications.
(b) Establish the detail design compatibility among the CI and other items of equipment, facilities, computer software and personnel.
(c) Assess CI risk areas (on a technical, cost and schedule basis).
(d) Assess the results of the producibility analyses conducted on system hardware.
(e) Review the preliminary hardware product specifications.

CRITICAL DEVIATION. A deviation shall be designated as critical when (5.3.1.3, 480B)

(a) A classification of defects (CD) utilizing the definitions of MIL-STD-109 exists, and the deviation consists of a departure from a characteristic in the documentation which is classified in the CD as critical; or
(b) The deviation consists of a departure involving safety.

CRITICAL ITEM. An item within a configuration item which, because of special engineering or logistic considerations, requires an approved specification to establish technical or inventory control. (3.1.22, 480B)

CRITICAL MANUFACTURING PROCESS. A process that is mandatory for use during the manufacturing of an item and without which, an acceptable item cannot be produced. (6.5.9, 31000)

CRITICAL WAIVER. A waiver shall be designated as critical when (5.4.1.3, 480B):

(a) A classification of defects utilizing the definitions of MIL-STD-109 exists, and the waiver consists of acceptance of an item having a critical defect; or
(b) The waiver consists of acceptance of an item having a nonconformance with contract or configuration identification requirements involving safety.

DATA ITEM DESCRIPTION (DID), DD FORM 1664. A completed form that defines the data required of a contractor. The form specifically defines the data content, preparation instructions, format and intended use. (3.1.24, 480B)

DATA LIST (DL). A data list is a tabulation of all engineering drawings, associated lists, specifications, standards, quality assurance procedures, and all other documents (contained within the drawing set) pertaining to the item for which the data list is prepared. (702, 100E)

DEBUG. The process of detecting and removing errors or faults from a computer program or from electronic equipment. (3.1.148, 1309C)

DEFECT.

(a) Any nonconformance of a characteristic with specified requirements. (109B)
(b) See fault.

DEFICIENCIES. Deficiencies consist of two types; (3.31, 973)

(a) Conditions or characteristics in any item which are not in accordance with the item's current approved configuration documentation; or

(b) Inadequate (or erroneous) item configuration documentation which has resulted, or may result, in units of the item that do not meet the requirements for the item.

DEPOT MAINTENANCE. Maintenance performed on material requiring major overhaul or a complete rebuild of parts, subassemblies, and end items, including the manufacture of parts, modification, testing, and reclamation as required. (3.1.157, 1309C)

DESIGN ACTIVITY. An activity having responsibility for the design of an item. (3.26, 100E)

DESIGN CHANGE. See engineering change.

DESIGN CHANGE NOTICE (DCN). A formal document prepared by a contractor or a government activity to notify the provisioning activity of a design change.

DESIGN FAULT. A fault due to inadequate hardware or software design. (3.1.158, 1309C)

DESIGN REVIEW. A formal, documented, comprehensive, and systematic examination of a design to evaluate the design requirements and the capability of the design to meet these requirements and to identify problems and propose solutions. (3.8, A3-1987)

DETAIL ASSEMBLY DRAWING. A drawing that depicts an assembly on which one or more parts are detailed in the assembly view or on detail views. (201.3.1, 100C)

DETAIL DRAWING. See paragraph 3 of ASME Y14.24M.

DEVELOPMENTAL CONFIGURATION.

(a) The contractor's software and associated technical documentation that defines the evolving configuration of a computer software configuration item under development. It is under the development contractor's configuration control and describes the software configuration at any stage of the design, coding and testing effort. Any item in the developmental configuration may be stored on electronic media. (3.15, 2167A)
(b) The contractor's design and associated technical documentation that defines the evolving configuration of a configuration item during development. It is under the developing contractor's configuration control and describes the design definition and implementation. The developmental configuration for a configuration item consists of the contractor's released hardware and software designs and associated technical documentation until establishment of the formal product baseline. (3.33, 973)

DEVELOPMENTAL DESIGN DRAWINGS. Drawings which describe the physical and functional characteristics of a specific design approach to the extent necessary to permit the analytical evaluation of the ability of the design approach to meet specified requirements and enable the development and manufacture of experimental hardware. (6.5.10, 31000)

DEVIATION. A specific written authorization, granted prior to the manufacture of an item, to depart from a particular requirement(s) of an item's current approved configuration documentation for a specific number of units or a specified period of time. (A deviation differs from an engineering change in that an approved engineering change requires corresponding revision of the item's current approved configuration documentation, whereas a deviation does not.) (3.34, 973)

DIAGRAMMATIC DRAWING. See paragraphs 9, 10 and 10.1 of ASME Y14.24M.

DIGITAL DATA PRODUCTION ENVIRONMENT. The set of automated tools and hardware necessary to transform digital data inputs into end products. The automated tools may include, but are not limited to, compilers, assemblers, operating system, debuggers, test tools, documentation tools, and data base management systems.

DOCUMENT. The term applies to the specifications, drawings, lists, standards, pamphlets, reports, and printed, typewritten, or other information, relating to the design, procurement, manufacture, test, or inspection of items or services (3.29, 100E)

DOCUMENT IDENTIFICATION NUMBER (DIN). This consists of numbers or combinations of letters, numbers and dashes. This number, in addition to the title and the CAGE Code, is assigned to a document for identification purposes. (402, 100E)

DRAWING. See "Engineering Drawing."

DRAWING FORM. A sheet of drafting material displaying the basic format features such as title block, general tolerance blocks and margins. (6.5.11, 31000)

DRAWING FORMAT. The arrangements and organization of information within a drawing. This includes such features as the size and arrangement of blocks, notes, lists, revision information, and the use of optional or supplemental blocks. (6.5.12, 31000)

DRAWING NUMBER. This consists of letters, numbers or a combination of letters and numbers, which may or may not be separated by dashes. The number assigned to a particular drawing and the CAGE Code provide a unique drawing identification. (403, 100E)

DRAWING TITLE. The name by which the part or item will be known and shall consist of a basic item name, government type designator, if applicable, and sufficient modifiers to differentiate like items in the same major assembly. (301, 100E)

ELEVATION DRAWING. See paragraph 7 of ASME Y14.24M.

END ITEM. See end product.

END PRODUCT (END ITEM). An item, either an individual part or assembly, in its final or completed state. (3.33, 100E)

ENGINEERING CHANGE. A change to the current approved configuration documentation of a configuration item at any point in the life cycle of the item. (3.35, 973)

ENGINEERING CHANGE NOTICE (ECN). See change notice.

ENGINEERING CHANGE PROPOSAL (ECP). A proposed engineering change and the documentation by which the change is described, justified, and submitted to the procuring activity for approval or disapproval. (3.38, 973)

ENGINEERING DATA. Engineering documents such as drawings, associated lists, accompanying documents, manufacturer specifications, and standards, or other information prepared by a design activity and relating to the design, manufacture, procurement, test or inspection of items. (3.34, 100E)

ENGINEERING DRAWING. An engineering drawing or digital data file(s) that discloses (directly or by reference) by means of graphic or textual presentations, or a combination of both, the physical and functional end-product requirements of an item. (3.30, 100E)

ENGINEERING MANAGEMENT. The management of the engineering and technical effort required to transform a military requirement into an operational system. It includes the system engineering required to define the system performance parameters and preferred system configuration to satisfy the requirement, the planning and control of technical program tasks, integration of the engineering specialties, and the management of a totally integrated effort of design engineering, specialty engineering, test engineering, logistics engineering, and production engineering to meet cost, technical performance and schedule objectives. (3.1, 499A)

ENGINEERING RELEASE. An action whereby configuration documentation or an item is officially made available for its intended use. (3.40, 973)

ENGINEERING SPECIALTY INTEGRATION. The timely and appropriate intermeshing of engineering efforts and disciplines such as reliability, maintainability, logistics engineering, human factors, safety, value engineering, standardization, transportability, etc., to insure their influence on system design. (3.4, 499A)

ENGLISH LEVEL LANGUAGE. A computer language in English terms which represent multiple binary instructions which can be processed directly by the machine (examples: ATLAS, BASIC, and so forth). Also called High Order Language. (3.1.189, 1309C)

ENVELOPE DRAWING. A drawing that depicts an item in a development (privately or Government) or pre-production stage. (204.2.2, 100E)

EQUIPMENT PLANNING DIAGRAM (EPD). A drawing prepared in block diagram or automated format which shows the assembly (top-down breakdown) in "family-tree" relationships of a system, set, group, unit, etc., or a portion thereof.

EQUIPMENT REPLACEABLE UNIT. The lowest assembly or individual part that can be fault detected, isolated, removed, replaced and verified functional at organization level without disassembly of the equipment to which it is attached in consonance with the maintenance concept. (3.1.192, 1309C)

ERASABLE PROGRAMMABLE READ-ONLY MEMORY (EPROM). A solid-state memory device which, after being programmed, can be re-programmed. (3.1.196, 1309C)

ERECTION DRAWING. A drawing that shows procedures and operation sequence for erection or assembly of individual items or assemblies of items. (201.8.1, 100C)

ERROR. The deviation of a computed, observed, or measured quantity from the true, specified or theoretically correct value of the quantity. (3.1.198, 1309C)

ERROR CORRECTING CODES. In the transmission of digital data, the use of additional (redundant) bits to permit the detection and correction of errors. (3.1.200, 1309C)

ERROR DETECTING CODES. In the transmission of digital data, the use of additional (redundant) bits to permit the detection of errors. (3.1.201, 1309C)

EVALUATION. The process of determining whether an item or activity meets specified criteria. (3.2, 2168)

EXAMINATION. An element of inspection consisting of investigation, without the use of special laboratory appliances or procedures, of supplies and services to determine conformance to those specified requirements which can be determined by such investigations. (109B)

EXPLODED ASSEMBLY DRAWING. A drawing that, using either isometric or perspective drawing techniques, depicts the individual items that make up a part in a manner whereby they are separated from each other but related to each other by the use of a center line. (201.3.6, 100C)

FAILURE. The state of inability of an item to perform its required function. Failure is the functional manifestation of a fault. (3.1.214, 1309C)

FAULT. A physical condition that causes a device, component, or element to fail to perform in a required manner; for example, a short-circuit or a broken wire. (3.1.235, 1309C)

FAULT ISOLATED REPLACEABLE UNIT. The replaceable subsystem, assembly, subassembly or component identified through diagnostic testing of a unit under test. (3.1.251, 1309C)

FIND NUMBER OR ITEM NUMBER. A reference number assigned to an item in lieu of the item's identifying number on the field of a drawing and entered as a cross reference to the item number of the parts list where the item name and identification number are given. (3.36, 100E)

FIRMWARE.

(a) The combination of a hardware device and computer instructions or computer data that reside as read-only software on the hardware device. The software cannot be readily modified under program control. (3.1.35, 480B)

The definition also applies to read-only digital devices other than digital computers. (5.1.n, 483A)

(b) Hardware components which contain embedded software, such as EPROMs, Programmable Read Only Memories (PROMS), and Read Only Memories (ROMs). (3.1.269, 1309C)

FIT. The ability of an item to physically interface or interconnect with or become an integral part of another item. (3.45, 973)

FORM. The shape, size, dimensions, mass, weight, and other visual parameters which uniquely characterize an item. For software, form denotes the language and media. (3.46, 973)

FORMAL QUALIFICATION REVIEW (FQR).

(a) The test, inspection, or analytical process by which a group of CIs comprising the system are verified to have met specific contracting agency performance requirements (specifications or equivalent). This review does not apply to hardware or software requirements verified at FCA for the individual configuration item (CI). (3.9, 1521B)

(b) A formal review, normally accomplished incrementally at the contracting facility, of test reports and test data generated during the formal qualification of a new group of CIs comprising a system to ensure that all tests required by Section 4 of the development specifications have been accomplished and that the system performs as required by Section 3. Usually held in conjunction with the FCA, it may be delayed until after the FCA/PCA if total system testing is required. (5.1.o, 483A)

FORMULATION DRAWING. A drawing that depicts the constituents of an explosive, propellant, pyrotechnic, filler, etc. (209.9.15, 100C)

FUNCTION. The action or actions which an item is designed to perform. (3.47, 973)

FUNCTIONAL BASELINE (FBL). The initially approved documentation describing a system's or item's functional, interoperability, and interface characteristics and the verification required to demonstrate the achievement of those specified characteristics. (3.49, 973)

FUNCTIONAL CHARACTERISTICS. Quantitative performance parameters and design constraints, including operational and logistics parameters and their respective tolerances. Functional characteristics include all performance parameters, such as range, speed, lethality, reliability, maintainability, and safety. (3.50, 973) See also characteristics and physical characteristics.

FUNCTIONAL CONFIGURATION AUDIT (FCA). The formal examination of functional characteristics of a CI, prior to acceptance, to verify that the item has achieved the performance specified in its functional and allocated configuration identification. (3.51, 973)

FUNCTIONAL CONFIGURATION DOCUMENTATION (FCI). The approved functional baseline plus approved changes. (3.52, 973)

FUNCTIONAL ITEM REPLACEMENT (FIR). A functional module which is replaced at the intermediate maintenance level. (3.1.280, 1309C)

GROUP. A collection of units, assemblies, or subassemblies which is a subdivision of a set or system, but which is not capable of performing a complete operational function. (Examples: antenna group, indicator group). (3.39, 100E)

HARDWARE. Items made of material, such as weapons, aircraft, ships, tools, computers, vehicles, and their components (mechanical, electrical, electronic, hydraulic, pneumatic). Computer software and technical documentation are excluded. (3.57, 973)

HIGH ORDER LANGUAGE (HOL). See english level language. (3.1.305, 1309C)

IMAGE FILE. A structured collection of software (computer instructions and/or data) files formatted in accordance with the requirements of the programming device that places the software in the solid-state microcircuit device.

INDEX LIST (IL). A tabulation of data lists and subordinate index lists pertaining to the item to which the index list applies. (703, 100E)

INSEPARABLE ASSEMBLY DRAWING. An inseparable assembly drawing delineates items (pieces) which are separately fabricated and permanently joined together (for example, welded, brazed, riveted, sewed, glued, etc.) to form an integral unit (part) not normally subject to disassembly. (204.2.1, 100E)

INSPECTION. The examination and testing of supplies and services (including, when appropriate, raw materials, components, and intermediate assemblies) to determine whether they conform to specified requirements. (109B)

INSTALLATION ASSEMBLY DRAWING. See paragraph 5 of ASME Y14.24M.

INSTALLATION COMPLETION NOTICE. A report of the accomplishment of one or more Class I changes for a system, computer software, equipment, and/or spares. (150.3, 483A)

INSTALLATION CONTROL DRAWING. A drawing that sets forth information on an item in terms of area, weight and space, access clearance, draining clearances, pipe and cable attachments required for the installation and co-functioning of the item to be installed with related items. (201.4.7, 100C)

INSTALLATION DRAWING. See paragraph 5 of ASME Y14.24M.

INSTRUCTION. A set of characters which define an operation, together with one or more addresses (or no address) and which, as a unit, causes the machine to operate accordingly on the indicated quantities. (3.1.324, 1309C)

INTEGRATED LOGISTIC SUPPORT (ILS). A composite of all the support considerations necessary to assure the effective and economical support of its system for its life cycle. (3.13, 881A)

INTERCHANGEABLE ITEM. One, which (3.2.1, 280A):

(a) Possesses such functional and physical characteristics to be equivalent in performance, reliability and maintainability, to another item of similar or identical purposes; and,
(b) Is capable of being exchanged for the other item:
    (1) Without selection for fit or performance, and,
    (2) Without alteration of the items themselves or of adjoining items, except for adjustment.

INTERCONNECTION DIAGRAM. See paragraph 10.5 of ASME Y14.24M.

INTERFACE. The functional and physical characteristics required to exist at a common boundary. (3.57, 973)

INTERFACE CONTROL. The process of identifying, documenting, and controlling all functional and physical characteristics relevant to the interfacing of two or more items provided by one or more organizations. (3.58, 973)

INTERFACE CONTROL DRAWING (ICD). See paragraphs 8.5 and 8.6 of ASME Y14.24M.

INTERFACE REQUIREMENTS SPECIFICATION (IRS). Specifies in detail the requirements for one or more computer software configuration items interfaces in the system, segment, or prime item. (20.4.6, 483A)

INTERMEDIATE MAINTENANCE. Maintenance which is the responsibility of and performed by designated maintenance activities for direct support of the using organizations. Its phases normally consist of calibration, repair or replacement of damaged or unserviceable parts, components or assemblies; the emergency manufacture of non-available parts and providing technical assistance to using organizations. (3.1.334, 1309C)

ISSUE. The act of distributing an approved item.

ITEM. A non-specific term used to denote any product, including systems, subsystems, assemblies, subassemblies, units, sets, accessories, computer programs, computer software or parts. (3.1.47, 480B)

ITEM LEVEL. Item levels from the simplest division to the more complex are as follows (3.1, 280A):

(a) Part
(b) Subassembly
(c) Assembly
(d) Unit
(e) Group
(f) Set
(g) Subsystem
(h) System

KIT DRAWING. See paragraph 11.6 of ASME Y14.24M.

LAYOUT DRAWING. See paragraph 2 of ASME Y14.24M.

LEVEL. Classification of engineering drawings as selected from DOD-D-1000. (727, 100C)

LEVEL 1, CONCEPTUAL AND DEVELOPMENTAL DESIGN. Engineering drawings and associated lists that, as a minimum, disclose engineering design information sufficient to evaluate an engineering concept and may provide information sufficient to fabricate developmental hardware. (3.3.1, 1000D)

LEVEL 2, PRODUCTION PROTOTYPE AND LIMITED PRODUCTION. Engineering drawings and associated lists that disclose a design approach suitable to support the manufacture of a production prototype and limited production models. (3.3.2, 1000D)

LEVEL 3, PRODUCTION. Engineering drawings and associated lists that provide engineering definition sufficiently complete to enable a competent manufacturer to produce and maintain quality control of item(s) to the degree that physical and performance characteristics interchangeable with those of the original design are obtainable without resorting to additional product design effort, additional design data or recourse to the original design activity. (3.3.3, 1000D)

LINE REPLACEABLE UNIT (LRU). An item which is replaced at the organizational maintenance level. (3.1.348, 1309C)

LOGIC DIAGRAM. See paragraph 10.7 of ASME Y14.24M.

LOGISTIC SUPPORT ANALYSIS (LSA). An analysis that leads to the definition of support needs (for example, maintenance equipment, personnel, spares, repair parts, technical orders, transportation and handling, etc. (10.2.5.1, 499)

LOT. A collection of units of product bearing identification and treated as a unique entity from which a sample is to be drawn and inspected to determine conformance with the acceptability criteria. (109B)

MACHINE CODE. An operation code that a machine is designed to recognize. (3.1.356, 1309C)

MACHINE INSTRUCTION. An instruction that a machine can recognize and execute. (3.1.357, 1309C)

MACHINE LANGUAGE. The set of instructions in the number system which is intelligible to a specific machine (for example, a computer or class of computers). (3.1.358, 1309C)

MAJOR DEFECT. A defect other than critical, that is likely to result in failure, or to reduce materially the usability of the unit of product for its intended purpose. (109B)

MANUFACTURER. A person or firm who owns or leases and operates a factory or establishment that produces (on the premises) materials, supplies, articles or equipment required under the contract (or of the general character described by the specifications, standards, and publications). (3.17, 130G)

MANUFACTURER'S IDENTIFICATION. The actual manufacturer's name, CAGE, or NSCM that identifies the place of manufacture. (3.18, 130G)

MATCHED PARTS DRAWING. See paragraph 11.8 of ASME Y14.24M.

MATERIAL. A generic term covering systems, equipment, stores, supplies and spares, including related documentation, manuals, computer hardware and software. (3.66, 973)

MATERIAL REVIEW BOARD (MRB).

(a) The formal Contractor-Government Board established for the purpose of reviewing, evaluating, and disposing of specific nonconforming supplies or services; and, for assuring the initiation and accomplishment of corrective action to preclude recurrence. (109B)
(b) A board consisting of representatives of contractor departments necessary to review, evaluate, and determine or recommend disposition of nonconforming material referred to it. (3.5, 1520C)

MECHANICAL SCHEMATIC DIAGRAM. See paragraph 9 of ASME Y14.24M.

MICROCODE. Software that directly controls the elementary operations of the target hardware.

MINOR DEFECT. A defect that is not likely to reduce materially the usability of the unit of product for its intended purpose, or is a departure from established standards having little bearing on the effective use or operation of the unit. (109B)

MODIFICATION DRAWING. See paragraph 6.3 of ASME Y14.24M.

MODULE. A component, or a complete subassembly combined in a single package, that is designed to be removed and replaced easily for maintenance or repair. (3.1.377, 1309C)

MONODETAIL DRAWING. See paragraph 3.1 of ASME Y14.24M.

MULTIDETAIL DRAWING. See paragraph 3.2 of ASME Y14.24M.

NATO SUPPLY CODE FOR MANUFACTURERS (NSCM). The five position alpha numeric code that is assigned to an organizational entity, located in a country other than the United States or Canada, that maintains design control or is a source of supply for items acquired by the Federal Government, NATO member nations, and other participating friendly Governments. (3.20, 130G)

NOMENCLATURE. The approved item name listed in the Cataloging Handbook H6 and the Government type designation, if assigned by the acquiring activity, plus such additional words as may be necessary for identification. (3.21, 130G)

NONCONFORMANCE.

(a) The failure of an item or product to conform to specified requirements. (3.67, 973)

(b) The failure of a unit of product to conform to specified requirements for any quality characteristic. (109B)
(c) The failure of a characteristic to conform to the requirements specified in the contract, drawings, specifications, or other approved product description. (3.6, 1520C)

NONCONFORMANCE MATERIAL. Any item, part, supplies, or product containing one or more nonconformances. (3.7, 1520C)

NON-DEVELOPMENTAL SOFTWARE (NDS). Deliverable software that is not developed under the contract but is provided by the contractor, the Government or by a third party. NDS may be referred to as reusable software, Government furnished software or commercially available software depending on the source. (3.22, 2167A)

NON-DELIVERABLE SOFTWARE. Software that is not required to be delivered by the contract. (3.3, 2168)

NON-GOVERNMENT STANDARDIZATION DOCUMENT. A standardization document developed by a private sector association, organization or technical society which plans, develops, establishes or coordinates standards, specifications, handbooks or related documents. (6.5.13, 31000)

NON-PART DRAWING. An engineering drawing that provides requirements, procedures, instructions, firmware, etc., applicable to an item, when it is not convenient to keep this information on the applicable part drawing. Examples include test requirements drawing, wiring diagram drawing, etc. (3.51, 100E)

NOTICE OF REVISION (NOR). A document used to propose revisions to drawings or associated lists, or other referenced documents which require revision after ECP approval. (3.69, 973)

NUMERICAL CONTROL DRAWING. A drawing that depicts complete physical and functional engineering and product requirements of an item to facilitate production by automated control means. (201.9.3, 100C)

OBJECT CODE. A series of "1s" and "0s" (machine language code) that can be used by a computer directly. (3.1.399, 1309C)

OBJECT PROGRAM. A computer program that is the output of an assembler or compiler. (610)

OPTICAL ELEMENT AND OPTICAL SYSTEMS DRAWINGS. See MIL-STD-34. (201.9.4, 100C)

ORGANIZATIONAL MAINTENANCE. Maintenance which is the responsibility of and performed by using organizations on its assigned equipment. Its phases normally consist of inspecting, servicing, lubricating, adjusting and the replacing of parts, minor assemblies and subassemblies. (3.1.415, 1309C)

ORIGINAL (DRAWING). The current design activity's document or digital data file(s) of record. (3.71, 973)

PART. One piece, or two or more pieces joined together which are not normally subject to disassembly without destruction or impairment of designated use. (Examples, outer front wheel bearing of a ¾ ton truck, electron tube, screw). (3.60, 100E)

PART OR IDENTIFYING NUMBER (PIN). A part or identifying number (PIN) is an alpha-numeric designator which identifies parts, items, or bulk materials, that are covered by a specification. (3.28, 961G)

PARTS LIST (PL). A tabulation of all parts and bulk materials (except those materials that support a process) required to manufacture the item to which the list applies. Reference documents may also be tabulated on a parts list. Items listed on a subordinate assembly parts list or specified in a referenced document need not be repeated in the using assembly parts list unless it is necessary to limit options in the subordinate document. (701, 100E)

PATCH. A modification made directly to an object program without reassembling or recompiling from the source program. (610)

PHYSICAL CHARACTERISTICS. Quantitative and qualitative expressions of material features, such as composition, dimensions, finishes, form, fit, and their respective tolerances. (3.72, 973) See also characteristic and functional characteristic.

PHYSICAL CONFIGURATION AUDIT (PCA). The formal examination of the "as-built" configuration of a CI against its technical documentation to establish or verify the CI's product baseline. (3.73, 973)

PIPING DIAGRAM. See paragraph 9 of ASME Y14.24M.

PLAN DRAWING. A drawing that depicts a horizontal projection of a structure, showing the layout of the foundation, floor, deck, roof, or utility system. (201.8.2, 100C)

PLOT (PLAT) PLAN DRAWING. A drawing that depicts areas on which structures are clearly indicated with detailed information regarding their relationship to other structures, existing and proposed utilities, topography, boundary lines, roads, walks, fences, etc. (201.8.3, 100C)

PRELIMINARY DESIGN REVIEW (PDR). This review shall be conducted for each configuration item (CI) or aggregate of CIs to (3.4, 1521B):

(a) Evaluate the progress, technical adequacy, and risk resolution (on a technical, cost and schedule basis) of the selected design approach;

(b) Determine its compatibility with performance and engineering specialty requirements of the HWCI development specifications;
(c) Evaluate the degree of definition and assess the technical risk associated with the selected manufacturing methods/processes; and,
(d) Establish the existence and compatibility of the physical and functional interfaces among the CI and other items of equipment, facilities, computer software and personnel.

For computer software configuration items, this review will focus on:

(a) The evaluation of the progress, consistency and technical adequacy of the selected top-level design and test approach;
(b) Compatibility between software requirements and preliminary design; and,
(c) The preliminary version of the operation and support documents.

PRELIMINARY REVIEW. An evaluation by contractor-appointed quality personnel, assisted by other personnel as required, to determine the disposition of nonconforming material after its initial discovery and prior to referral to the material review board (MRB). Preliminary review may result in an authorized disposition of the nonconforming material without referral to the MRB for final disposition. (3.10, 1520C)

PRINTED WIRING MASTER DRAWING. See paragraph 11.3 of ASME Y14.24M.

PRINTED WIRING MASTER (STABLE BASE ARTWORK) PATTERN DRAWING. See paragraph 11.3 of ASME Y14.24M.

PROBLEM ORIENTED LANGUAGE. A language designed for the convenient solution of a given class of problems. (3.1.474, 1309C)

PROCEDURE ORIENTED LANGUAGE. A programming language designed for the convenient expression of procedures used in the solution of a wide class of problems. (3.1.475, 1309C)

PROCESS SPECIFICATION. A specification that defines the specific processes and/or procedures required to ensure that a satisfactory result may be achieved.

PRODUCT BASELINE (PBL). The initially approved documentation describing all of the necessary functional and physical characteristics of the configuration item and the selected functional and physical characteristics designated for production acceptance testing and tests necessary for support of the configuration item. In addition to this documentation, the product baseline of a configuration item may consist of the actual equipment and software. (3.74, 973)

PRODUCT CONFIGURATION DOCUMENTATION (PCD). The approved product baseline plus approved changes. (3.75, 973)

PRODUCT DRAWINGS. Engineering drawings that provide the necessary design, engineering, manufacturing and quality support information necessary to permit a competent manufacturer to produce an interchangeable item which duplicates the physical and performance characteristics of the original design without additional design engineering or recourse to the original manufacturer. (6.5.14, 31000)

PRODUCTION READINESS REVIEW (PRR). This review is intended to determine the status of completion of the specific actions which must be satisfactorily accomplished prior to executing a production go-ahead decision. (3.10, 1521B)

PROFILING. The process of writing a program into a read-only memory. This is also referred to as programming the unprogrammed PROM.

PROGRAM. To write a computer program (610).

PROGRAMMABLE LOGIC DEVICE (PLD). An integrated circuit chip containing arrays of logic elements which can be configured (programmed) by the user to perform a complex logic function.

PROGRAMMABLE READ-ONLY MEMORY (PROM). A solid-state memory storage device which is not programmed at the time of manufacture, but once programmed cannot be reprogrammed. (3.1.480, 1309C)

PROGRAMMING.

(a) The design, the writing and testing of a program. It involves analyzing the problem, flowcharting, coding, debugging, and documentation. (3.1.485, 1309C)
(b) See profiling.

PROGRAMMING LANGUAGE. The language in which a computer program is written for processing by a computer. (3.1.486, 1309C)

QUALIFICATION. The entire process by which products are obtained from manufacturers or distributors, examined and tested, and then identified on a qualified products list. (109B)

QUALIFIED PRODUCT. A product which has been examined and tested and listed on or qualified for inclusion on a qualified product list. (109B)

QUALIFIED PRODUCT LIST (QPL). A list of products, qualified under the requirements stated in the applicable specification, including appropriate product identification and test reference with the name and plant address of the manufacturer or distributor, as appropriate. (109B)

QUALITY ASSURANCE PROVISIONS. Quality assurance requirements documented and annotated in accordance with appendix B of MIL-T-31000. (6.5.15, 31000)

QUALITY ASSURANCE REQUIREMENTS. The tests and inspections necessary to verify that an end item meets the physical and functional requirements for which it was designed, or verify that a component, part, or subassembly will perform satisfactorily in its intended application. (6.5.16, 31000)

QUICK REPLACEABLE ASSEMBLY (QRA). A preferred form of shop replaceable assembly which is easily removable from the weapons replaceable assembly without complex operations or special tools and is typified by a plug-in design. (3.1.1.1, 2084AS)

READ ONLY MEMORY (ROM). A solid-state memory storage device which is programmed upon manufacture and cannot be reprogrammed. (3.1.506, 1309C)

REFERENCE DOCUMENTS. Documents referred to in a TDP element that contain information necessary to meet the design disclosure requirements of that TDP element. (6.5.17, 31000)

REFERENCED DOCUMENTS. Design activity standards, drawings, specifications or other documents referenced on drawings or lists. (3.69, 100E)

RELEASE.

(a) A configuration management action whereby a particular version of software is made available for a specific purpose (for example, released for test). (3.24, 2167A)

(b) A configuration management action whereby a particular drawing or a revision of a drawing is made available for a specific purpose (such as released for fabrication).

REPAIR. A procedure which reduces but does not completely eliminate a nonconformance resulting from production, and which has been reviewed and concurred in by the material review board and approved for use by the Government. The purpose of repair is to reduce the effect of the nonconformance. Repair is distinguished from rework in that the characteristic after repair still does not completely conform to the applicable specifications, drawings, or contract requirements. (3.1.58, 480B)

REPLACEMENT DRAWING. A replacement drawing is a new original drawing substituted for the previous original drawing of the same drawing number. (3.72, 100E)

REPLACEMENT ITEM. An item which is interchangeable with another item but which differs physically from the original item in that the installation of the replacement item requires operations such as drilling, reaming, cutting, filing, or shimming, in addition to the normal methods of attachment. (3.31, 961C)

REUSABLE SOFTWARE. Software developed in response to the requirements for one application that can be used, in whole or in part, to satisfy the requirements of another application. (3.25, 2167A)

REVIEW. A process or meeting during which a work product or set of work products, is presented to project personnel, managers, users, customers, or other interested parties for comment or approval. Types include code review, design review, formal qualification review, requirements review, test readiness review (610). See also audit.

REVISION. Any change to an original drawing which requires the revision level to be advanced. (3.73, 100E)

REVISION AUTHORIZATION. A document such as a Notice of Revision, Engineering Change Notice, or Revision Directive which describes the changes to be made to the drawing in detail and is issued by the activity having the authority to revise the drawing. (3.74, 100E)

REWORK. A procedure applied to a nonconformance that will completely eliminate the nonconformance and result in a characteristic that conforms completely to the specifications, drawings, or contract requirements. (3.1.61, 480B)

ROUTINE. A subdivision of a program consisting of two or more instructions that are functionally related. (3.1.531, 1309C)

SCHEMATIC DIAGRAM. See paragraph 10.3 of ASME Y14.24M.

SCRAP. Nonconforming material that is not usable for its intended purpose and which cannot be economically reworked or cannot be repaired in a manner acceptable to the Government. (3.14, 1520C)

SCREENING INSPECTION. An inspection in which each item of product is inspected for designated characteristics and defective items are removed. (109B)

SCREENED PART. A part that has successfully passed a screening inspection.

SELECTED ITEM DRAWING. See paragraph 6.2 of ASME Y14.24M.

SERIAL NUMBER. The unique notation which identifies a single unit of a family of like units, normally assigned sequentially. (3.26, 130G)

SET. A unit or units and necessary assemblies, subassemblies, and parts connected or associated together to perform an operational function. (Set is also used to denote a collection of like parts such as a tool-set, or a set of tires.) (3.76, 100E)

SHIP EQUIPMENT (MARINE ITEM) DRAWING. A drawing that depicts components, equipment and systems, for example, pumps or radar systems that may be used on one or more than one ship. (201.9.12, 100C)

SHOP REPLACEABLE ASSEMBLY (SRA).

(a) An item which is designated to be removed or replaced upon failure from a higher level assembly in the shop (intermediate or depot maintenance activity), and is to be tested as a separate entity. Also called FIR. (3.1.557, 1309C)

(b) A generic term which includes all the packages within a weapons replaceable assembly including the chassis and wiring as a unit. (3.1.1, 2084AS) See also bench replaceable assembly.

SHOP REPLACEABLE UNIT (SRU). See shop replaceable assembly (SRA). (3.1.558, 1309C)

SINGLE-LINE OR ONE-LINE DIAGRAM. See paragraph 10.2 of ASME Y14.24M.

SOFTWARE. A combination of associated computer instructions and computer data definitions required to enable the computer hardware to perform computational or control functions. (3.7, 2167A)

SOFTWARE CONFIGURATION MANAGEMENT PLAN. A configuration management plan whose coverage is restricted to software.

SOFTWARE DEVELOPMENT LIBRARY (SDL). A controlled collection of software, documentation, and associated tools and procedures used to facilitate the orderly development and subsequent support of software. The SDL includes the developmental configuration as part of its contents. A SDL provides storage of and controlled access to software and documentation in human-readable form, machine-readable form, or both. The library may also contain management data pertinent to the software development project. (3.27, 2167A)

SOFTWARE ENGINEERING. The application of a systematic, disciplined, quantifiable approach to the development, operation, and maintenance of software; that is, the application of engineering to software. (610)

SOFTWARE ENGINEERING ENVIRONMENT. The set of automated tools, firmware devices, and hardware necessary to perform the software engineering effort. The automated tools may include but are not limited to compilers, assemblers, linkers, loaders, operating system, debuggers, simulators, emulators, documentation tools and data base management system(s). (3.28, 2167A)

SOFTWARE REQUIREMENTS SPECIFICATION (SRS). A document that defines the complete set of engineering requirements for one computer software configuration item. (5.2.2.1, 2167A)

SOFTWARE SPECIFICATION REVIEW (SSR). A review of the finalized computer software configuration item requirements and operational concept. (3.3, 1521B)

SOURCE CODE. The code in which a program is prepared. Generally a high order language code (such as BASIC, ATLAS, and so forth). (3.1.575, 1309C)

SOURCE CONTROL DRAWING. See paragraph 8.3 and 8.4 of ASME Y14.24M.

SPECIAL INSPECTION EQUIPMENT. Either single or multipurpose integrated test units engineered, designed, fabricated or modified to perform special purpose testing of an item. It consists of items or assemblies of equipment that are interconnected and interdependent so as to become a new functional entity for testing purposes (FAR 45.101) (6.5.18, 31000)

SPECIAL PURPOSE DRAWING. See paragraph 1.10 of ASME Y14.24M.

SPECIAL TOOLING. Unique tooling which is mandatory to the manufacture of an item. It differs from tooling designed to increase manufacturing efficiency in that the use of the special tool imparts some characteristic to the item that is necessary for satisfactory performance and cannot be duplicated through other generally available manufacturing methods. (6.5.19, 31000)

SPECIFICATION. A document intended primarily for use in procurement, which describes the essential technical requirements for items, material or services, including the procedures for determining whether or not the requirements have been met. (3.1.63, 480B)

SPECIFICATION CHANGE NOTICE (SCN). A document used to propose, transmit and record changes to a specification. (3.84, 973)

SPECIFICATION CONTROL DRAWING. See paragraph 8.2 of ASME Y14.24M.

SPECIFICATION TREE. A reference diagram depicting the indentured relationships of the various specifications and other documents that define a configuration item or a system.

STANDARD. A document that establishes engineering and technical requirements for items, equipments, processes, procedures, practices, and methods that have been adopted as standard. Standards may also establish requirements for selection, application and design criteria for material. (3.79, 100E)

STANDARD REPAIR PROCEDURE (SRP). A documented technique for repair of a type of nonconformance which has been demonstrated to be an adequate and cost-effective method for repair when properly applied. SRPs are developed by the contractor, reviewed and concurred in by the material review board, and approved by the Government for recurrent use under defined conditions. Defined conditions shall include an expiration date or a finite limit on the number of applications, or both. (3.15, 1520C)

STANDARDIZED MILITARY DRAWING. A standardized military drawing (SMD) is a control drawing and shall disclose the applicable configuration, envelope dimensions, mounting and mating dimensions, interface dimensional characteristics, specified performance requirements, and inspection and acceptance test requirements for microcircuits in a military application. (204.2.3, 100E)

STATEMENT OF WORK (SOW). A document that defines those work tasks that cannot be contained in a specification, a CDRL, or a DID. (4.3.1, 245A)

SUBASSEMBLY. Two or more parts which form a portion of an assembly or a unit replaceable as a whole, but having a part or parts which are individually replaceable. (3.84, 100E)

SUBPROGRAM. A part of a larger program which can be converted into machine language independently. (3.1.589, 1309C)

SUBROUTINE. A subprogram that may be used at more than one place in the program (such as, processing different sets of data in a common way). (3.1.590, 1309C)

SUB-SHOP REPLACEABLE ASSEMBLY (SUB-SRA). A modular item packaged in a shop replaceable assembly (SRA). (3.1.1.3, 2084AS)

SUBSTITUTE ITEM. An item which possesses such functional and physical characteristics as to be capable of being exchanged, for another, only under specified conditions or in particular applications, and without alterations of the items themselves or the adjoining items. (3.39, 961C)

SUBSYSTEM. A combination of sets, groups, etc., which performs an operational functional within a system and is a major division of a system. (3.1.7, 280A)

SUPPLIER. The terms subcontractor, supplier, vendor, seller, or any other term used to identify the source from which the prime contractor obtains support are considered to be synonymous for the purpose of this standard. (3.17, 1520C)

SUPPORT SOFTWARE. Software which aids in preparing, analyzing, editing, and maintaining operational or test computer programs. (3.1.593, 1309C)

SYSTEM. A composite of equipment, skills, and techniques capable of performing or supporting an operational role (or both). A complete system includes all equipment, related facilities, material, software, services and personnel required for its operation and support to the degree that it can be considered a self-sufficient item in its intended operational environment. (3.1.68, 480B)

SYSTEM ALLOCATION DOCUMENT. A document which identifies the aggregation of configuration items by serial number and the system configuration at each location. (5.1.u, 483A)

SYSTEM DESIGN REVIEW (SDR). This review shall be conducted to evaluate the optimization, correlation, completeness, and risks associated with the technical requirements. (3.2, 1521B)

SYSTEM ENGINEERING PROCESS. A logical sequence of activities and decisions transforming an operational need into a description of system performance parameters and a preferred system configuration. (3.3, 499A)

SYSTEM LIFE CYCLE. Phases through which a system progresses from conception through disposal. (3.1.602, 1309C)

SYSTEM REQUIREMENTS REVIEW (SRR). The objective of this review is to ascertain the adequacy of the contractor's efforts in defining system requirements. (3.1, 1521B)

SYSTEMS ENGINEERING. The application of scientific and engineering effort to (3.11, 881A):

(a) Transform an operational need into a description of system performance parameters and a system configuration through the use of an iterative process; for example, definition, syntheses, analysis, design, test and evaluation, etc.
(b) Integrate related technical parameters and assure compatibility of all physical, functional, and program interfaces in a manner which optimizes the total system definition and design, and
(c) Integrate reliability, maintainability, safety, human, and other such factors into the total engineering effort.

TABULATED DETAIL DRAWING. A drawing that depicts similar items, which as a group, have constant and variable characteristics. Each item is uniquely identified. (201.3, 100C)

TASK CHANGE PROPOSAL (TCP). See contract change proposal.

TECHNICAL DATA PACKAGE (TDP). A technical description of an item adequate for supporting an acquisition strategy, production, engineering and logistics support. The description defines the required design configuration and procedures required to ensure adequacy of item performance. It consists of all applicable technical data such as drawings and associated lists, specifications, standards, performance requirements, quality assurance provisions, and packaging details. (6.5.20, 31000)

TECHNICAL PERFORMANCE MEASUREMENT (TPM). The continuing prediction and demonstration of the degree of anticipated or actual achievement of selected technical objectives. It includes an analysis of any differences among "achievement to date," "current estimate," and the specification requirement. "Achievement to date" is the value of a technical parameter estimated or measured in a particular test and/or analysis. "Current estimate" is the value of a technical parameter predicted to be achieved at the end of the contract within existing resources (3.5, 499A)

TECHNICAL PROGRAM PLANNING AND MEASUREMENT. The management of those design, development, test, and evaluation tasks required to progress from an operational need to the deployment and operation of the system by the user. (3.2, 499A)

TEST. A procedure or action taken to determine under real or simulated conditions the capabilities, limitations, characteristics, effectiveness, reliability or suitability of a material, device, system or method. (3.1.612, 1309C)

TEST READINESS REVIEW (TRR). A review conducted for each computer software configuration item (CSCI) to determine whether the software test procedures are complete and to assure that the contractor is prepared for formal CSCI testing. (3.6, 1521B)

TESTING. An element of inspection and generally denotes the determination by technical means of the properties or elements of supplies, or components thereof, including functional operation, and involves the application of scientific principles and procedures. (109B)

TOLERANCE. The total permissible deviation of a measurement from a designated value. (3.1.654, 1309C)

TUBE BEND DRAWING. See paragraph 11.7 of ASME Y14.24M.

TYPE DESIGNATOR. Type designators, a combination of letters and/or numbers assigned by the Government for the purpose of item identification, are assigned in accordance with a approved type designator—nomenclature systems such as . ... (301.2, 100E)

UNDIMENSIONED DRAWING. See paragraph 11.5 of ASME Y14.24M.

UNIT. An assembly of any combination of parts, subassemblies and assemblies mounted together which are normally capable of independent operation in a variety of situations. (3.1.72, 480B)

UNIT OF PRODUCT. The thing inspected in order to determine its classification as defective or non-defective or to count the number of defects. (109B)

UNSCREENED PART. A part that has not been subjected to a screening inspection.

USE-AS-IS. A disposition of material with one or more minor nonconformances determined to be usable for its intended purpose in its existing condition. (3.18, 1520C)

VALIDATION.

(a) The process of evaluating software to determine compliance with specified requirements. (3.32, 2167A)
(b) The process of evaluating a system or component during or at the end of the development process to determine whether it satisfies specified requirements. (610)
(c) The contractor's procedure for proving that the deliverable item meets its contractual requirements. (3.1.668, 1309C)

VENDOR SUBSTANTIATION DATA. The quality conformance inspections, tests, evaluation criteria and procedures to be followed to approve a potential supplier as a qualified source for a product, material or process used in an aerospace propulsion system. (6.5.21, 31000)

VERIFICATION.

(a) The process of evaluating a system or component to determine whether the products of a given development phase satisfy the conditions imposed at the start of that phase. (610)
(b) The process of evaluating the products of a given software development activity to determine correctness and consistency with respect to the products and standards provided as input to that activity. (3.33, 2167A)
(c) The Government's procedure for verifying that the deliverable item meets its contractual requirements. (3.1.670, 1309C)
(d) The act of reviewing, inspecting, testing, checking, auditing, or otherwise establishing and documenting whether items, processes, services, or documents conform to specified requirements. (A3-1987)

VERSION. An identified and documented body of software. Modifications to a version of software (resulting in a new version) require configuration management actions by either the contractor, the contracting agency, or both. (3.34, 2167A)

VERSION DESCRIPTION DOCUMENT (VDD). A document that identifies and describes a version of a computer software configuration item. (5.7.5.1, 2167A)

VICINITY PLAN. A vicinity plan or site drawing (or vicinity map used with construction drawings) delineates the relationship of a site to features of the surrounding area, such as towns, bodies of water, railroads, highways, etc. (201.8.4, 100C)

WAIVER. A written authorization to accept an item, which, during manufacture or after having been submitted for inspection, is found to depart from specified requirements, but nevertheless is considered suitable for use "as is" or after repair by an approved method. (3.96, 973) See use-as-is.

WEAPON REPLACEABLE ASSEMBLY (WRA). A generic term which includes replaceable packages of a system installed in the weapon system with the exception of cables, mounting provisions, and fuse boxes or circuit breakers. See also bench replaceable assembly, quick replaceable assembly, and shop replaceable assembly. (3.1.675, 1309C)

WIRING HARNESS DRAWING. See paragraph 11.1 of ASME Y14.24M.

WIRING LIST. See paragraph 10.6 of ASME Y14.24M.

WORK BREAKDOWN STRUCTURE (WBS). A product-oriented listing, in family tree order, of the hardware, software, services, and other work tasks which completely define a product or program. The listing results from project engineering during the development and production of a defense material item. A WBS relates the elements of work to be accomplished to each other and to the end product. (3.4, 881A)

APPENDIX B

ACRONYMS AND ABBREVIATIONS

B.1 INTRODUCTION

The acronyms listed below are in common use in various segments of the configuration management community.

To avoid confusion, if an item has been abstracted from a particular standard, the reference in brackets ( ) after each item identifies the source of the item.

(a) The first number is the number of the section in the document from which the item was abstracted.
(b) The second number is the abbreviation of the document from which the item was abstracted. This second number itself is an acronym and its complete name is available in this appendix. Complete identification of referenced documents is provided in Appendix C.
    For example, (3.1, 973) after the acronym ABL indicates the definition of the acronym was abstracted from section 3.1 of MIL-STD-973.
(c) If only one number is provided, it is the document number. For example, (109B) after the acronym AQL indicates that the definition of the acronym was abstracted from MIL-STD-109B.

B.2 ACRONYMS AND ABBREVIATIONS

ABL: Allocated Baseline (3.1, 973)
ACSN: Advance Change Study Notice (3.1, 973)
ADP: Automatic Data Processing
aka: also known as
ANSI: American National Standards Institute
AQL: Acceptable Quality Level (109B)
ASME: American Society Of Mechanical Engineers
A3-1987: ANSI/ASQC Standard A3-1987
BOM: Bill of Materials
BRA: Bench Replaceable Assembly (3.1.1.2, 2084AS)
CAB: Corrective Action Board (3.4, 1520C)
CAGE: Commercial and Government Entity Code (6.5.2, 31000)
CALS: Computer-Aided Acquisition and Logistics Support
CASE: Computer Aided Software Engineering
CCB: Configuration Control Board (3.1, 973)
CDR: Critical Design Review (10.2, 2167A)
CDRL: Contract Data Requirements List (10.2, 2167A)
CFE: Contractor Furnished Equipment (3.2, 480B)
CI: Configuration Item (3.1, 973)
CIDS: Critical Item Development Specification (10.2, 2167A)
CII: Configuration Item Identification (5.1.i, 483A)
CM: Configuration Management (3.1, 973)
CN: Change Notice
COTS: Commercial Off-The-Shelf (3.6, 130G)
CRISD: Computer Resources Integrated Support Document (10.2, 2167A)
CSA: Configuration Status Accounting (3.1, 973)
CSAR: Configuration Status Accounting Report (3.1, 973)
CSC: Computer Software Component (10.2, 2167A)
CSCI: Computer Software Configuration Item (10.2, 2167A)
CSU: Computer Software Unit (10.2, 2167A)
CWBS: Contractor Work Breakdown Structure (3.7, 881A)
DCN: Design Change Notice (3.2, 480B)
DEC: Digital Equipment Corporation
DFD: Data Flow Diagram
DID: Data Item Description (3.1, 973)
DL: Data List (3.1, 100E)
DOD: Department of Defense (10.2, 2167A)
DODISS: Department of Defense Index of Specifications and Standards (10.2, 2167A)

ECN: Engineering Change Notice
ECP: Engineering Change Proposal (3.1, 973)
EEPROM: Electronically Erasable Programmable Read-Only Memory
EIA: Electronic Industries Association
EPD: Equipment Planning Diagram
EPROM: Erasable Programmable Read-Only Memory (3.1.196, 1309C)
ER: Engineering Release
EWBS: Expanded Work Breakdown Structure
FIR: Functional Item Replacement (3.1.280, 1309C)
FQR: Formal Qualification Review (3.9, 1521B)
FSCM: Federal Supply Codes for Manufacturers
GFE: Government Furnished Equipment (3.1, 973)
GFI: Government Furnished Information
GFS: Government Furnished Software (10.2, 2167A)
HOL: High Order Language (3.1.305, 1309C)
HWCI: Hardware Configuration Item (10.2, 2167A)
I/O: Input/Output (3.1.100, 1309C)
iaw: in accordance with
ICD: Interface Control Drawing (3.1, 973)
ICWG: Interface Control Working Group (3.1, 973)
IEEE: Institute of Electrical and Electronic Engineers
IL: Index List (3.1, 100E)
ILS: Integrated Logistic Support (3.1, 973)
IRS: Interface Requirements Specification (10.2, 2167A)
LRU: Line Replaceable Unit (3.1.348, 1309C)
MIL: Military
MRA: Mission Requirements Analysis
MRB: Material Review Board (3.1, 973)
MTEP: Master Test and Evaluation Plan
NATO: North Atlantic Treaty Organization
NC: Numerical Control (201.9.3, 100C)
NDI: Non-Developmental Item (3.1, 973)
NDS: Non-Developmental Software (10.2, 2167A)
NOR: Notice of Revision (3.1, 973)
NSCM: NATO Supply Code for Manufacturers (3.20, 130G)
PA: Product Assurance
PBL: Product Baseline (3.1, 973)
PCA: Physical Configuration Audit (3.1, 973)
PDR: Preliminary Design Review (10.2, 2167A)
PIC: Product Integration Center

PIDS: Prime Item Development Specification (10.2, 2167A)
PIN: Part or Identifying Number (3.28, 9616)
PL: Parts List (3.1, 100E)
PM: Program Manager
PMO: Program Management Office
PR: Problem Report
PROM: Programmable Read-Only Memory (3.1.480, 1309C)
PRR: Production Readiness Review (3.10, 1521B)
QPL: Qualified Products List (109B)
QRA: Quick Replaceable Assembly (3.1.1.1, 2084AS)
RFP: Request for Proposal
ROM: Read Only Memory (3.1.506, 1309C)
SCCB: Software Configuration Control Board
SCM: Software Configuration Management
SCMP: Software Configuration Management Plan
SCN: Specification Change Notice (3.1, 973)
SDD: Software Design Document
SDL: Software Development Library (10.2, 2167A)
SDP: Software Development Plan (10.2, 2167A)
SDR: System Design Review (3.2, 1521B)
SMD: Standardized Military Drawing (3.1, 100E)
SOW: Statement of Work (10.2, 2167A)
SQL: Standard Query Language
SRA: Shop Replaceable Assembly (3.1.1.3, 2084AS)
SRP: Standard Repair Procedure (3.15, 1520C)
SRR: System Requirements Review (10.2, 2167A)
SRS: Software Requirements Specification (10.2, 2167A)
SSPM: Software Standards and Procedures Manual
SSR: Software Specification Review (3.3, 1521B)
SSS: System/Segment Specification (10.2, 2167A)
sub-SRA: Sub-Shop Replaceable Assembly (3.1.1.3, 2084AS)
S/W: Software
TBD: To be determined
TBP: To be provided
TBR: To be resolved
TBS: To be supplied
TCP: Task Change Proposal (5.1.w, 483A)
TDP: Technical Data Package (6.5.20, 31000)
TPM: Technical Performance Measurement (3.5, 499)
TRR: Test Readiness Review (3.6, 1521B)
VDD: Version Description Document (10.2, 2167A)

WBS: Work Breakdown Structure (3.1, 973)
WRA: Weapon Replaceable Assembly (3.1.675, 1309C)
61: MIL-HDBK-61 (Draft)
100C: DOD-STD-100C
100E: MIL-STD-100E
109B: MIL-STD-109B
130G: MIL-STD-130G
245A: MIL-HDBK-245A
280A: MIL-STD-280A
480B: DOD-STD-480B
481B: MIL-STD-481B
483A: MIL-STD-483A
490A: MIL-STD-490A
499A: MIL-STD-499A
610: ANSI/IEEE Std 610
828: ANSI/IEEE Std 828-1990
881A: MIL-STD-881A
961C: MIL-STD-961C
973: DOD-STD-973
1000B: DOD-D-1000B
1028: ANSI/IEEE Std 1028-1988
1063: ANSI/IEEE Std 1063-1987
1309C: MIL-STD-1309C
1042: ANSI/IEEE Std 1042-1986
1456A: MIL-STD-1456A
1520C: MIL-STD-1520C
1521B: DOD-STD-1521B
1063: ANSI/IEEE 1063-1987
2084AS: MIL-STD-2084AS
2167A: DOD-STD-2167A
2168: DOD-STD-2168
31000: MIL-T-31000

APPENDIX C

REFERENCES

C.1 INTRODUCTION

C.1.1 Purpose

This provides complete identification of documents that are either referenced elsewhere in this text or that provide significant information bearing on the topic of configuration management.

C.1.2 Sources

Sources for specific standards are identified in the appropriate sections. Sources from which to obtain standards in general are:

(a) Global Engineering Documents
TEL: 1-800-854-7179
1990 M Street, NW
Suite 400
Washington, DC 20036

(b) Information Handling Services
TEL: 1-800-525-7052,
FAX: 303-790-0686.
P.O. Box 2220
Englewood, CO 80130

C.2 ANSI STANDARDS

C.2.1 American Society of Mechanical Engineers (ASME)

(Copies of ASME standards may be obtained from the American Society of Mechanical Engineers, 345 East 47th St., New York, NY 10017.)

ASME Y14.24-1989, "Types and Applications of Engineering Drawings."

C.2.2 American Society for Quality Control (ASQC)

(Copies of ASQC standards may be obtained from the American Society for Quality Control, 310 West Wisconsin Avenue, Milwaukee, WI 53203.)

ANSI/ASQC Standard A3-1987, "Quality Systems Terminology."

C.2.3 Institute of Electrical and Electronics Engineers (IEEE)

(Copies of IEEE standards may be obtained from the IEEE Service Center, 445 Hoes Lane, Piscataway, NJ 08855-1331.)

(a) ANSI/IEEE Std 610, "IEEE Computer Dictionary," Jan. 18, 1991.
(b) ANSI/IEEE Std 828-1990, "IEEE Standard for Software Configuration Management Plans."
(c) ANSI/IEEE Std 830-1984, "IEEE Guide For Software Requirements Specifications."
(d) ANSI/IEEE Std 1028-1988, "IEEE Standard for Software Reviews and Audits."
(e) ANSI/IEEE Std 1042-1986, "IEEE Guide for Software Configuration Management."
(f) ANSI/IEEE Std 1063-1987, "IEEE Standard for User Documentation."

C.3 ELECTRONIC INDUSTRY ASSOCIATION (EIA) PUBLICATIONS

(Copies of EIA standards may be obtained from the Electronic Industry Association, 2001 Pennsylvania Avenue NW, Washington, DC 20006)

(a) CMB4-1A, "Configuration Management Definitions for Digital Computer Programs."
(b) CMB4-2, "Configuration Identification for Digital Computer Programs."
(c) CMB4-4, "Configuration Change Control for Digital Computer Programs."
(d) CMB5-A, "Configuration Management Requirements for Subcontractors/Vendors."
(e) CMB6-1B, "Configuration and Data Management References."
(f) CMB6-2, "Configuration and Data Management In-House Training Plan."
(g) CMB6-3, "Configuration Identification."
(h) CMB6-4, "Configuration Control."
(i) CMB6-5, "Textbook for Configuration Status Accounting."
(j) CMB6-9, "Configuration and Data Management Training Course."
(k) CMB6-10, "Education in Configuration and Data Management."
(l) CMB7-1, "Electronic Interchange of Configuration Management Data."
(m) CMB7-2, "Guideline Management to an Automated Environment."

C.4 U.S. DEPARTMENT OF DEFENSE PUBLICATIONS

(Unless otherwise stated, copies of these publications may be obtained from the Commander, Naval Publications and Forms Center, Code 3013, 5801 Tabor Avenue, Philadelphia, PA 19120.)

C.4.1 Department of Defense Standards

(a) DOD-STD-100C, "Engineering Drawing Practices," Dec. 22, 1978. (This has been superseded by MIL-STD-100E.)
(b) DOD-STD-480B, "Configuration Control—Engineering Changes, Deviations and Waivers w/Notice 1," July 15, 1988.
(c) DOD-D-1000B, "Drawing, Engineering and Associated Lists, 28 Oct 1977 with Amendment 4," Aug. 18, 1987. (This has been superseded by MIL-T-31000.)
(d) DOD-STD-1521B, "Technical Reviews and Audits for Systems, Equipments and Computer Software," June 4, 1985.
(e) DOD-STD-2167A, "Defense System Software Development," Feb. 29, 1988.

(f) DOD-STD-2168, "Defense System Software Quality Program," Apr. 29, 1988.

C.4.2 Military Handbooks

(a) MIL-HDBK-61, "Configuration Management (Draft)."
(b) MIL-HDBK-245A (NAVY), "Preparation of Statement of Work (SOW)," Aug. 1, 1978.

C.4.3 Military Standards

(a) MIL-STD-100E, "Engineering Drawing Practices," with Notice 2, Sept. 4, 1992.
(b) MIL-STD-109B, "Quality Assurance Terms and Definitions," Apr. 4, 1969.
(c) MIL-STD-130G, "Identification Marking of U.S. Military Property."
(d) MIL-STD-280A, "Definition of Item Levels, Item Exchangeability, Models and Related Terms," July 7, 1969, with Notice 1, July 30, 1986.
(e) MIL-STD-454M, "Standard General Requirements for Electronic Equipment, with Notice 1," Aug. 15, 1990.
(f) MIL-STD-481B, "Configuration Control—Engineering Changes (Short Form), Deviations and Waivers," July 15, 1988.
(g) MIL-STD-483A, "Configuration Management Practices for Systems, Equipment, Munitions and Computer Programs," June 4, 1985.
(h) MIL-STD-490A, "Specification Practices," June 4, 1985.
(i) MIL-STD-499A, "Engineering Management," May 1, 1974. (This is currently under revision.)
(j) MIL-STD-881A, "Work Breakdown Structures for Defense Material Items," Apr. 25, 1975. (This is currently under revision.)
(k) MIL-STD-961C, "Military Specifications and Associated Documents, Preparation Of," May 20, 1988.
(l) MIL-STD-973, "Configuration Management," with Notice 1, Dec. 1, 1992.
(m) MIL-STD-1309C, "Definition of Terms for Test, Measurement and Diagnostic Equipment," Nov. 18, 1989.
(n) MIL-STD-1456A, "Configuration Management Plan," Sept. 11, 1989.

(o) MIL-STD-1520C, "Corrective Action and Disposition System for Nonconforming Material," June 27, 1986.
(p) MIL-STD-2084AS, "General Requirements for Maintainability of Avionic and Electronic Systems and Equipment," Apr. 6, 1982.
(q) MIL-T-31000, "Technical Data Packages, General Requirements For," Dec. 15, 1989.

C.4.4 Department of Defense Other Publications

(Copies of these documents are available from the Defense Quality and Standardization Office, 5203 Leesburg Pike, Suite 1403, Falls Church, VA 22041-3466.)

(a) DOD Standardization Program Plan, "Configuration Management (CMAN)," Revision 1, Aug. 10, 1990.
(b) Joint DOD Services/Agency Regulation, "Configuration Management."

C.5 OTHER STANDARDS

C.5.1 British Standards Institute (BSI)

(Copies of this document are available from the British Standards Institute, Linford Road, MK 146LE, Milton Keynes, U.K.)

BS 6488, "Code of Practice For Configuration Management of Computer-Based Systems."

C.5.2 Canadian National Defense Standards

(a) C-05-002-001/AG-00, "Aerospace Engineering Change Proposal Procedures."
(b) D-02-006-008/SG-001, "The Design Change, Deviation and Waiver Procedure."
(c) D-01-100-215/SF-000, "Specification for Preparation of Material Change Notices."

C.5.3 European Computer Manufacturers Institute (ECMA)

(Copies of this document are available from the European Computers Manufacturing Association, Rue de Rhone 114, Geneva, 01204, Switzerland.)

ECMA-TR 47, "Configuration Management Service Definition."

C.5.4. European Space Agency

(Copies of these documents are available from the European Space Agency, ESTEC, Noordwijk, The Netherlands).

(a) ESA BSSC (85) 1, "Software Configuration Management."
(b) ESA BSSC 1B, "ESA Software Configuration Management Standards."

C.5.5 Federal Aviation Administration

(Copies of this document are available from the Federal Aviation Administration, Department of Transportation, 800 Independence Ave., S.W., Washington, DC 20591.)

FAA-STD 021, "Software Configuration Management."

C.5.6 North Atlantic Treaty Organization (NATO) Standard

(Copies of the below-identified documents are available from the Defense Quality and Standardization Office, 5203 Leesburg Pike, Suite 1403, Falls Church, VA 22041-3466.)

(a) NATO Standardization Agreement, STANAG 4159, "NATO Material Configuration Management Policy and Procedures For Multinational Joint Projects."
(b) NAT-PRC-2, "Software Project Configuration Management Procedures."
(c) NAT-STAN-4, "Software Configuration Management Requirements."

C.5.7 United Kingdom Ministry of Defense Standards

(Copies of these standards can be obtained from the Directorate of Standardization (Stan 1), Kentigern House, 65 Brown Street, Glasgow G2 8EX, United Kingdom.)

(a) 00-22, "The Identification and Marking of Programmable Items," May 3, 1991.
(b) 05-57, "Configuration Management Policy and Procedures for Defense Material," Sept. 2, 1985.
(c) AVP 38: SEC 3, "Configuration Control."
(d) NES 41, "Requirements for the Configuration Management and Ship Fit Definitions," Issue 3, May 1989.

C.6 OTHER REFERENCE DOCUMENTS

This is a very short list of publications. The literature is vast, and to mention one item is to slight all the others. However, these listed items will provide a starting point from which individuals can proceed based on their interests.

C.6.1 Articles

(This was previously referenced in the text.)

S. Dart, "Adopting An Automated Configuration Management Solution," *Software Technology Center Conference*, April 1994, Hill Air Force Base, Utah.

C.6.2 Books

(a) H. Berlack, *Software Configuration Management*, John Wiley & Sons, 1992.
(b) D. Whitgift, *Software Configuration Management: Methods and Tools*, John Wiley & Sons, 1991.

C.6.3 Proceedings

Third International Workshop on Software Configuration Management, IEEE Computer Society Press, June 1991.

C.6.4 National Institute For Standards and Technology

(Copies of this document are available from the National Institute For Standards and Technology, Standards and Codes Information, Room A163, Bldg. 411, Gaithersberg, MD 20899.)

S. P. 500-161, "Software Configuration Management: An Overview."

C.6.5 Magazines

(a) *CALS/CE Report*, Knowledge Base International, 5700 Northwest Central Dr., Suite 160, Houston, TX 77092 (713) 690-7644.
(b) *CALS Journal*, 14407 Big Basin Way, Saratoga, CA 95070-6008, (408) 997-7394.

C.6.6 Reports

Software Configuration Management Technology Report, Software Technology Support Center, Attn: Customer Service, Ogden ALC/TISE, Hill AFB, UT 84056, (801) 777-7703.

APPENDIX D

PROJECT CONFIGURATION MANAGEMENT PLAN EXAMPLE

The purpose of providing this configuration management plan example is to assist those who are charged with initiating and implementing a configuration management effort for the first time. This plan provides one detailed implementation example of the concepts discussed in the text. This plan is not perfect and reflects only one way to achieve the desired end.

This plan is not complete (for example, a number of items are assumed to be expressed in corporate or lower organization instructions). Furthermore, certain sections and tables are incomplete; these are items that would be too lengthy for inclusion and at a level of detail that would be very specific to the implementing organization.

The user of this example plan should refer to the index of the book for the exact locations of specific points in the plan that require detailed discussion.

Footnotes are provided in the plan when additional discussion on specific points in the text is appropriate.

Additional example CM plans are available in the Appendices to IEEE Standard 1042-198, "Guide To Software Configuration Management."

31 Aug 199X
SPP-CMP

PROJECT CONFIGURATION MANAGEMENT PLAN
FOR
THE STEAM POWER PROJECT

CONTRACT NO. EPU-000567SPP

D. Boss
Steam Power Project Manager

Date

TABLE OF CONTENTS

LIST OF FIGURES

LIST OF TABLES

D.1 INTRODUCTION

D.1.1 Purpose

This document establishes the plan to maintain the integrity of the products to be produced as part of the Steam Power Project (SPP).

D.1.2 Scope

This does not include the software used by manufacturing. That is covered separately in TZA 4570.

D.1.3 Background

The EPU Corporation is building a co-generation conventional power plant to provide both electric power and steam for their large manufacturing complex located at Red River, IL. As part of that effort, the EPU corporation has awarded a contract to the TZA Company to provide a process control system to provide on-line control of this power plant. This system, the Steam Power System, consists of the two subsystems shown in Figure D-1.

(a) The automatic data processing (ADP) subsystem provides real-time control of the co-generation power plant through interaction with the remote sensor and control (RSC) subsystem.
(b) The remote sensor and control subsystem contains all the sensors and automatic controls throughout the co-generation power plant. These are interfaced to the ADP subsystem through the interface control cabinet (ICC), a part of the RSC subsystem.

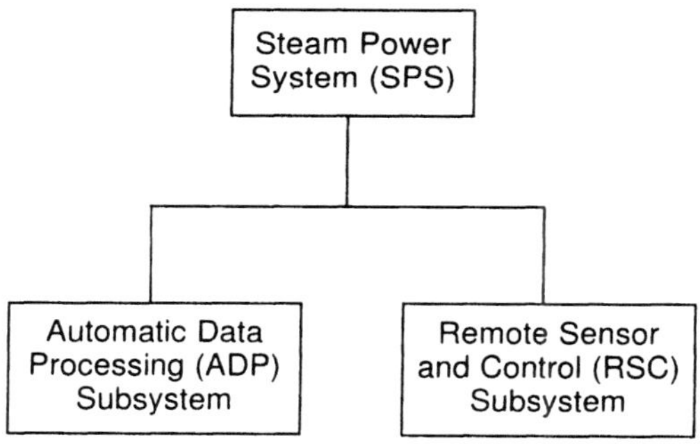

FIGURE D-1. Steam Power System Structure.

D.1.4 Introduction to the Rest of this Document

The remainder of this document is organized as follows:

(a) ...

D.2 REFERENCED DOCUMENTS

The following documents, of the exact issue shown, form a part of this document to the extent specified herein.

(a) Statement of Work ...
(b) ...

D.3 CONFIGURATION IDENTIFICATION

The items that form a part of the Steam Power System (SPS) are identified in the steam power equipment planning diagram (EPD) in accordance with the requirements of TZA 2550. This equipment planning diagram is a controlled drawing and provides a further breakout of the individual items of the SPS.

D.3.1 Baseline Identifications

The baselines established for this project are shown in Table D-I.

(a) The functional baseline consists of the SPP system specification, the top-level agreement on the requirements for the power plant. This is established when it is approved by the customer.
(b) The subsystem allocated baselines are the two subsystem specifications and the subsystem interface control document. These are established on completion of the system design review when approved by the SPP project manager.
(c) The allocated baselines consist of the individual unit specifications (for hardware), the individual software requirements specifications and the subsystem interface requirements specifications (one per

subsystem).[1] These are established at the completion of the individual requirements reviews when approved by the subsystem managers.

The hardware unit specifications include the requirements for the software portion of any firmware included in those units.

(d) The hardware design baseline consists of hardware design documents and engineering drawings. This baseline is established incrementally as the design documents and drawings are released.

TABLE D-I. STEAM POWER PROJECT BASELINES

Baseline	Components	Establishment
Functional	System specification	Customer approval
Subsystem allocated	Subsystem specifications, Subsystem interface control document	Completion of system design review
Allocated	Unit specifications, Software requirements specifications Interface requirements specifications	Completion of requirement reviews
Hardware design	Hardware design documents	Design activity approval
	Engineering drawings	Release of drawings
Developmental configuration	Sections 1, 2, and 3 of the SDD	Completion of PDR
	Sections 4 and 5 of the SDD	Completion of CDR
	Category I and II software	Completion of unit test
Test	Test plans, test procedures, test data	Subsystem manager approval
	Category I, II, and IV software	Start of qualification test dry run
Product	Technical data package Software product specifications User manuals Maintenance manuals	Completion of PCA

[1]The reason for two interface requirements specifications is to ease the control problem. Each subsystem interface requirements specification identifies the interfaces that are inside that subsystem. This enables the subsystem managers to authorize changes to interfaces that are inside their subsystems without a requirement for further approvals.

Interfaces that are common to two subsystems are documented in the subsystem interface control document (a part of the subsystem allocated baseline).

(e) The developmental configuration baseline is established incrementally. The first increment, the top-level design (Sections 1 through 3.2 of the software design documents), is established at the completion of the preliminary design review (PDR). The second increment, the detailed design (the rest of the sections of the software design documents), is established at the completion of the critical design review (CDR). The third increment, Category I and II software, becomes part of this baseline when it completes its unit tests. (See Section 3.3.1 of this plan for the definitions of software categories.)
(f) The test baseline is also established incrementally. The initial increment consists of the approved qualification test plans, the associated test procedures and test data, and the Category I and II software being used as part of those tests. The documents become part of this baseline as they are approved by the subsystem manager. The software code itself becomes part of this baseline at the initiation of the first formal dry run of a qualification test in which this software participates.
(g) The product baseline consists of the technical data package, software product specifications, user manuals, and maintenance manuals. This is established on completion of the physical configuration audit (PCA).

D.3.1.1 Document Tree

Figure D-2 shows the SPP document tree. As shown therein:

(a) The system is decomposed into subsystems, and further into hardware and software configuration items.
(b) The top-level design of the hardware configuration items is documented in hardware design documents, while the lower levels of the design are carried forth into engineering drawings. At the end of the development, the complete design of the hardware configuration items is documented in the technical data package.
(c) The design of the software configuration items (and the software component of firmware) is reflected in the software design documents.
(d) Each level of decomposition (system, subsystem, and configuration item) contains its own test plans, test procedures, and test reports.
(e) Operator and maintenance manuals are collected at the system level.

D.3.1.2 Contract Data Requirements List

The complete list of data items that will be placed under configuration management is provided in Table D.3.1.2-I.[2]

D.3.1.3 Configuration Items

Table D-II provides a list of all the configuration items. As shown therein:

(a) Each configuration item has a complete name (for example, Interface Control Cabinet), an acronym (for example, ICC), and a number (for example, 2010).
(b) Hardware configuration item numbers start with 2, software configuration item numbers start with 4, and firmware configuration item numbers start with 6.

System Specification

- *System Test Plans Procedures Reports*
- *Operator and Maintenance Manuals*
- *Subsystem Specifications*
    - *Subsystem Test Plans Procedures Reports*
    - *Unit Specifications*
        - *Hardware Design Documents*
        - *Engineering Drawings*
        - *Hardware Test Plans Procedures Reports*
        - *Technical Data Package*
    - *Software Requirements Specifications*
        - *Software Design Documents*
        - *Software Product Specifications*

FIGURE D-2. SPP Document Tree.

---

[2]This table is not provided as a part of this example.

D.3.2 Hardware Identification

D.3.2.1 General

Unless otherwise stated, hardware shall be identified using the TZA manufacturing code and the drawing number of the item. See Volume 8 of the "TZA Corporate Engineering Documentation Manual," as modified by the SPP Project Drafting Instruction, SPP-PI-0019, for details.

D.3.2.2 Serial Numbers

Serial numbering requirements, to include those for line replaceable units (LRUs), will be provided as part of an SPP project instruction.

D.3.2.3 Erasable Electronic Media

D.3.2.3.1 Labels

Electronic media labels shall be attached to all containers containing media (tapes, hard disks, and floppy disks) on which information from the configuration management library has been placed. These labels shall contain the following information:

(a) Name of the contents including the system identification, computer software configuration item acronym and number (or other distinguishing name), and build identification
(b) The date when the tape or disk was prepared
(c) The name, telephone number, and mail stop of the person who prepared the tape or disk.
(d) The number of the version description document (VDD) that specifies the detailed contents of the media.

An example is shown in Figure D-3.

TABLE D-II. SPP CONFIGURATION ITEMS

Name	Acronym	Number
1. Interface control cabinet	ICC	2010
⋮		
25. Real-time control	RTC	4040
⋮		

D.3.2.3.2 Version Description Documents

Version description documents shall be used to delineate the detailed software contents on this media. See TZA 4050 for details associated with the format and content of version description documents.

D.3.3 Software

D.3.3.1 Software Categories

All the software for the SPP project has been placed in one of the categories shown in Table D-III.

(a) Category I software is all the software being developed as part of this project and delivered as computer software configuration items. These are listed in Table D.3.3-II.[3]

TZA SPP
RTC_4040
Incremental Build 5
15 Sept 199X
D. Brown, (709) 424-6489
MS 71-4
VDD: TSA__SPP__RTC__IB__05.12

FIGURE D-3. Electronic Media Label Example.

TABLE D-III. SPP SOFTWARE CATEGORIES

Category	Description
Category I	New deliverable software, to be developed and designated as a configuration item.
Category II	The software component of deliverable firmware.
Category III	Vendor-provided and -maintained software.
Category IV	Test software, the software used to support the qualification tests of deliverable hardware, software, and firmware.
Category V	Product support software, the software developed to support the formal process of producing Categories I, II, IV, and VI software.
Category VI	Informal software, this is software developed to support informal tests and other items.

[3] Tables 3.3-II and 3.3-III are not provided as part of this example.

(b) Category II software is the software component of deliverable firmware being developed as a part of this project. These are listed in Table D.3.3-III.
(c) Category III software is commercially available software, purchased for this project and maintained by the vendor. These are listed in Table D-IV.
(d) Category IV software is the software developed to support qualification tests of deliverable items (hardware, software, and firmware). This consists of the test data, test drivers, test analysis software, and other test support software required to execute and analyze the output data of the qualification tests of those items.
(e) Category V software is the software developed to support the formal process of producing Categories I, II, IV, and VI software. This includes software tools to check the software units for standards compliance, compile and link the resulting software, and so on.
(f) Category VI software is software developed to support informal tests and other development activities.

D.3.3.2 Software Identification

The identification requirements for the software are stated below.

D.3.3.2.1 Category I Software Identification

D.3.3.2.1.1 Source File Identification: All source files shall be identified as follows:

(a) The first line of each source file shall provide the source file name, file type, version number, and date of last revision beginning at character 10. The file name, file type, and version number on the first line of the source file shall be identical to the external file name, file type, and version number (for example, the one printed on the flag sheet). The dates may be different.
(b) The following conventions shall be used for the assignment of source file names:

TABLE D-IV. CATEGORY III SOFTWARE

1.	VAX/VMS operating system software
	⋮

(1) The first two letters of each source file name shall begin with a standard letter keyed to the computer software configuration items to which it belongs. These are specified in Table D-V. As shown in that table, source files that are common to more than one configuration item shall begin with the letters "XX."[4]

(2) Specific naming conventions for each source file inside each computer software configuration item shall be specified by the manager responsible for that configuration item.

(c) The file type shall follow standard VAX naming conventions. See Table D.3.2 of the VAX/VMS DCL Concepts Manual.

(d) The version number shall be initialized at "1" and incremented by one for each approved change. Version numbers shall be reset to "1" only with the approval of the SPP configuration control board (CCB).

(e) The date of the last revision shall be the date when the last revision was implemented in the configuration management library, and shall be stated as day-month-year (for example, 5 Jan 199X). It should be noted that the date of the last revision as shown in the first line of the source file may differ from the date shown in the directory listing of the same source. This is due to the reissuing of dates by the VAX/VMS operating system when files are shifted from one subdirectory to another.

D.3.3.2.1.2 Object File Identification: Object file names shall be identified with the same name used for their source file. Version numbers shall not be controlled.

D.3.3.2.1.3 Executable File Identification: File names shall use the computer software identification number and the purpose of the build separated by underscores (for example, 6080__FQT10). Additional qualifiers

TABLE D-V. CATEGORY I SOURCE FILE FIRST LETTER ASSIGNMENTS

Computer Software Configuration Item	First Two Letters
Real-time control (4040)	AA
⋮	
Common to more than one configuration item	XX

[4] Alternately, the three-character acronym for the computer software configuration item could be used for the unique files.

may be added for clarity. The version number associated with each executable file name shall be incremented by one for each issue. Version numbers may be reset with the concurrence of the SPP configuration control board.

D.3.3.2.2 Category II Software Identification

This shall be identified in the same manner as Category I software, with the following addition: image files shall be produced to format 15 as specified in TZA 2133.

D.3.3.2.3 Category III Software Identification

This shall use the vendors' identifications.

D.3.3.2.4 Category IV, V, and VI Software Identification

This shall be identified as specified by the design activity.

D.3.3.3 Firmware

D.3.3.3.1 Software Component

See Section D-3.3.2.2.

D.3.3.3.2 Unaltered Hardware Component

This shall be identified in the same manner as any other hardware item. See Section D-3.2.

D.3.3.3.3 Altered Hardware Component

These are divided into types for the purpose of identification.

D.3.3.3.3.1 Type 1 Programmable Parts: These are programmed at the time of manufacture and cannot be reprogrammed.

(a) Type 1 programmable parts acquired from suppliers with embedded commercial software shall be identified using the suppliers' part numbers.

(b) Type 1 programmable parts acquired as part of a higher-level assembly from suppliers shall be acquired together with the appropriate supplier documentation that provides complete identification of the embedded software.
(c) Custom software to be placed on Type 1 programmable parts being manufactured by suppliers should be identified as part of a specification control drawing or a source control drawing.
(d) Custom software to be placed on Type 1 programmable parts being manufactured by this organization shall be identified as part of a software drawing.

D.3.3.3.3.2 Type 2 Programmable Parts: These are programmed after the time of manufacture and cannot be reprogrammed.
Custom software to be placed on these devices shall be identified on an altered item drawing. See Sections 3.2 and 3.5 of this plan.

D.3.3.3.3.3 Type 3 Programmable Parts: These are programmed after the time of manufacture and can be reprogrammed only by removing the individual devices from the next higher assembly.

Custom software to be placed on these devices shall be identified on an altered item drawing.

D.3.3.3.3.4 Type 4 Programmable Parts: These are programmed after the time of manufacture and are programmed and reprogrammed only while mounted in the next higher assembly.

Software to be placed on these parts shall be identified using a software drawing, and the software drawing itself shall be a referenced drawing to the next higher assembly. Further lower-level drawings (to identify the software on each chip) should not be required.

D.3.3.3.3.5 Type 5 Programmable Parts: Type 5 are programmed after the time of manufacture, are initially programmed as individual parts, and are reprogrammed only while mounted on the next higher assembly.

The programmed part shall be handled as an altered item during the assembly of the board. The software that is to be loaded while the parts are mounted on the board, shall be identified using a software drawing. The software drawing shall state whether or not the software on the type 5 part is being replaced. Further lower-level drawings (to identify the software on each chip) should not be required.

D.3.4 Document Identification

SPP project instruction SPP-PI-0001 establishes a control and disseminating procedure for documents generated for this project. Each of these documents is identified with a unique identification issued by TZA Information Control. Information Control uses this number to store, reproduce, and issue these documents in accordance with their approved distribution.

D.3.4.1 Deliverable Document Identification Requirements

Documents that are deliverable to the customer will follow the additional documentation identification requirements specified in SPP-PI-001.

D.3.4.2 Document Source File Identification

Document source files in the configuration management library shall have a file name that consists of the following fields, which shall be separated by underscores:

(a) Group Identification Codes:

  (1) For documents that are unique to one and only one configuration item, this shall be the four numbers of the configuration item identification number. These are provided in Table D-II.
  (2) For documents that apply to more than one configuration item (for example, this plan), this shall be "SPP," indicating the Steam Power Project.

(b) Document Acronyms. These are listed in Table D-VI.
(c) Revision Identification. This shall consist of revision letters. The first revision shall be indicated by the use of the letter "A," the second by the use of the letter "B," and so forth.

TABLE D-VI. DOCUMENT ACRONYMS

Document	Acronym
⋮	
7. Software requirements specification	SRS
⋮	

2010__US__C

FIGURE D-4. An Example of a Document Source File Name.

An example of a document file name is provided in Figure D-4. This identifies the source file for the third revision of the unit specification for the ICC.

If the document is produced from a master source file and one or more secondary source files (for example, using the REQUIRE command of RUNOFF or the BOOK facility of VAX DOCUMENT), then the master file shall be named as indicated above. The names of the secondary source files shall begin with the name of the master document source file (for example, 2010__US__C__XYZ).

D.3.5 Drawings

The drawing practices for application to this program are defined in accordance with TZA 7017. As stated herein, the overall reference is the "TZA Corporate Engineering Documentation Manual," as modified by the SPP Project Drafting Instruction, SPP-PI-0019.

D.4 CONFIGURATION CONTROL

D.4.1 Overview

Table D-VII identifies the configuration change control authority for the baselines established as part of this project. Each of these is discussed in the subsections that follow.

D.4.1.1 Functional Baseline Changes

All engineering changes, deviations, and waivers to the functional baseline shall be documented using engineering change proposals (ECPs), together with proposed specification change notices (SCNs) and proposed specification change pages, and shall be provided to the customer for approval.

D.4.1.2 Subsystem Allocated Baseline Changes

All changes to the subsystem allocated baseline shall be documented using engineering change proposals together with proposed specification change notices and proposed specification change pages, and shall be provided to the SPP project manager for approval. Copies of these items shall be provided for information only to the customer at the customer's request.

D.4.1.3 Allocated Baseline Changes

Changes to the allocated baseline shall be documented using engineering change proposals (pages 1 and 2 only), together with proposed specification change notices and proposed specification change pages, and shall be provided to the appropriate SPP subsystem manager for approval.

D.4.1.4 Hardware Design Baseline

Changes to the hardware design baseline are in two parts:

(a) Changes to hardware design documents shall be by revisions to those documents and shall be approved by the design activity.
(b) Changes to released drawings shall be by engineering change notices (ECNs).

D.4.1.5 Developmental Configuration Baseline Changes

Changes to the developmental configuration baseline are in three parts:

(a) Changes to software design documents after they become part of the developmental configuration shall be by revisions to those documents and shall be approved by the design activity.

TABLE D-VII. CONFIGURATION CHANGE APPROVAL AUTHORITY

Baseline	Approval Authority	Documentation
Functional	Customer	ECP/SCN/change pages
Subsystem allocated	Project manager	ECP/SCN/change pages
Allocated	Subsystem manager	ECP/SCN/change pages
Hardware design		
Design documents	Design activity	Revisions
Type 2 drawings	Design activity	ECN
Type 1 drawings	Project manager	ECN
Developmental configuration	Design activity	Revisions
Test		
Configuration item	Subsystem manager	ECP/SCN/ECN
Subsystem	Project manager	ECP/SCN/ECN
System	Customer	ECP/SCN/ECN
Product	Customer	ECP/SCN/ECN

(b) Changes to Category I and II software after they become part of the developmental configuration shall be by revisions to the source files and shall be approved by the design activity.
(c) If the changes in Category II software will require a drawing change, changes to that hardware will be processed concurrently and in accordance with Section D.4.1.4 above.

D.4.1.6 Test Baseline

D.4.1.6.1 Normal Changes

Changes to the test baseline are as follows:

(a) Changes to the configuration item test plans, test procedures, and test reports shall be submitted in the form of revisions to those documents and shall be approved by the subsystem manager concerned.
(b) Changes to the subsystem test plans, test procedures, and test reports shall be submitted in the form of revisions to those documents and shall be approved by the SPP project manager.
(c) The system test plans, test procedures, and test reports are submitted to the customer as specified in the associated contract data requirements list items. After initial approval of those documents, changes to those items will be submitted to the customer for approval. These changes will be in the form of revisions to the documents.
(d) Changes to the Category I and II software that are part of configuration items, subsystem, or system shall be by ECP/SCN (and ECN as appropriate). These shall be approved by the subsystem manager (for configuration item qualification tests), and the customer (for system qualification tests).
(e) Changes to the Category IV software that support these tests shall be by revisions. These shall be approved by the subsystem manager (for configuration item qualification tests), the project manager (for subsystem qualification tests), and by the customer (for system qualification tests).

D.4.1.6.2 Expedited Changes

D.4.1.6.2.1 Documentation: Test plans and test procedures may also be changed by "red-lining" the individual document.

(a) Such changes require the consent of the organization responsible for the item under test and the organization that approved the document being changed. Each such change shall be initialed and dated by the individuals concerned, signifying such agreement.
(b) A copy of the initialed "red-lined" copy of the changed document, together with a retyped version of the changed document reflecting such changes, shall be provided with the associated test report.

D.4.1.6.2.2 Software: Category I, II, and IV software may be changed by the authority of the appropriate test director.

(a) Such changes require the consent of the organization responsible for the item under test and the organization that approved the software being changed. Each such change shall be initialed and dated by the individuals concerned, signifying such agreement.
(b) Any such changes are considered temporary and require submission of an appropriate change package for formal approval at the next configuration control board.

D.4.1.7 Product Baseline Changes

All engineering changes to the product baseline shall be documented using engineering change proposals. Proposed specification change notices, proposed specification change pages, and/or engineering change notices, revised source files, and DIFFERENCE files, shall be attached as appropriate, depending on the items being changed.

D.4.2 Software Change Control

D.4.2.1 Change Levels

Control of software changes shall be at the source file level. Code will not be controlled at the source line of code level.

D.4.2.2 Approval of Entry of New Source Files

The entry of new source files (for example, source files that have not been previously entered in the configuration management library) shall require the approval of the design activity. The authorization to make these entries shall be documented using a source file entry request (see TZA 7043).

D.4.2.3 Category I, II, and IV Software Changes

These are covered as baseline changes.

D.4.2.4 Category III Software Changes

Category III software (for example, VAX/VMS 11.7) shall be controlled by the SPP project manager. Proposed changes and proposed upgrades to this software shall be submitted to the SPP project manager by memo, identifying the name and version proposed to be installed. These changes shall only be made after approval of the SPP program manager.

D.4.2.5 Category V Software Changes

Changes to Category V software will be revisions and will be approved by the design activity.

D.4.3 Problem Reporting System

...

D.4.4 Corrective Action System

There are a number of documents used to implement changes:

(a) Approved changes to baselined documents are distributed using approved specification change notices and approved specification change pages.

(b) Approved changes to released drawings are made using approved engineering change notices only.

  (1) When authorization is required outside of TZA to change a released drawing, a copy of the draft engineering change notice will be attached to the engineering change proposal requesting such changes.

  (2) When direction is received from the customer to implement a change that will require change in a released drawing, the SPP project manager will initiate an engineering change notice to accomplish that change.

D.4.4.1 Processing of Approved Request for Waivers and Requests for Deviations

These items are processed as approved changes to the contract and are handled as contract changes.

D.4.5 Configuration Control Boards

D.4.5.1 SPP Configuration Control Board

All changes for which the SPP project manager has responsibility or that the SPP project manager reviews prior to forwarding to the customer shall be processed through the SPP configuration control board. Details of that process are specified in SPP-PI-057, which is the specific implementation of TZA 2910 for this project.

D.4.5.2 Other Configuration Control Boards

...

D.4.6 Expedited Processing

D.4.6.1 CCB Action

The chair of the SPP configuration control board (or a designee) may, for good and sufficient reasons, act directly for the SPP configuration control board. In such cases, the determinations that are made by the Chair shall be reduced to writing and shall be provided to the SPP configuration control board at their next meeting.

D.4.6.2 Delegations of Authority

Delegations of the authority for actions in this plan (for example, to the SPP test director to approve interim software changes, or by the design activity manager to lower-level manager to approve hardware design changes) may be made for good and sufficient reasons. Any such delegations shall be made by SPP project instruction.

D.5 CONFIGURATION STATUS ACCOUNTING

D.5.1 TZA Configuration System Reports

As specified in TZA 2858, a mechanized system, the TZA configuration system, is used to record and retrieve all TZA documentation assigned a drawing number.

(a) Sample reports available from this system for the SPP effort are as follows:

(1) The title file project bulletin provides a list of all drawings and all non-TZA parts for the SPP, together with an indication of the release status of all outstanding engineering change notices.
(2) The assembly status listing provides a list of all assemblies on the SPP, the associated reference drawings for all the assemblies, and the drawing release status of each drawing.
(3) The generation breakdown provides a breakdown in list form of an assembly and all its subassemblies to the level requested with each indenture indicated (for example, complete breakdown or assemblies only).
(4) The parts variation report provides a list of parts from a given assembly breakdown, which indicates quantity variations compared with the previous breakdown of the same assembly.
(5) The parts applications list provides a list of all the parts contained within a given breakdown in numerical sequence, including the quantity of the item used in each assembly and a summary of the total quantity used in the particular breakdown.
(6) The parts list provides a tabulated list of all parts, materials, subordinate assemblies, and referenced data required to fabricate, assemble, or install the items delineated on the drawing to which the list applies.
(7) The problem report status provides a list of open/closed problem reports in either problem report numbers or drawing number sequences.

(b) In accordance with TZA 2856 and as indicated in Table D-VIII, an SPP program instruction is to be prepared to specify unique SPP requirements for configuration status accounting purposes.

D.5.2 SPP Configuration Status Accounting Report

This is a formal report and provides the complete status of:

(a) The contract, including the statement of work and other contract documents
(b) The SPP system specification and the other documents identified in the SPP document tree (see Section D.3.1)
(c) The SPP equipment planning diagrams
(d) Program plans
(e) Problem reports
(f) Proposed changes
(g) Implementation of approved changes

D.6 CONFIGURATION AUDITS AND REVIEWS

D.6.1 Common Actions

The following subsections are common to all configuration audits and reviews.

D.6.1.1 Location

Unless otherwise specified, all reviews and audits will be held at the TZA facility in Red Rock, WI.

D.6.1.2 Pre-Meeting Actions

Prior to the meeting:

(a) TZA shall provide to the customer an agenda, which describes the sequence of topics to be covered in the conduct of the meeting. This initial agenda shall be provided 60 days prior to the start of the meeting.
(b) The customer will provide comments by fax 30 days prior to the start of the meeting.
(c) TZA will provide a revised agenda to the customer by fax 15 days prior to the start of the meeting.

D.6.1.3 TZA Meeting Actions

TZA shall:

(a) Provide facilities, personnel, and documentation to conduct the meeting.
(b) Be given the opportunity to prove to the audit team that any potential discrepancy is in fact an allowable difference. If the audit team chair concurs, the potential discrepancy shall be omitted from the audit work sheet.

D.6.1.3.1 Customer Actions

The customer will:

(a) Provide the meeting chair
(b) Conduct the meeting in accordance with the agenda
(c) Complete and sign the meeting audit forms

D.6.1.4 Post-Meeting Actions

On completion of the meeting, TZA shall prepare a meeting report. This report shall document the meeting findings and planned corrective actions for reported discrepancies.

D.6.2 Level 3 Drawing Review

The purpose of the Level 3 drawing review is to verify that the Level 3 drawing package conforms to requirements (see Section 6.2.1 of the statement of work).

D.6.2.1 Initiating Actions

When at least 50% of the Level 3 drawings have been completed, TZA shall initiate the actions leading to the review.

D.6.2.2 Pre-Level 3 Drawing Review Actions

(a) TZA shall provide the following material to the customer not later than 60 days prior to the Level 3 drawing review:

(1) A list of completed Level 3 drawings
(2) A copy of the first of each document type

(b) The customer will identify to TZA, not later than 30 days prior to the review, a maximum of 30% of the drawings listed to be reviewed.

D.6.3 Concept of Formal Audits

The concept is as follows:

(a) Functional configuration audits (FCAs) and physical configuration audits (PCAs) will be conducted on the hardware and firmware configuration items in Table D-II.
(b) Following successful conclusion of a functional configuration audit on an individual item, the physical configuration audit will be conducted.
(c) Functional configuration audits and physical configuration audits:

(1) On a particular item will be serial.
(2) May be interleaved across the entire set of items for cost effectiveness. For example, it will not be necessary to complete the functional configuration audits on all items before beginning the physical configuration audit on an item that has successfully completed its functional configuration audit.

(d) Traceability of the configurations after the successful completion of the functional configuration audits and physical configuration audits will be maintained through the submission to the customer of engineering change proposals.

D.6.4 Functional Configuration Audits

The purpose of the functional configuration audits is to verify that the hardware is compliant with the requirements of the development specifications and to confirm the satisfactory completion of the hardware qualification tests.

D.6.4.1 Pre-FCA Actions

Prior to the functional configuration audit, TZA shall provide the following material to EPU:

(a) A copy of the approved qualification test plans, approved test procedures, and approved test reports for each of the hardware configuration items.
(b) A copy of all problem reports written during the conduct of the qualification tests that were identified in the approved test report as "OPEN." Accompanying each of these discrepancy reports shall be the follow-up actions taken since the issuance of the approved test report to resolve those discrepancies, together with any documentation associated with any further testing.
(c) A list of all outstanding changes made to the hardware and the hardware documentation. This listing shall include all changes in the process of being incorporated in the hardware and documentation and any requests for waivers and/or deviations.

D.6.5 Physical Configuration Audits

D.6.5.1 Scope

The scope of the physical configuration audit is as follows:

(a) The audit will be conducted on the hardware and the hardware component of firmware.
(b) The audit will be a comparison of the hardware to the documentation identified in Section 4.9.2 of the statement of work.
(c) The level of the audit is such that disassembly of the hardware will not be required, but removal of modular replaceable assemblies shall be accomplished to make all assemblies for the audit visible.

D.6.5.2 Additional Pre-PCA Actions

Prior to the physical configuration audit, TZA shall provide the following material to EPU:

(a) Certificate of completion and EPU approval of the functional configuration audit.
(b) Product baseline engineering drawings.
(c) A list of outstanding changes to hardware and hardware documentation, including all changes in the process of being incorporated in the hardware and documentation.

D.7 ARCHIVING

See TZA 6666.

D.8 SUBCONTRACTOR/VENDOR CONTROL

Subcontractors and vendors are controlled at the same level as TZA internal activities. The administrative process of subcontractor and vendor selection, monitoring, control, and communication are described in detail in the TZA SPP acquisition plan.

D.8.1 Subcontractors

Each subcontractor is required to provide a disciplined environment and the administrative procedural framework necessary to accomplish configuration change control. As a part of this activity, each subcontractor is required to provide a subcontract configuration management plan to state in detail how the configuration management activities specified in the subcontract statement of work will be organized, managed, and executed.

D.8.2 Vendors

Vendor procurements are specified by part numbers, specification control drawings, or source control drawings. Vendor material is inspected at the vendor's plant by TZA field quality control or upon receipt at TZA by the purchased material quality inspection activity.

D.8.3 Non-Developed Items Change Control

These will be handled as follows:

(a) Changes will be proposed by the subcontractors/vendors as part of their normal enhancement process as revisions.
(b) All changes to items baselined with EPU will be handled through the use of engineering change proposals in accordance with the requirements of Sections D.4.3.7, D.4.4.1, and D.4.5 of this plan.
(c) All changes to items on which drawings have been released inside TZA but that are not baselined with EPU shall be processed using engineering change notices in accordance with the requirements of Sections D.4.3.7, D.4.4.1, and D.4.5 of this plan.

D.9 PROGRAM PHASING

Major milestones for the implementation of configuration management are shown in Table D-VIII.

D.10 RESOURCES AND ORGANIZATION

D.10.1 Organizational Structure

The TZA SPP program manager has total responsibility for the SPP project. As part of the SPP planning effort, the TZA SPP configuration management plan has been produced to provide overall policy and planning guidance for configuration management throughout this project.

D.10.2 Staff Support

Generalized support is provided by the following organizations:

(a) TZA Quality Assurance provides independent staff support to this configuration management effort in accordance with the approved TZA quality assurance plan.
(b) TZA Information Control provides a centralized point of document distribution and retention. As a part of that effort, Information Control provides a list of all the internal data generated in compliance with the work effort described in the statement of work.
(c) The TZA Computer Program Library provides secure storage facilities for electronic media (tapes and disks).

D.10.3 SPP Configuration Management Organization

D.10.4 Personnel

This identifies the numbers and skill levels of the personnel required to implement this plan.

TABLE D-VIII. CONFIGURATION MANAGEMENT—MAJOR MILESTONES

Item	Date
⋮	⋮

APPENDIX E

PLAN FOR A GENERIC CM PLAN

E.1 INTRODUCTION

Current management direction at XYZ Company is that each project will have a configuration management (CM) plan that will establish the policies and procedures by which the integrity of the products will be maintained. In the implementation of that direction it appears that it would reduce overall costs by preparation of a generic plan which could be then be tailored on a project-by-project basis.

E.1.1 Purpose

The purpose of this document is to provide a plan for the creation of a generic configuration management plan.

E.1.2 Scope

The scope of this plan includes the software component of firmware and the associated test software to include the documentation and the code. This plan does not cover the hardware aspects of firmware (for example, altered-item drawings) except where such items are necessary for coverage of the software aspects.

E.1.3 Use

The output of this plan would be a generic CM plan that could be tailored with minimum efforts to development projects inside XYZ Company.

E.2 REFERENCES

MIL-STD-973, *Configuration Management,* 17 April 1994

E.3 GUIDANCE

The generic CM plan should:

(a) Use the format provided in Appendix A of MIL-STD-973.

   (1) Where a section heading in Appendix A of MIL-STD-973 is not applicable to this plan, the section heading will be kept and the words "This section does not apply to this effort" will be placed as the only contents in that section.

   (2) It will be recommended in the tailoring portion of the generic plan that when the generic plan is tailored for application to a specific project, that these unused sections be placed in the tailored plan. This will ease the tailoring of generic CM procedures for that project. (Otherwise the references in the generic CM procedures will not be accurate.)

(b) Assume that there is a project management plan (PMP) for the project and refer to the PMP for organizational details.

(c) Be organized so that it would fit various size projects. The manner in which it should approach this requirement is to place the details of such items as specification trees, configuration change control authorities, and so forth in numbered generic CM procedures, which themselves can be tailored to the project specifics.

(d) Comply with the current XYZ Engineering Instructions (EIs) and management policies.

(e) Successfully pass an audit by Quality Assurance (QA).

(f) Build on the current project CM plans and others as appropriate.

(g) Be coordinated extensively with the projected users, and QA.

(h) Be composed using a commercial word processor.

(i) Be annotated, where appropriate, to provide:

(1) A reference to requirements placed by other documents; for example, EIs. This would provide the rationale for the requirement and ease the preparation of an explicit Request For Deviation if the requirement in the EI should not be implemented on a specific project.
(2) The reasons why certain statements are made in the generic plan.

E.4 APPROACH

The approach to be used to produce this generic CM plan is as follows:

(a) Produce a draft outline to the third level. (This outline will change as the plan proceeds but will provide a stable platform for the development of the details.)
(b) Initiate the coordination of the draft outline with the projected users and QA. This should be done on a walk-around basis, contacting the individuals directly and leaving hard copy for review. Concurrently with this coordination, the person doing the coordination (assumed to be the CM plan writer) should ask for other views, insights, and suggestions.
(c) Review existing CM plans to ascertain what approaches are in use at this time and which have been successful.
(d) Fill in the draft outline.
(e) Initiate a second round of coordination similar item (b) above. This would be a formal coordination with written comments requested. This would further require a meeting with those who have provided comments to ensure that the comments have been understood and the thoughts behind the comments correctly implemented.
(f) Initiate the formal approval cycle.

E.5 SCHEDULE

See attached schedule.

E.6 COSTS

The costs associated with this are estimated as 2.5 man-months of effort.

E.7 ADDITIONAL EFFORTS

Follow-on efforts will be required to provide a set of generic implementing CM procedures. This would require three activities:

(a) Development of a format for the procedures.
(b) Development of a set of generic procedures for interfaces outside of the CM activity.
(c) Development of a set of step-by-step objective procedures for the activities inside the CM group such that they could be correctly executed by a person who had no direct knowledge of the project.

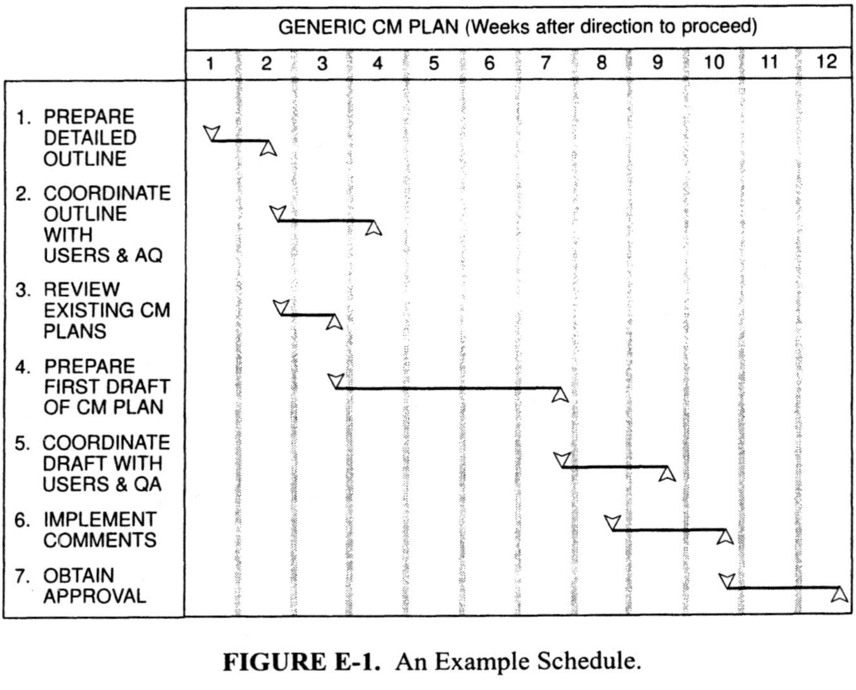

FIGURE E-1. An Example Schedule.

APPENDIX F

A GENERIC CONFIGURATION MANAGEMENT PLAN EXAMPLE

This appendix provides an example generic configuration management plan. This plan:

(a) Is designed to be tailored to provide a project configuration management plan.

(b) Is composed to minimize the project funds required to: (1) tailor it to a specific project, and, (2) participate in third-party audits and respond to action items. Realizing it is much more cost-effective to delete than to add, this document provides a complete CM plan. If an item is not to be done by CM (for example, control of the functional baseline), then: (1) that part of the plan dealing with the functional baseline should be deleted, and, (2) a corresponding statement placed in Section F.1.2 stating that actions involving the functional baseline are beyond the scope of this plan.

(c) Uses the format provided in Appendix A of MIL-STD-973.

(1) When a section heading in Appendix A of MIL-STD-973 is not applicable to this plan, the section heading has been kept and the words "This section does not apply to this effort" or equivalent words have been placed as the only contents in that section.

(2) When the generic plan is tailored for application to a specific project, the unused section titles should be identified in the tai-

lored plan. This will ease the tailoring of generic CM procedures for that project. (Otherwise the references in the generic CM procedures will not be accurate.)

(d) Assumes that there is a project management plan (PMP), a software or firmware development plan, or other project planning documentation that identifies for the project the tasks to be performed, funding, the schedule, and the organizations and individuals responsible. If one of those higher-level documents is not available, then this plan will require augmentation.
(e) Is organized so that it will fit various size projects. The manner in which it approaches this requirement is to place the majority of the details in numbered generic CM procedures which can be tailored to the project specifics.

18 JULY 19XX
GEN-SYS-SCMP

GENERIC CONFIGURATION MANAGEMENT PLAN

FOR

XYZ CORPORATION

(TBD)-SYS-CMP

CONFIGURATION MANAGEMENT PLAN

For The

(PROJECT NAME OR CI NOMENCLATURE AND NUMBER)

CONTRACT NO. (TBD)
CDRL SEQUENCE NUMBER (TBD)
1 AUGUST 199X

Prepared For:
(TBD)

Prepared By:

XYZ Company
...

DRAFT

RECORD OF REVIEW AND HISTORY

Change No.	Date Approved	List Of Changed Pages
1.		

TABLE OF CONTENTS

LIST OF FIGURES

LIST OF TABLES

F.1 INTRODUCTION

This is the configuration management plan for the (TBD) project and follows the format and content instructions of Appendix A of MIL-STD-973. This plan is accompanied by and makes reference to the SCM procedures manual for this project which specifies additional details associated with this effort.

F.1.1 Purpose

The purpose of this plan is to describe the methods and techniques for maintaining the integrity of the designated products.

F.1.2 Scope

(This is an example set of scope statements. These should be tailored to explicitly identify what is included in this plan and what is not included in this plan.)

The scope of this plan includes:

(a) The deliverable hardware and software products.
(b) The software component of the deliverable firmware products.
(c) The software component of firmware embedded in test system equipment.
(d) The test software used to determine that the software component of the firmware meets its requirements.
(e) The requirements and design documentation used to develop the software component of the designated firmware and the associated test software.
(f) The vendor-provided and other software in the associated software development environments.

This plan does not include:

(a) Configuration management of the hardware component of the deliverable firmware products, nor the preparation and control of the altered item drawings used to document the firmware products.
(b) Staff supervision or audit of CM aspects of subcontracts.

F.1.3 Contractual Applicability

This plan is produced in accordance with the requirements of CDRL (TBD) of the contract and is fully compliant with the requirements of that CDRL.

F.1.4 Program Phases

This plan applies to the actions of the Engineering Department in the development phases of this effort as defined in section (TBD) of the (TBD) project management plan (*or software development plan, and so forth*).

F.1.5 System Description

(Provide a brief description of the system with a figure that shows the relationships from the system level down to the configuration items. Then provide a reference to the document where additional details are provided.)

The DO_MORE radar provides simultaneous surveillance and tracking functions on multiple targets. As shown in Figure F-1, the DO MORE system consists of five HWCIs and three CSCIs. The Signal Processor Firm-

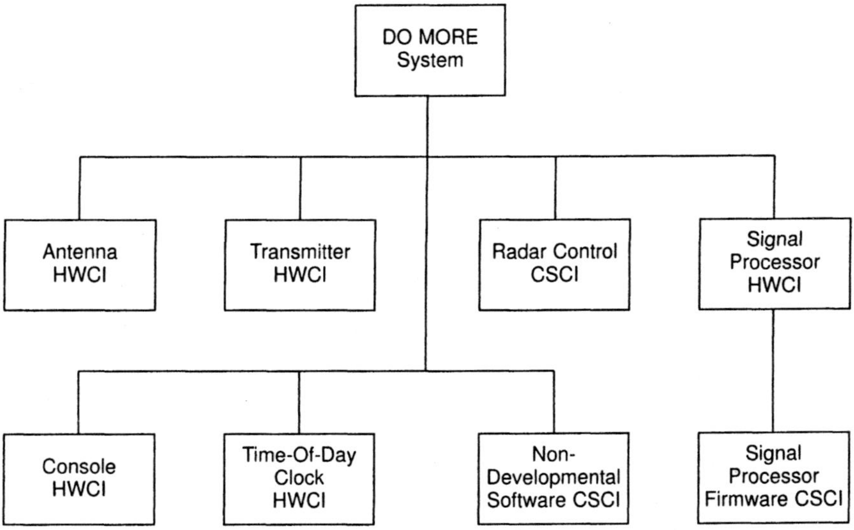

FIGURE F-1. DO MORE System Components.

ware CSCI is shown as proceeding from the Signal Processor HWCI as it derives its requirements from the Signal Processor HWCI. For additional details on the DO MORE system, see the *System Specification For The DO MORE Radar.*

(This view of the CIs may be tailored to show the further decomposition down to additional firmware entities.)

F.1.6 Definitions and Acronyms

(a) Unless otherwise noted in the body of this plan, the definitions and acronyms used in this plan are found in Section 3 of MIL-STD-973, *Configuration Management,* and Section 3 of DOD-STD-2167A, *Defense System Software Development.*

(b) The use of the term *firmware* in this plan is implied to mean the software component of firmware unless otherwise: (1) explicitly stated in this plan to apply to the combination of both the software and the hardware components of firmware, or, (2) clear from the context of its use.

F.1.7 Plan Description

This section provides a description of the plan's major features and objectives and a concise summary of XYZ's approach to CM, including any special conditions applicable to this effort.

F.1.7.1 Major Features And Objectives

The major feature of this plan is the cost-effective application of configuration management techniques to maintain the integrity of the designated items. The objective is to apply these techniques in a manner that will be as unobtrusive as possible to the system developers.

This CM plan is the governing document for the configuration management activities on this project. When this plan is approved by the appropriate section and project managers, this is the authority and approval to tailor downward (deviate) from any other requirements specified in the XYZ Company policies and engineering instructions.

F.1.7.2 Summary Of XYZ's Approach To CM

XYZ's approach to CM is to provide CM services from entities that are separate from and not under the control of the developing organization. This ensures that the maintenance of the integrity of the products will not be compromised under the pressure of development schedules.

F.1.7.3 Special Conditions

Special conditions that bear on the configuration management activities are as follows: (Some examples are provided in the following subsections. if none, then state "None" and delete the sections.)

F.1.7.3.1 Security Constraints

(For example, this would have to be consistent with the plans for a classified project; this may involve physically separating parts of the SCML, etc.)

F.1.7.3.2 Interoperability Constraints

(This may include considerations associated with the situation when the host and target machines are different.)

F.1.7.3.3 Non-Developmental Items

(These may require different handling from a CM viewpoint.)

F.2 REFERENCE DOCUMENTS

The following documents of the exact issue shown, apply to the extent specified elsewhere in this plan.

F.2.1 DoD Standards And Specifications

(a) MIL-STD-973, *Configuration Management*, w/Notice 1 Dec 1992
(b) DOD-STD-2167A, *Defense System Software Development*, 29 February 1988
(c) MIL-S-83490, *Specifications, Forms And Types*, 30 October 1968

F.2.2 Contract Documents

F.2.3 XYZ Standard Procedures And Engineering Instructions

(a) ...

F.2.4 Other XYZ Documents

(a) ...

F.2.5 (TBD) Project Documents

(a) (Project Management Plan)
(b) (Software Development Plan For Product Software)
(c) (Software Development Plan For Test Software)
(d) (Firmware Development Plan)
(e) (QA Program Plan)
(f) [(TBD) Project CM Procedures Manual]

F.3 ORGANIZATION

This section describes the relationship of XYZ Government Electronic System's project management to configuration management, and the integration of CM activities with other project management activities.

F.3.1 XYZ Functional Organization

This section provides an overview of the functional organization of XYZ Company with emphasis on the CM activities. For additional details, see the (TBD) project management plan (or software development plan, etc.).

As shown in Figure F-2, XYZ is organized functionally with elements of the functional organizations assigned to specific project teams as needed.

(a) The (TBD) project office tasks other elements of Government Electronics Systems for support as appropriate.
(b) The Engineering Department provides a centralized skill base for engineering efforts and will provide specific engineering skills as they are required as the (TBD) project progresses through development, production, and life-cycle support.

(c) Product Assurance develops, implements and maintains contractually-compliant product/quality assurance systems that assure product quality at optimum costs and that satisfy contractual and internal requirements.

As shown in Figure 3, the Engineering Department is organized into skill centers functionally with elements assigned to specific projects as needed.

(a) ...

F.3.2 (TBD) Project Office

(Reference Figure F-4 and provide a brief statement of the duties of each of the organizational elements that interface with SCM.)

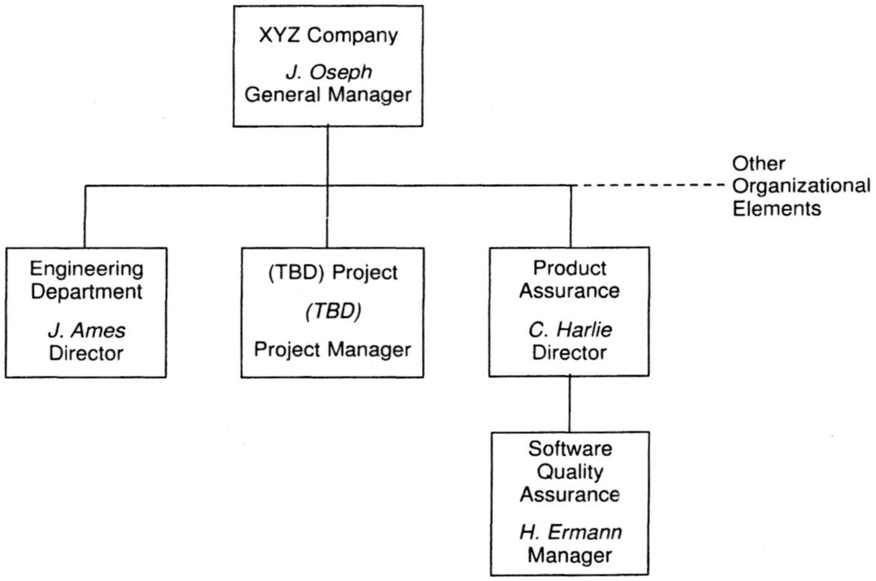

FIGURE F-2. The XYZ Functional Structure for (TBD) Project.

. . . .

FIGURE F-3. The Engineering Department Organization.

For additional details, see the Project Management Plan, CDRL XXX (or the software development plan, etc.)

F.3.3 (TBD) Project CM Organization And Responsibilities

As shown in Figure F-4, the SCM manager reports operationally for this project to the (TBD) manager while Figure F-5 shows the detailed organization of the SCM activity for the (TBD) project.

The software CM organization has the following responsibilities:

(a) The identification element prepares and updates this CM plan, supporting procedures and associated CM project instructions. This is an ongoing effort that documents the objective processes by which the SCM organization performs its tasks. The procedures are continually updated on a "red-lined" basis as operations evolve and changes are made to resolve ambiguities, reflect productivity improvements, or implement project instructions. The "red-lined" plan, procedures, and instructions are kept in the SCM area for reference for all concerned and for use in preparing official updates as appropriate. See SCM Procedure (TBD).

(b) The change control element receives in draft form from the originator and prepares in final form all Engineering Change Proposals (ECPs), Specification Change Notices (SCNs), Change Pages, Differences (the results of running a buffered-compare program between old and new files), Requests For Deviations (RFDs), Requests For Waivers (RFWs) and Notices Of Revisions (NORs) to be processed by the Configuration Control Board (CCB).The change control element is also the secretariat for the (TBD) project CCB. *(If ECPs are controlled elsewhere; for example, by a production PMO, then that should be stated in this subparagraph.)*

(c) The status accounting element prepares and distributes configuration status accounting reports (CSARs), metrics, and coordinates with Data Management (DM) for the delivery of all CM items that are inside the scope of this plan and that are required by the Contract Data Requirements List (CDRL). Status accounting information associated with engineering drawings and associated lists will be provided by the hardware configuration management element.

(TBD)

FIGURE F-4. The (TBD) Project Management Office.

(d) The audits element is responsible for the coordination and support of physical configuration audits (PCAs) and functional configuration audits (FCAs) conducted by the customer.

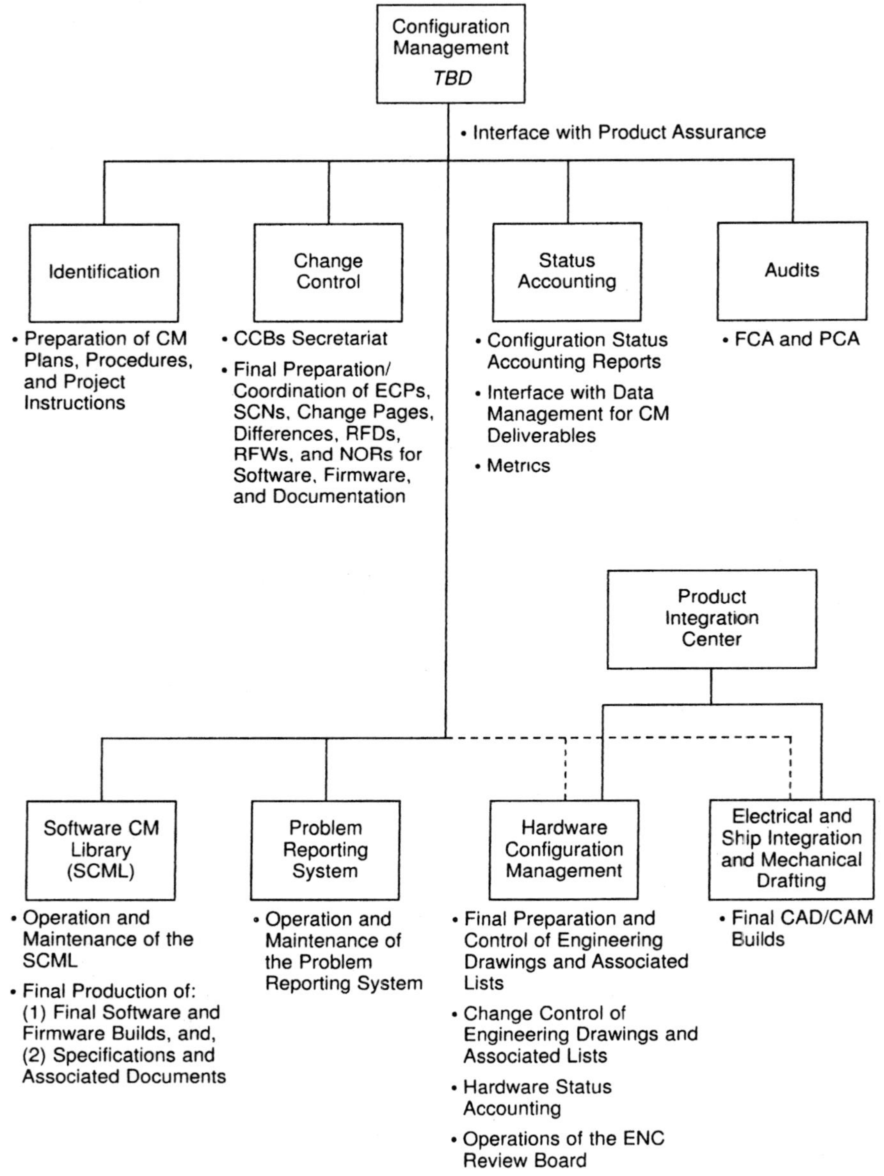

FIGURE F-5. Configuration Management Organization.

(e) The software configuration management library (SCML) element operates and maintains the SCML, which is the controlled access repository for all software and firmware to be controlled by SCM. The SCML element receives from the responsible individuals (RI)s, the source material and *(depending on the project)* the command files (scripts) necessary to produce the final products under controlled, objective conditions. Using that material, the SCML element controls, produces and releases:

   (1) The development builds and the QA builds.
   (2) The final software builds (including the builds of the software component of firmware) for all formal testing and delivery.
   (3) All software configuration documentation (except engineering drawings and associated lists). (This may be released to a specific group; for example, in NSD, that is responsible for CDRL processing. If so, that group should be identified in this subparagraph.)

(f) The problem reporting system element is responsible for the operation and maintenance of the problem reporting system. This includes training developers in the operation of the system and ensuring that a smooth interface exists between the developers and the associated tool.

(g) Hardware CM support is provided on a plant-wide basis by Hardware Configuration Management to all ongoing projects. As noted on Figure F-5, that organization is part of the Product Integration Center and not part of the scope of this CM plan.

To accomplish these tasks, the SCM activities will be staffed with the following personnel: (TBD) *(provide levels and durations against tasks in an accompanying figure).*

F.3.4 Other Organizational Interfaces

F.3.4.1 Data Management

Figure F-4 shows the organizational placement of the (TBD) project data management organization. Data management is responsible for obtaining approval, and for the delivery and distribution of all CDRL items to the customer. The direct interface between configuration management and data management is that configuration management will deliver one copy of the required CDRL item to data management. Data management will arrange for duplication and distribution of the items in accordance with the CDRL requirements.

{If CM is to do the DM task [for example, (1) establish across-the-project document numbering schemes, (2) maintain hard-copy record, restricted access storage of all project documentation, (3) provide duplication and distribution services, and the like], then these tasks need to be separately identified, estimated, and funded. They should be in the CM plan if the work is to be done by the CM organization; however, the funds for these tasks should not be mixed with the funds allocated for CM tasks.}

F.3.4.2 Subcontractor Relationships

There are no subcontractors for which the SCM organization has responsibility.

F.3.4.3 Configuration Control Boards

As shown in Figure F-6, the (TBD) project includes a number of configuration control boards (CCBs). The roles of CM in these boards is shown in Table F-I. The functions, responsibilities and authorities of these boards are covered in Section F.8.1.

F.3.4.4 Integration Of CM Functions With Other Project Activities

Table F-II shows the integration of CM activities with other project activities such as technical reviews. *(This table should be reviewed against the project design reviews to be held in accordance with other project documents to ensure that it reflects any other reviews; for example, firmware requirements reviews.)*

TABLE F-I. THE CM ROLE IN PROJECT CCB

CCB	CM Role
Project CCB	Acts as secretariat
Software CCB	Acts as secretariat
Hardware CCB	Acts as secretariat
ECN review board	None
Problem report board	Acts as secretariat

F.3.4.5 Interfaces Between (TBD) Project CM And The Government

None

F.3.4.6 Interfaces Between (TBD) Project CM And Subcontractors

None

F.3.4.7 Interfaces Between (TBD) Project CM And Associate Contractors

None

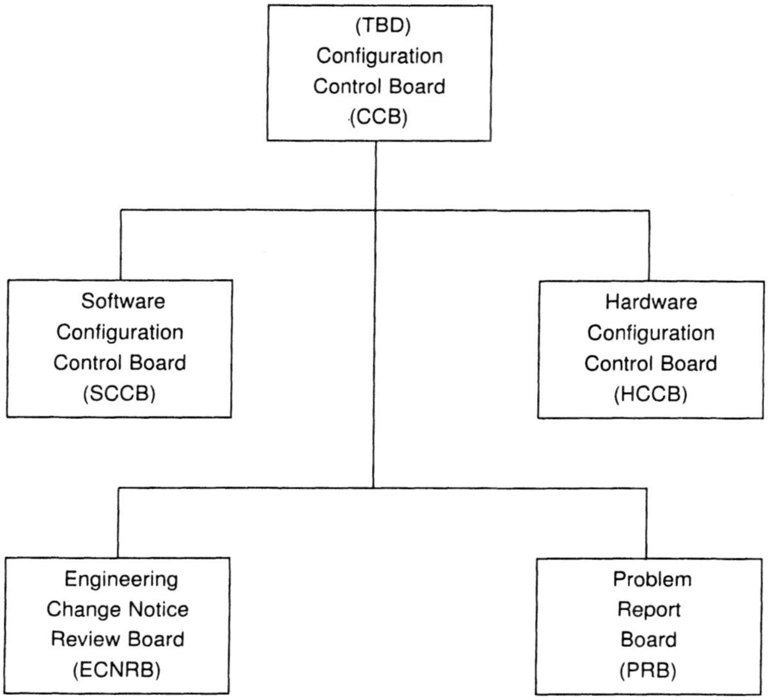

FIGURE F-6. (TBD) Project Configuration Control Boards.

TABLE F-II. SCM INTEGRATION WITH OTHER PROJECT ACTIVITIES

Item No.	Project Activity	SCM Functions
1.	System requirements review	(1) Provide a controlled copy of the functional configuration documentation to data management for duplication and distribution (TBD) days prior to the start of the scheduled review. (2) Provide a revision of the functional configuration documentation to data management for duplication and distribution (TBD) days.
2.	System design review	(1) Provide a controlled copy of the functional configuration documentation to data management for duplication and distribution (TBD) days prior to the start of the scheduled review. (2) Provide a revision of the functional configuration documentation to data management for duplication and distribution (TBD) days after the end of the scheduled review and establish these documents as the functional baseline.
3.	Software requirements review	(1) Provide a controlled copy of the allocated configuration documentation to data management for duplication and distribution (TBD) days prior to the start of the scheduled review. (2) Provide a revision of the allocated configuration documentation to data management for duplication and distribution (TBD) days after the end of the scheduled review and establish these documents as the allocated baseline.
4.	Preliminary design review	(1) Provide a controlled copy of the developmental configuration documentation to data management for duplication and distribution (TBD) days prior to the start of the scheduled review. (2) Provide a revision of the developmental configuration documentation to data management for duplication and distribution (TBD) days after the end of the scheduled review.
5.	Critical design review	(1) Provide a controlled copy of the developmental configuration documentation to data management for duplication and distribution (TBD) days prior to the start of the scheduled review. (2) Provide a revision of the developmental configuration documentation to data management for duplication and distribution (TBD) days after the end of the scheduled review.
6.	Formal tests	(1) Provide a controlled copy of the draft and final formal test plans and test procedures to data management for duplication and distribution prior to the start of the scheduled test. (2) Receive from the test manager a copy of the "red-lines" to the formal test plan and test procedures immediately after completion of the formal test. (3) Provide a witnessed controlled copy of the image file and the associated test software prior to the start of the scheduled test to (a) QA for use in test activities. (b) The IIS computer library for archiving.
7.	Internal review	(1) Provide a controlled copy of the appropriate configuration documentation to data management for duplication and distribution (TBD) days prior to the start of the scheduled review. (2) Provide a revision of the appropriate configuration documentation to data management for duplication and distribution (TBD) days.

F.4 CONFIGURATION MANAGEMENT PHASING AND MILESTONES

Table F-III describes the sequence of events and milestones for the implementation of CM under this plan. (This table should be reviewed against the project design reviews to be held in accordance with the other project documents to ensure that it reflects any other reviews; for example, firmware requirements reviews.)

Figure F-7 graphically portrays the sequence of milestones for implementing CM in phase with major program milestones.

F.5 DATA MANAGEMENT

There are no computer-aided acquisition and logistic support (CALS) requirements in this contract.

F.6 CONFIGURATION IDENTIFICATION

F.6.1 Selection Of Configuration Items

The selection of configuration items has already been completed and is beyond the scope of this plan. See Section F.1.5. for identification and description of the configuration items. *(This is a system engineering responsibility and by the time the CM plan is published, the CIs have already been chosen.)*

F.6.2 Establishment And Management Of The Developmental Configuration

See CM procedure (TBD).

F.6.3 Establishment Of The Project Baselines

See CM procedure (TBD).

(TBD)

FIGURE F-7. Sequence of CM Events and Milestones.

TABLE F-III. CONFIGURATION MANAGEMENT MILESTONES AND PHASING

Milestone Number	Major Project Milestone	SCM Milestone	Phasing
CM-1.	System requirements review	Submittal of draft functional configuration documentation	(TBD) days prior to start of review
CM-2.	System design review	Submittal of draft functional configuration documentation	(TBD) days prior to start of review
CM-3.		(1) Release of functional configuration documentation (2) Establishment of: (a) The functional baseline (b) The project CCB (c) Customer control of the functional baseline. (3) Initiation of configuration status accounting reports	(TBD) days after completion of review
CM-4.	Software specification review	Submittal of draft allocated configuration documentation	(TBD) days prior to start of review
CM-5.		(1) Release of allocated configuration documentation (2) Establishment of: (a) The allocated baseline (b) Internal control of the allocated baseline	(TBD) days after completion of review
CM-6.	Preliminary design review	Provision of draft developmental configuration documentation	(TBD) days prior to start of review
CM-7.		(1) Release of developmental configuration documentation (2) Establishment of: (a) The initial developmental configuration (b) Internal control of the initial developmental configuration	(TBD) days after completion of review
CM-8.	Critical design review	Provision of draft developmental configuration documentation	(TBD) days prior to start of review
CM-9.		(1) Release of developmental configuration documentation (2) Establishment of: (a) The subsequent developmental configuration (b) Internal control of the subsequent developmental configuration	(TBD) days after completion of review
CM-10.	Physical configuration audits	Submittal of draft product baseline configuration documentation	(TBD) days prior to start of audit
CM-11.		(1) Release of product baseline configuration (2) Establishment of: (a) The product baseline (b) Government control of the product baseline.	(TBD) days after completion of audit

F.6.4 Engineering Release And Correlation Of Manufactured Products

See CM procedure (TBD).

F.6.5 Assignment And Application Of Configuration Identifiers

See CM procedure (TBD).

F.6.6 Forms

Unless otherwise stated in project documentation, all configuration documentation will be produced to form 1b requirements as specified by MIL-S-83490. As part of this, the pagination will not necessarily be in accordance with Section A.4.1, Appendix A, MIL-STD-973.

F.7 INTERFACE MANAGEMENT

F.7.1 Identification Of Interface Requirements

Interface requirements will be identified in interface requirements specifications (IRSs) and interface control drawings.

F.7.2 Establishment Of Interface Agreements

This does not apply to this plan.

F.7.3 Participation In Interface Control Working Groups (ICWGs)

This does not apply to this plan.

F.8 CONFIGURATION CONTROL

F.8.1 Functions, Responsibilities and Authorities Of CCBs

See CM procedure (TBD).

F.8.2 Classification Of Changes

See CM procedure (TBD).

F.8.3 Change Approval Authorities

See CM procedure (TBD).

F.8.4 Processing Of Class I ECPs and VECPs

See CM procedure (TBD).

F.8.5 Processing Of Class II ECPs

See CM procedure (TBD).

F.8.6 Processing Of Requests for Deviations And Requests for Waivers

See CM procedure (TBD).

F.8.7 Processing Of Specification Change Notices

See CM procedure (TBD).

F.8.8 Processing Of Notices Of Revision (NORs)

See CM procedure (TBD).

F.8.9 Problem Reporting System

Three anomaly-reporting systems will be applied to this project.

(a) The failure and discrepancy report (FDR) is the primary means of recording hardware, system, or documentation discrepancies that occur in acceptance testing. These will be processed in accordance with the requirements of XYZ Standard Procedure 777.
(b) The problem sheet (PS) is the primary means of of recording discrepancies associated with systems, equipment, material and parts,

and the associated documentation that arise during ordering, procurement, manufacturing, operation, inspection, and test as well as installation of equipment at local or remote sites. These will be processed in accordance with XYZ Standard Procedure 778.

(c) The problem report (PR) is the primary method of recording discrepancies associated with hardware, software, firmware, or documentation not covered by either of the other two forms.

F.8.9.1 Problem Report Contents

See CM procedure (TBD).

F.8.9.2 Procedures For Processing Problem Reports

See CM procedure (TBD).

F.8.10 Software Archiving Requirements

This identifies the requirements for archiving software in the SCML.

F.8.10.1 Overall Requirements

Archiving will be performed in accordance with the requirements of:

(a) ...

F.8.10.2 Backup Requirements

Backups will be performed daily, weekly, and monthly.

(a) Daily backups will be incremental backups; that is, only the changes from the previous backup will be recorded. These will normally take place on Monday, Tuesday, Wednesday and Thursday. Daily backups will be overwritten every week.

(b) Weekly backups will be complete backups and will normally take place on Fridays. Weekly backups will be kept for a period of 8 weeks and may then be recycled.

(c) Monthly backups will be made on the last workday of the month. Monthly backups will be stored in the XYZ Computer Library.

Monthly backups will be kept for the lifetime of the project but may be recycled by written authorization of the project CCB.

F.8.10.3 Additional Archiving Requirements

See CM procedure (TBD).

F.9 CONFIGURATION STATUS ACCOUNTING

F.9.1 CSA Data Collection, Recording, Processing and Maintenance

See CM procedure (TBD).

F.9.2 CSA Report Description

See CM procedure (TBD).

F.9.3 CSA Reporting Frequency And Distribution

See CM procedure (TBD). There will be no on-line access to this status accounting information.

F.9.4 Metrics

F.9.4.1. CM Metrics

See CM procedure (TBD).

F.9.4.2 Project Metrics

(These are metrics that can be provided from material in the SCML; for example, number of problem reports per unit time, causes of problems, etc. This is not part of the CM task and this effort should be discussed with the PMO before beginning, and separately funded. Funds to support these tasks should not be mixed with funds for the CM tasks.)

See CM procedure (TBD).

F.10 CONFIGURATION AUDITS

F.10.1 Functional Configuration Audits

See CM procedures (TBD) for FCA plans, procedures, documentation and schedules.

Table F-IV tailors the requirements of MIL-STD-973 to this project.

F.10.2 Physical Configuration Audits

See CM procedures (TBD) for PCA plans, procedures, documentation and schedules.

Table F-V tailors the requirements of MIL-STD-973 to this project.

F.10.3 In-Process Configuration Audits

There will be no subcontractor/vendor audits as part of this plan. In-process audits on the execution of this plan will be performed by:

(a) The CM group using CM engineers not associated with this project [see CM procedure (TBD)], and,
(b) QA in accordance with its approved QA program plan.

TABLE F-IV. APPLICATION OF MIL-STD-973 REQUIREMENTS FOR SOFTWARE FCAS

MIL-STD-973		Applicable To This Project?	Comments
Section Number	Requirement		
5.6.2.3.a	Review test procedures and results for compliance with specification requirements.	No	Test procedures and test results are deliverable items and are reviewed and accepted by the customer separately.
5.6.2.3.b	N/A		Does not apply
5.6.2.3.c	Audit test plans, specifications and test procedures against test data.		(1) The test plans, specifications, procedures and input test data are audited at the time they are approved. (2) Output test data is approved as part of the test report.
...	...	...	...

F.11 SUBCONTRACTOR/VENDOR CONTROL

This does not apply to this effort.

TABLE F-V. APPLICATION OF MIL-STD-973 REQUIREMENTS FOR SOFTWARE PCAS

MIL-STD-973		Applicable To This Project?	Comments
Section Number	Requirement		
5.6.3.3.a	N/A (hardware only)	No	Does not apply.
5.6.3.3.b	N/A (hardware only)		
5.6.3.3.c	N/A (hardware only)		
5.6.3.3.d	N/A (hardware only)		
5.6.3.3.e	(1) Review of all records of baseline configuration for the CI by direct comparison with the contractor's engineering release system and change control procedures to verify that the configuration being produced accurately reflects released engineering data. (2) This includes interim releases of spares/repair parts provisioned prior to PCA to ensure delivery of currently configured spares/repair parts.	(1) No (2) No	(1) CSCIs are CDRLs and are not processed through the release of engineering drawings. The letter of transmittal is accompanied by a VDD which states the content of the media being transmitted. (2) N/A (hardware only).
...	...	...	...

Index and Further References

As previously noted in Chapter 1, this index not only provides pages in the text where specific topics are discussed but also includes references to the government standards where additional guidance is provided on those topics. For example, details on Ada Complications are found on page 182, while details on ACSN are provided in Section 5.4.2.3.3.1.2. of MIL-STD-973.

D

N

O

P

T

U

V

W

9 780818 689321